Fight Right

Fight Right

How Successful Couples
Turn Conflict Into Connection

Julie Schwartz Gottman, PhD
and John Gottman, PhD

HARMONY
NEW YORK

Published in the United States by Harmony Books, an imprint of
Random House, a division of Penguin Random House LLC, New York.
harmonybooks.com

Harmony Books is a registered trademark, and the Circle colophon is a
trademark of Penguin Random House LLC.

Library of Congress Cataloging-in-Publication Data
Names: Gottman, John Mordechai, author. | Gottman, Julie Schwartz, author.
Title: Fight right : how successful couples turn conflict into connection /
Dr. Julie Schwartz Gottman & Dr. John Gottman.
Description: First edition. | New York : Harmony, [2023] |
Includes bibliographical references. | Identifiers: LCCN 2023023993 (print) |
LCCN 2023023994 (ebook) | ISBN 9780593579657 (hardcover) |
ISBN 9780593579664 (epub)
Subjects: LCSH: Couples therapy—Popular works. | Couples—Psychology—
Popular works. | Interpersonal communication—Popular works. | Interpersonal
relations—Popular works. | Conflict management—Popular works.
Classification: LCC RC488.5 .G6785 2023 (print) | LCC RC488.5 (ebook) |
DDC 616.89/1562—dc23/eng/20230807
LC record available at https://lccn.loc.gov/2023023993
LC ebook record available at https://lccn.loc.gov/2023023994

ISBN 978-0-593-57965-7
Ebook ISBN 978-0-593-57966-4

Printed in the United States of America

Book design by Andrea Lau
Jacket design by theBookDesigners

10 9 8 7 6 5 4 3 2 1

First Edition

CONTENTS

INTRODUCTION

What Are We Fighting For?

They were perfectly matched in so many ways. She was a young lawyer (land use law) and so was he (media rights). They were both Midwest transplants to Seattle. They were busy and ambitious, and loved to pack their free time with new experiences. When they first met, they'd venture out someplace new every weekend. They hopped in the car and drove up to Vancouver for the weekend to wander the open-air market or pop in for some late-night sushi. They headed off into the mountains for an overnight camping trip. Or they grabbed last-minute tickets to a play. They both worked long hours but loved to be spontaneous in their time off.

There was just one tiny problem. She wanted a puppy. He didn't.

A year later, there was indeed a puppy—one that had grown into a big, happy, playful dog. But the marriage was ending. Divorce papers were signed. The two moved out of the house they'd bought together before they got married, the one they came home to the night of their wedding, still shaking the sparkly confetti the guests had tossed out of their hair and clothes, laughing. They split up all their furniture, books, pots and pans. She, of course, took the dog.

How did a *puppy* break up this marriage?

The fight started out simply: with a difference of opinion. He thought dogs were too much responsibility, too much work, too much commitment. You couldn't leave a dog home for very long—you couldn't even go away for the day. And dogs could get expensive. Didn't they want to use their extra money in other ways? Hadn't they talked about traveling?

But his job required frequent business trips, and he was gone a lot, leaving her alone in the house, where she worked long hours from home. She felt lonely, and when he was away overnight, she got spooked. They hadn't really been traveling like they'd once talked about—why *not* get a puppy, a buddy for her to keep her company? She imagined the dog accompanying them on weekend hikes, riding in the car with its head out the window. It was nice to picture them as a threesome: a couple with their dog.

They weren't getting anywhere. They just kept looping around inside the same argument, with no resolution. His concerns about time, money, and commitment seemed so overblown—if he would just *try* it, she was sure, he'd see it wasn't that much work! So, she decided: she would just get a puppy and give it to him as a gift. Once there was a real, live, adorable fuzzball in his lap, how could he resist? He'd come around.

He did not come around.

The conflict escalated. He was upset that she'd ignored him and done what she wanted to. She was upset that he continued to dig his heels in, even after she'd told him how important this was to her. To him, the puppy in the house was a constant reminder of how she'd completely disregarded how he felt and what was important to him.

To her, his refusal to accept the dog felt like a rejection of her and her needs. Every little thing about the dog sparked a fight: Who would take him out. The vet bill. Having to add his food to the grocery list. Worse, they were fighting about other stuff now too—*more than they ever had before.*

She started to notice how little he did around the house. Okay, fine, she thought, she'd do most of the dog stuff—it had been her idea. But he seemed to leave the rest of the housework to her too. Either he didn't care, or he just expected it—is that what it would be like, she wondered, if they had a baby? For his part, the way she brought stuff up grated on him. She never just asked for help. She'd say, "I guess I'm doing the dishes again tonight," and some little flash of anger inside him would make him snap, "Yeah, I guess so." Later, feeling bad, he'd try to do more—he'd put a few loads of laundry through, clean the bathroom—but she never noticed.

They were spending less and less time together. And one Friday afternoon, when he reminded her that he was going away for the weekend on a camping trip with an old high school buddy, she felt overwhelmed by anger and sadness.

"Oh, so you're just going to take off," she said, suddenly on the verge of tears, "and I can stay home with this dog you never wanted."

Blindsided, he blew up. "What is the matter with you?" he shouted. "I've had this trip planned for months! It has nothing to do with the stupid dog!"

There was fuel behind this fight, just under the surface, like underground oil feeding a fire: each of them had a hidden agenda.

His hidden agenda: he wanted freedom and adventure.

Her hidden agenda: she wanted a family.

But they barely acknowledged these deeper truths to themselves, much less to each other.

They retreated further and further from each other, each digging into his or her own separate foxhole, from which they lobbed accusations and criticisms like grenades. One day, she caught a bad cold and couldn't take the dog out—he had to do it. He was filled with resentment every time he had to stop doing something important to clip the leash on—he hadn't signed up for this! On another day, the puppy made his own sign of protest: he did his little dump right under the husband's desk, where he worked when he was home.

He said he wasn't cleaning it up.

She said she wasn't cleaning it up.

That tiny pile of poo marked the line nobody would cross—to cross it would be to admit defeat, to let the other side win.

When they sold the house in the divorce, they had a cleaning service come in. The cleaners moved from room to room, washing away all the evidence of this couple's life together—their fingerprints and cooking spices, dust and left-behind papers—to make the space spotless for the prospective buyers who would be coming through, imagining themselves living there instead. And then they came to the desk.

Do you know what happens when you leave dog poop for a long time?

It turns into a hard, white lump.

Yes, the punchline of this story is . . . *mummified dog poop*. And we're sorry! But we're telling you this story because it's so universal: every couple has some small disagreement that won't go away, snowballs, and turns into a huge blockage. And it seems so trivial! It's easy to hear this story and think: What a terrible reason to break up a good marriage—over a *puppy*?

Well, the fight wasn't really about the puppy. Or the poop. The puppy represented major life philosophies for each person. When they fought about taking the dog out, or the vet bill, or who should perform the errand of shopping for dog food, they weren't really fighting about those things. They were fighting about their values, their dreams, their vision of what they wanted out of marriage and out of life. They were fighting about some really foundational stuff—stuff that would have been good for them to dig into and might even have saved their marriage if they had. But they never got there. They never really figured out what they were actually fighting about or how to talk to each other about it. Their fights became destructive, and eventually that strong relationship they'd once had splintered apart.

This was a long time ago, before John started his work studying couples. He didn't fully understand the depths of their conflict until much later, when his research taught him more about the science of relationships. In the end, he wasn't able to help them. They did unfortunately split up. But since then, we have helped thousands of other couples who were just as gridlocked, just as stuck, just as desperately out of sync.

In writing this book, we thought about that long-ago couple a lot. We wish we'd known then what we know now, with fifty years of research under our belts. If we could go back in time, this is the book we would write for them.

We Need to Fix the Way We Fight

It's never been easy to partner up with someone for the long haul and gracefully navigate all the ups and downs that come with that kind of commitment. We've been working with couples for decades, and we'll tell you this: people have always sought help in this arena. But the last several years have been unusually excruciating for many of the couples we see.

Couples have been dealing with enormous levels of stress and intensity. For a long stretch of the COVID-19 pandemic, many people were homebound, or even if not, they were cut off from the normal routines, recreational outlets, and social connections that once sustained them. Boundaries between work and home dissolved as the bedroom became the workplace. We've long studied the ways couples carry stress home from work—now there was even less distance to carry it. It was all there, overlapping in the same space. Couples struggled to figure out finances, childcare, work schedules. Many clashed over how to handle pandemic safety recommendations. Was it necessary to fold family and friends into your bubble? Or was it not worth the risk? A spouse feeling desperate for community and connection partnered with one experiencing deep anxiety over exposure was often a recipe for destructive and polarizing conflict.

For many, the home, which may once have been a refuge, became a kind of crucible where every small issue was magnified and every hairline fracture split into a painful crack.

Data is still emerging from this period, but preliminary observations suggest that the COVID-19 pandemic drove couples to extremes: couples who were doing well pre-pandemic largely did all right. But couples who had some issues they were working on—and let's be real, that's a lot of us[1]—did much worse. Fault lines in the relationship, which under normal circumstances might have been more easily repaired, became critical.

We may not even have a full picture of how much people are struggling. Researchers in this field often conduct surveys to assess marital satisfaction, but these surveys can be biased. When people are really having trouble, they hang up when the interviewer calls. They don't want to talk about it. So we may be missing information from couples in crisis.

For many of us, the last few years have been a period of turmoil and questioning. People have been reevaluating their priorities and how they allocate their time and resources. Couples may be wondering: Do we still share the same goals? Is all this friction a sign that we weren't meant to be together? Are we actually compatible?

But here's the thing. Pandemic or no pandemic, couples have always gone through these kinds of "pressure cooker" times. Times when things, for whatever reason, get especially hard. When every little thing seems to spark a fight. When the fights feel awful. When you say things you regret. When you wish you could have a do-over.

No matter what phase you and your partner are in, whether you're in a bad patch or a great patch, whether your love is young or decades old, there's one thing for sure: you don't want to leave any "poop under the desk" in your relationship.

No Conflict Is Not the Answer

Let's get one thing out of the way: We're not going to teach you how to *not* fight, ever. It might sound nice—a life with no conflict? Bliss! But it's probably not in your best interests. Intimacy inevitably creates conflict.

Take another couple we worked with. According to these two, they didn't fight at all. This couple tended to avoid hot-button issues—they didn't want to hurt feelings or get embroiled in a tough discussion. What was the point, they figured, when such discussions never seemed to end with any kind of solution to the problem? To them, it seemed better to just skirt around issues that they probably wouldn't be able to solve anyway and avoid all the stress and drama.

Seems reasonable. But by the time they were in our office, sitting side by side on the couch, we saw that emotionally they were miles apart. Yes, they'd been polite to each other—there were no raised voices in that household. There were no slammed doors, no snapping in frustration, no small pile of dog poo petrifying under a desk. But they'd also, at some point, lost track of each other.

When they came to see us, we had them do an activity together that we often do with couples, where each person takes stock of what they know about their partner. Questions such as: *Who are your partner's best friends? What are some stresses your partner is facing right now? What are some of your partner's life dreams?* And so on.

As they each went down the list, it quickly became clear: they could barely answer any of them. And in a facilitated conversation, tensions and resentment slowly leaked out. At one point, the husband confessed something that had been bothering him for months but that he hadn't raised with his wife: that she'd gotten in the habit of going out for drinks with a work friend every Friday evening after work instead of coming straight home. It bothered him because they themselves hadn't gone out on any kind of date in . . . well, he couldn't remember the last time.

She was shocked. "But I asked you if you'd mind and you said 'no'!" she said. "Why didn't you just tell me?"

"Well," he replied, "I didn't want to fight."

Conflict is a natural part of every human relationship. And it's a *necessary* part of every human relationship. We tend to equate low levels of conflict with happiness, but that just isn't true. The absence of conflict doesn't indicate a strong relationship—in fact, it can lead to exactly the opposite.

A study run by the Divorce Mediation Research Project found that the vast majority of couples who divorced (80 percent) described growing apart and losing a feeling of closeness as some of the main reasons for their split.[2] And our own research has found that couples can have happy, long-lasting unions across multiple types of "conflict styles." It's not *whether* there's conflict in your relationship that makes it or breaks it. Even the happiest couples fight. It's *how you do it.*[3]

Conflict is connection. It's how we figure out who we are, what we want, who our partners are and who they are becoming, and what *they* want. It's how we bridge our differences and find our similarities, our points of connection. The problem is, we haven't been taught how to do it right. We don't get "Fighting 101" in high school, before we launch into our first relationships. We go in blind. Our beliefs about and approach to conflict come from our childhood, our upbringing and culture, and our past relationships, and they shape the way we fight in ways we may not even be aware of. No matter how many relationships we might have had, or how many years we've been partnered, many of us are still feeling our way, trying to figure it out as we go—and we make a lot of mistakes.

We stew on resentments for far too long before bringing up a problem.

We start harshly, with criticism.

We don't know how to self-soothe, and we get overwhelmed and flooded with emotion.

We get defensive.

We don't stop to figure out what the fight is really
about.

We miss or reject the attempts our partners make to
repair and meet in the middle.

We can't seem to compromise without feeling that
we've given up too much.

We apologize too fast because we just want the fight
to be over.

And here's a huge one: we ignore past fights—or, as we like to call
them, "regrettable incidents." We don't talk about them, heal from
them, or learn from them, we just *move on.*

The end result: we hurt each other. We end up wounded by our
conflicts and further apart from our partners than we were before.
Or, afraid of being wounded, we avoid conflict entirely, and that gap
grows even wider.

We're doing conflict all wrong, and we urgently need an intervention.

Uncovering the Science of Helping People "Fight Right"

We've been studying the science of love for a while now—five decades! John as a researcher and, originally, a mathematician; Julie as
a practicing clinician. Our life's work has been developing interventions for couples who love each other and want to make it work but
need real tools to keep their relationship thriving and on the right

track. Often, it's not the relationship itself that's the problem—it's that you simply haven't been given the tools you need. Every relationship is distinct, its own unique, unrepeatable chemistry project of love and attraction, conflict and connection, personalities and pasts that mix, collide, and create something new. Our relationship is not exactly like yours or any other. But we've discovered that there *are* universal interventions that work across the board. And what we most want is to get these out into the world. We all need them.

It's been fifty years since John, along with his research partner, Robert Levenson, ran his first studies on couples, applying the scientific method, for the first time, to love. It's been three decades since we (John and Julie) started working together, launching our "Love Lab" on the campus of the University of Washington in Seattle, where we ourselves met and fell in love. Like all couples, we too had to figure out our own conflict culture as we combined lives, married, and became parents. We had to work through the fights that started wrong, the ones that came out of nowhere, the ones that we seemed to have repeatedly about the same topics. And we did figure it out— we've gotten pretty good at fighting! We've found that you *can* fight with kindness, with love, and with peace at the end. But we had an edge: we had the Love Lab data.

Over three thousand couples have passed through the Love Lab, where our goal as researchers is to get as granular as possible about what specific behaviors lead to lasting love and happiness. We've had couples come in and stay for a weekend in a comfy, Airbnb-like apartment where we videotape their interactions and analyze them, then follow them for years, even decades, to track the status of their relationship as well as their happiness and satisfaction. And because it's so important to the health of a relationship, we've zeroed in on conflict and how partners interact before, during, and after fights. In one study, we had couples come in, sit down, and talk about one of their points of conflict, something they hadn't resolved yet. We recorded the interaction so that we could analyze those tapes down to the one one-hundredth of a second. We coded every gesture, sigh, smile, and pause; we coded body language, tone of voice. Nothing was too small or insignificant. We had participants hooked up to biofeedback devices so we could simultaneously track heart rate and breathing, those physiological markers that can tell us so much about how and why a conflict unfolds the way it does.

We did this with straight couples, gay and lesbian couples, couples with children and without, wealthy couples and couples in poverty, couples that came from various demographics across race and culture. And then, after getting this incredibly deep and thorough picture of each couple's interaction during one moment in time, we brought these couples back, year after year, and had them do it all again. Would they change? Would they stay together? Would the union be a happy one? And when it came to conflict, we urgently wanted to know: Why were some couples broken apart by their conflicts? And how did others find peace? So, what did we find out?

We found that by observing and coding behaviors, we were able to predict, with over 90 percent accuracy, which couples would stay together,[4] even through ups and downs, and overall feel satisfied with their union (we called these the "masters" of love), and which would divorce, split, or stay together unhappily (the relationships that unfortunately turned out to be "disasters").

We found that the first *three minutes* of a fight can predict the status of the relationship six years later.[5]

We found that couples needed to hit a certain ratio of positive to negative interactions during conflict in order to stay in love for the long haul—and that *outside* of conflict, that ratio jumped even higher.[6]

We found that during conflict, couples who exhibited four key behaviors we call "the Four Horsemen of the Apocalypse" (criticism, contempt, stonewalling, and defensiveness) were likely to split an average of five years post-wedding.[7]

But we also found that "no conflict" wasn't the answer—because there was another wave of divorces, about a decade after that five-year mark. These couples did not have the Four Horsemen. What they had was nothing. No major conflict, sure. But also no humor. No question asking. No interest in one another.

We found that the masters of love didn't avoid conflict. But they had a certain interactive skill set that allowed them to go into conflict as a collaboration, not a war; and when someone got hurt (as can happen to the best of us in conflict), they knew how to repair.[8]

We found all this—and a *lot* more. And we're going to lay it all out for you in this book. We're going to start by talking about the context for our conflicts—the "setting" for them, if you will—which basically boils down to everything that leads up to a fight, starting with how we were raised, the culture we came from, and our meta-emotions, or "feelings about feelings," which shape our relationships in surprising ways. We'll talk about how the casual, day-to-day interactions with our partners set us up for certain dynamics within conflict. We'll talk about how mystifying it can be to figure out what we're *really* fighting about below the surface (in other words, you're not fighting about a puppy!). And then we'll take you through five fights that show clearly where we go wrong during conflict and how to do it right instead. Because we also found that people could turn relationships around—fight right, love better, and connect more deeply—when they were given practical, science-based interventions to use in conflict.

When our daughter was a little girl, she said something once that clarified our mission for us, as we thought about how and why we were doing the work we were doing with couples. She was asking us about our work at the Love Lab—maybe she was irritated that we were going to be gone for a weekend, running a couples' retreat, when she would have preferred we stay home and take her for a ferry ride and an ice cream cone. In any case, she pressed us on what *exactly* we were doing out there with all this "love science." We explained that we'd been working to isolate the most powerful interventions couples could do to stay in love and stay happy—if that's what they wanted—so we could share them with people. We told her that a lot of couples—ourselves included, at certain points—go through a time where they just can't seem to get along.

"What do you think happens," we asked her, "if mommies and daddies are fighting all the time?"

"Well," she said, "I guess there are no rainbows in the house."

We were both quiet. *No rainbows in the house.* This little four-year-old had just articulated the perfect way to think about the mission of our work. Storms will come—they inevitably do. But in the aftermath, there can be something beautiful. But you only get to the rainbow by going through a storm.

Conflict Is a Human Constant

We've written a lot about love: what makes it, what breaks it, what keeps it alive. But recently, we've felt an urgent push to home in on *how we do conflict.* One of the big reasons is that our conflicts aren't going anywhere. The data tells us that whatever you're fighting about, you'll very likely always be fighting about. Overwhelmingly, the conflicts we have with our partners are not fleeting, situational, or easily fixable—they are *perpetual.*

There are two basic types of fights that couples have: **solvable** and **perpetual**. Your solvable fights are the ones that have some kind of solution. They are fixable. Let's say you're feeling put upon because you always have to load the dishwasher after your partner makes a mess preparing dinner. You and your partner might fight about this once you finally reach your boiling point (side note: talking about these types of things *before* you hit critical mass is definitely something we'll be talking about!), but in the end you can probably find a solution of some kind: you'll swap dinner prep and cleanup, or he'll do the cleanup too while you take care of other household tasks that need doing. It's a logistical problem, one that can be figured out once everybody has a cool head.

Perpetual fights are different. These are the issues that don't go away. These are the things we end up fighting about time and time again, because they tap into some of the deeper differences between us: differences in personalities, priorities, values, and beliefs. And no matter how perfect someone is for you, *these are always going to be there*. We don't fall in love with our clones. In fact, we're often drawn to people who are very different from us in certain ways: people who don't replicate us but complement us.

It comes down to this: the vast majority of our problems—69 percent, to be precise—are perpetual, not solvable. That's a lot! That means that most of the time, whatever you and your partner are fighting about is not going to have a simple solution or any easy fix. And of these perpetual fights, 16 percent become gridlocked: the partners go round after round on the same topics, not only not getting anywhere, but causing more hurt, anger, and distance. And this is why fixing the way we fight is such an urgent issue. *How we fight* is, as we've said, how we communicate and connect. But (and we feel comfortable saying this, because of the sheer number of couples we've studied and tracked over the years) *we are doing it wrong.* We're rushing in, wounding each other, missing opportunities, and then repeating the cycle again, the next time we fight about the same old thing.

This particular moment in human history also demands a different approach to conflict. Couples are more in distress now, in the COVID era, than ever before. Rates of domestic violence are up: in our international study with over forty thousand couples, we found that in couples seeking therapy, *60 percent* were experiencing some degree of domestic violence. And there were other concerning statistics. In these couples, we found high rates of anxiety (27 percent), depression (46 percent), and suicidality (29 percent). Almost a third of all couples were struggling with issues surrounding substance abuse. And 35 percent were dealing with the fallout of an affair.[9]

Our world seems to become more and more uncertain, and so often, we end up taking out our stress and anxiety on the people closest to us. When we fight with a partner, we aren't fighting in a vacuum. The world gets in. By the time we arrive at a point of conflict with a partner, we're often already carrying so much—our emotional bandwidth is short, we're cognitively overloaded, and that shrinks our capacity to be gentle with each other. We carry the residue of the day with us when we interact—the worries and the pressures that we've experienced and that weigh on us in ways we might not be aware of. And beyond the walls of our homes, conflict abounds. It proliferates in the virtual world, where the format of the interaction makes true understanding vanishingly rare. Our world has never been as polarized.

We are at a critical point in human history—a point where across the board, in every arena, we need to learn to set aside our defenses, open up, and fight for peace and understanding. This starts within the four walls of the home. Our romantic partnerships are the building blocks of our larger communities. They have ripple effects on our children, our friendships and extended families, our collaborations in the workplace. They influence our capacity to give back to the world and make change; they affect how we come together as a society. As we learn to fight better in our homes, we can learn to fight better in our communities, across political divides, in our society, and even as a human race.

It's only human to have conflicts. It's even *humane* to have conflicts—often, it's exactly the right thing to do. But we need to bring our best humanity to our conflicts.

When we fight, we should be trying to create something better. That's the ultimate goal of conflict: to create something better for yourself, for you and your partner as a couple, and for the world. Conflict doesn't have to break us apart. Conflict and peace are not mutually exclusive. We can arrive at peace through conflict. We can combine kindness and gentleness with fighting. We can grow closer *because* of conflict. But to do this, we need to get to the heart of our conflicts.

We are so deep as human beings. We're not just what you see on the surface—the hair and skin and clothing. We're not even the personalities we project. We are subterranean. We have rivers and waterfalls and rocky cliffs inside us, deep valleys that perhaps even we haven't fully explored. And we're often afraid to show those parts of ourselves in relationships. We feel like we have to be on our "best behavior" to win the heart of another. So we keep the door closed on that complicated inner world. Then, once we're into the thick of a relationship, those parts start to leak out. And they most often leak out through conflict, surprising not only our partners but us too. These long-buried or suppressed parts of ourselves—these needs and dreams and emotions we've held down—flare up in the heat of the moment. And they can burn down the house.

But they don't have to.

Fights can get intense and messy. People relive old pain and trauma. We so easily fall into old patterns—we get hijacked by our emotions, our pasts, our old hurts. But if you can get at what's underneath, there's so much compassion and understanding.

Our hope for you and your partner, as you read this book, is that you can come to see your conflicts as a profound opportunity. That you'll gain a deeper understanding of your own conflict culture and where it comes from. That you'll learn how to uncover what you're *really* fighting about, so you can get to the heart of the matter and understand each other better through your fights. We hope you'll walk away with a clear understanding of the five major ways we go wrong when fighting with the one we love most, and how to pivot, *even in the heat of the moment,* and do it right. And we hope you'll be able to inject some humor and levity into your fights—it can go a long way.

Conflict isn't always fun, but we hope this book will be.

part 1

Conflict 101

WHY WE FIGHT

"What's going on?" he says, as she says at the same time, "So what do you want to talk about?"

They both laugh.

The couple is sitting close together, propped up against crisp white pillows on their comfy bed, facing the camera. They're angled toward each other; so far, they both seem warm and relaxed—maybe a little nervous about being filmed. We've asked them to turn on the camera of their laptop, begin recording, and then simply talk about how their day is going. That's all.

Meanwhile, our AI system is watching them. This system was built to assist our Gottman-trained therapists and couples wanting to assess their relationship at home—to gather illuminating data about how partners respond to each other in casual interactions and in conflict. The AI can read their heart rate from the video feed, without any other devices. Using machine learning, it does emotion coding, pinpointing each partner second by second on a wide range of possible emotional categories. And it rates each person's trust level in their partner on a scale of 0 to 100 percent.

The AI—designed by our brilliant colleagues, Rafael Lisitsa and Dr. Vladimir Brayman—gathers all this data as this couple chats briefly about their workweek, how they're looking forward to the weekend and having the chance to relax. So far, the AI has coded their interaction as progressing from "neutral" to "interested." Both are relaxed—heart rate is around 80. Trust metric is fairly high.

Then, she says, "Oh, by the way. I told my parents they could stay in our room this weekend when they come to visit. We'll sleep on the couch."

There's a pause.

"You already told them?" he says.

"Well, yeah," she says, a bit dismissively. "They're my parents. I—"

"You know I don't sleep well on the couch."

"Oh, come on." *(Eye roll)* "It's just for the weekend. What's the big deal?"

"Well, I want to be at my best with your parents. I don't want to be grumpy because I didn't—"

"Like you're ever at your best with my parents anyway, so . . ."

"Wow." His voice is laced with hurt and sarcasm. "Okay."

"Why are you making that face? You know it's true!"

"Hey, I'm trying to make an effort for your parents, and—"

"Oh yeah? Well, why has it taken three years for you to do that? Why is *this* the weekend?"

"Three years? You don't think that I've made an effort for three years?"

From here the temperature of the interaction spikes rapidly. They interrupt, talk over each other. She accuses him of making her dad cry during a phone conversation recently; he tries to defend himself.

"You just *had* to slip in a snide little comment, didn't you," she says, "while I was just trying to say, 'Happy Birthday' to him."

"I was just trying to be funny!" he shouts.

The AI has clocked both partners' heart rates rising—his more significantly, to 107 beats per minute. The trust metric has plummeted; his goes critically low, to below 30 percent. Emotion rating nosedives for both. The interaction rapidly skews negative; she attacks, he defends, both speak to each other with contempt. Less than thirty seconds later, the couple turns away from each other, exhausted and angry, giving up on the conversation completely. As the video captured by the AI cuts off, they each stare off in opposite directions.

"Coding" Conflict

The couple above is a real couple who agreed to participate in a new platform we set out to build, designed to help other couples just like them: normal couples who had hit a tough patch (or a tough year . . . or a tough decade) and needed some support and guidance.

In recent years—and accelerated by the COVID-19 pandemic—the demand for skilled therapists has overwhelmed the existing network. Plus, for busy couples who are working full time and perhaps caring for young children or other family, getting in to see someone can be difficult. A lot of couples who really could use some professional guidance are going without for various reasons. We wanted to figure out a way for couples who are struggling to get immediate relief. And we saw that a *lot* of couples were struggling. So we went to work on a platform that couples could access through a phone, laptop, or tablet—a place they could go to find guidance and tools. And for this to work, we needed an AI that could observe couples interacting and, like the most skilled and experienced trained professional, identify the signs and signals of a conversation going into toxic territory. Therapists are trained to look for these signs: subtle cues in body language and physiology, vocal tone, language choices, and more. Could a computer be programmed to be this sensitive?

In short: yes. And when it comes to the coding of conflict, not only has the AI matched its human counterparts, it's actually outperformed them.

Much of the data and observations about couples in conflict in this book comes from our decades of work in the Love Lab and from other important and groundbreaking observational studies by ourselves and other researchers. But now we are getting even more sophisticated and granular information from the AI we trained with John's emotional coding system, called SPAFF, short for *Specific Affect Coding System*.[1]

When John was first beginning his research into couples, the field of psychology was struggling to nail down consistent patterns when it came to the personality and behavior of *one* individual, much less two. The general belief in the field was that studies of couples would be too unreliable to be scientifically useful. Studying a single individual was already so unreliable, the thinking went, that studying two would simply square that unreliability, making it exponentially worse. John, ever the mathematician, set out to prove that false.

He began searching for patterns of behavior in individuals and couples—specifically, *sequences of interactions* that could be indicative of the couple's overall happiness and the success (or not) of their relationship.[2] Across a series of observational research studies, he and his colleagues worked out a coding system that measured every possible nuance of an interaction between two people: facial expressions, tone of voice, language and rhetoric, physical cues, and more.

He and his research partner, Robert Levenson, developed ways for couples participating in the studies to actually rate their own experiences during conflict conversations, offering even more essential data about how people experienced conflict and whether or not their intentions matched their impact. Following couples over time, they were able to track how these coded sequences of interactions between couples aligned with the outcome of their relationship: Did they break up? Did they stay together? If together, were they happy or miserable?

John studied all three groups, gathering data from couples who divorced, couples who stayed happily together, and couples who stayed unhappily together. That data was anything but unreliable.

John found that interactions between couples were incredibly stable over time and highly predictive of the future of their relationship. Using SPAFF to code a couple's interactions, John was able to predict, *with over 90 percent accuracy,* the future of that couple's relationship.[3] And a huge part of that prediction was how these couples behaved in conflict.

One of the key pieces to John's studies on relationships was the "conflict task," where couples were asked to choose a topic of ongoing conflict and discuss it. Their fight would be taped, and a team of researchers would then pore over the footage, working to code every expression and interaction, down to the hundredth of a second. It's demanding work, and our researchers needed to be highly trained in order to do this accurately. Before SPAFF, the other coding systems for looking at behavior and interactions were *cue based*—they looked at actions and expressions, elements of human behavior that you could note visually. The problem is, that left out a ton of essential context. What about vocal tone? A major key will suggest positive emotion, while a minor key indicates the opposite. What about emphasis on certain words versus others? We call that a *paralinguistic cue:* the same sentence, read with an emphasis on different words, could communicate either frustration or flexibility—you have to take that into account. And what about cultural differences in the use of language and physicality? Our coding system accepts that emotion is conveyed in an interactive way across *all* communication channels.

We are so complex as humans, and any system for coding our behavior has to be equally complex. In order to code emotion during a fight, you have to be incredibly sensitive. You have to know the meaning of words, understand the words in context, understand the culture you're operating within. You have to hear the music in words: tone, loudness, pitch, tempo, emphasis. It's a lot! But amazingly, the AI, trained with John's coding system, can duplicate exactly what culturally informed observational researchers can do. From the beginning, the AI matched what human coders could do. And over time, through machine learning, it got better and better, until it was as good as the best humans.

All this is to say: *Our AI is extremely good at this.* When we have a couple sitting there, like our young couple above having their fight about a foldout couch with the laptop propped up and the video camera on, the AI is gathering irreplaceable data and doing it better than most seasoned professionals—it even synchronizes affect coding with each partner's physiology. The "breakdown" of this fight that we got from the AI was highly accurate. And this fight in particular is a great one to dissect, since it manages to encapsulate just about everything we tend to do in conflict.

A "Textbook" Fight

We chose this fight to feature here, at the beginning of this book, for a simple reason: it's a classic. It illustrates all the major features of typical couples' conflict:

- **It's about almost nothing.** One minute, we're having a nice conversation about our week; the next we're in a full-blown war.
- **It moves very quickly into difficult conflict (escalation).** The AI recorded this interaction upgrading to escalated conflict in less than a minute.
- **There's no listening.** In this dialogue, we see absolutely no space for understanding. It's all attack and defend. It looks less like a conversation and more like two people dueling with swords.
- **It contains every single one of the "Four Horsemen of the Apocalypse":** the negative communication patterns that, over time, predict the end of a relationship:
  - Criticism (Why has it taken you three years to make an effort with my parents?)
  - Contempt (You just had to slip in a snide little comment, didn't you . . .)
  - Defensiveness (I was just trying to be funny!)
  - Stonewalling (At the end of the fight, the male partner shuts down, completely disconnects, and stops responding.)
- **There's "flooding."** This is the emotional hijacking of the nervous system in conflict that leads to overwhelm and eventually the stonewalling we saw above. The AI

clocked a rapid and intense physiological response in the
male partner in particular as the conflict escalated—on
average with men, this looks like a spike from about 80
beats per minute (bpm) to 107 bpm (and it can go even
higher)—a major indicator of flooding.

- **Negative interactions rapidly outnumber the positive.**
  For couples to be successful long-term, they need to
  maintain a certain ratio of positive to negative
  interactions in conflict. That ratio is *5:1:* five positive
  interactions for every negative interaction. In this fight,
  the interaction becomes 100 percent negative almost
  immediately.

- **There are very few—if any—repair attempts.** One of the
  major ways the masters of love keep conflict on track is
  through *repair,* not only after a fight but during a fight.
  Like so many of us when things get heated and emotions
  run high, these two are not willing or even able to
  attempt repair. It is all damage.

- **And finally . . . it's about in-laws!** We can probably all
  relate to that.

To give you a visual image of this couple: they are in their late
twenties. Relatively speaking, theirs is a young relationship—they've
been married for about two years. She has long blonde hair, Joni
Mitchell style, and a slim gold nose ring. He has dark hair, shoulder
length, which he runs his hands through, first calmly as he reclines
on the bed at the beginning of their chat, then faster and faster as he
gets agitated. As she gets angry, she leans toward him. Her body language is aggressive. She looks at him intently, laser focused on his
face as she lobs criticisms, and can barely wait for his response be-

fore making the next accusation—she is "kitchen sinking," or dumping pent-up resentments that she hasn't found a way to express previously. On the defensive, he defaults to sarcasm. He appears to feel boxed in by conversation: it's almost as if you can see the mental wheels turning as he realizes, "There's no way out of this."

By the end of this fight, they have gotten nowhere.

They both go silent, shaking their heads in defeat.

But they're here, on the app, because they aren't defeated. They know that something is wrong, and they're trying to fix it. They don't want to give up on each other or their life together. They want it to get better. But they are plagued with the question that so many couples come to us with: *Why are we like this?*

We could give you a hundred reasons why we fight. But let's take a look at the big ones.

"Opposites Attract" and Other Reasons We Are Doomed to Fight

It's a famous phrase: *opposites attract*. And, it turns out, a scientifically accurate one.

We really do have "chemistry," as one Swiss zoologist proved in a study on sense of smell, attraction, and genetic differences.[4] Klaus Wedekind recruited a hundred heterosexual participants—half male, half female—specifically selected to have genetic diversity. The men were given clean T-shirts and sent home; after wearing them to sleep for two nights, they returned the unwashed shirts to the lab. When the female participants were brought in, they were each offered an array of seven different shirts to smell. (Would you sign up for this study?) As they progressed from shirt to shirt, taking a whiff of each, they were asked to describe each one in terms of "intensity, pleasantness, and sexiness" and say which T-shirt's scent they found most appealing overall.

The results were fascinating. Overwhelmingly, the women preferred the scent of the shirts worn by the men who had a particular gene sequence that was *most different from their own.* The particular gene Wedekind was homing in on was called the MHC gene, or *major histocompatibility locus.* Why is it important? It's a key part of the immune system. When parents have very different MHC genes, their offspring will have an edge in fighting off viruses and diseases. It gives them more of a shield. In other words, mating with someone genetically *different* from you is a deeply entrenched, biological human survival mechanism.

So, we may find ourselves frequently in conflict with our partners because we've picked someone very different from us—we're programmed to do so! In fact, **personality differences** account for the vast majority of couples' conflict. As we said in the introduction, most of our conflicts (69 percent of them) are *perpetual,* not solvable—we'll be managing them for the entirety of the relationship.[5] Perpetual problems between partners typically stem from differences in personality and lifestyle preferences. The more couples can be accepting of each other's differences, the better, but where we often go wrong is when we try to turn our partners into ourselves and then criticize them when that doesn't work. Those differences that were once so alluring and magnetic become long-lasting points of friction.

"I was drawn to him because of his spontaneity" turns into "Why can't you make a plan and stick to it?"

"I fell for her outgoing personality and great sense of humor" turns into "Do you really have to talk to every single person at the party? And were you flirting with that guy?"

Even if you're not a classic "opposites attract" couple, you aren't immune to this category of conflict. We see so many instances of what we'll call "opposites uncovered": you and your partner seem so similar, it takes a while longer to bump into those differences. But they're there. Take this couple we worked with: Both were artists—he a painter and she a singer—and they bonded over art making and the creative process. But she was an extrovert who got so much energy and creative spark from interacting with others; he was an introvert who needed a lot of solitude and downtime. These are people who were drawn together because of shared interests, background, and lifestyles, but then had oppositional personalities and needs—a very common scenario.

Another predictor of conflict we see is **major life changes,** for instance, becoming parents. The arrival of a baby is supposed to be a joyous event, but our research on newlyweds found that three years after a baby was born, a staggering 67 percent of couples had experienced a plummeting in overall happiness and a spike in hostility toward each other[6]—in other words: a whole lot more fighting. A baby's a big one, but any kind of life shift can spark conflict with your partner, especially if that shift is something that presses up against your needs, dreams, beliefs, values. Stuff like: Moving an aging parent in with you. Taking a new demanding job. Moving. A big shift in your financial circumstances. All of this is the stuff of life, of course—which makes it even more essential that we learn to do conflict well.

And we aren't fighting in a vacuum. **Life stress** is a huge factor in how often we fight and how those fights go. Whether we go to an office, Zoom from a bedroom desk, or spend all day taking care of kids, we bring stress and worry from the day into our interactions with our partner. In 2004, our colleague Robert Levenson ran a study he called "The Remains of the Workday," looking at how the "residue" of the day seeps into marital interactions.[7] The study focused on "police couples"—officers and their spouses. Policing, as a high-stress job, offered a particularly illuminating window into how work stress and exhaustion can affect both *physiological and subjective components* of marital interactions: In other words, how the body measurably responds to conflict and how participants assessed their own experiences during that conflict after the fact. Levenson had participating couples keep daily "stress diaries" for a month; meanwhile, once a week, they came into the lab and interacted normally—having a conversation about their respective days, for instance—while he and researchers observed.

What they found: On higher-stress days, the interactions between partners were more heavily tinged with discord. Both spouses were more physiologically aroused (or "flooded," with a higher heart rate, blood pressure, stress hormone levels, and more signs of nervous system overdrive) and in their self-assessment reported more negative emotions and fewer positive ones. Men in particular were affected by physical exhaustion—they experienced even more of a spike in flooding when they were more wiped out. This all points pretty clearly to the fact that our daily experiences out there in the world (or inside our bedrooms and offices as we work remotely) most definitely do spill over into our relationships. When we're stressed at work (or parenting, if that is the work you do), we're more likely to have conflict with our partners *and* in that conflict more likely to become physiologically flooded and overwhelmed and to struggle to regulate our emotions.

For all of these reasons—and more—we are set up to have conflict. But one of the big reasons that conflicts escalate, no matter what the cause or topic, is a single common factor: we have a tough time dealing with negative emotions. Especially our partner's. We feel attacked, we get defensive; we suppress negative emotions until they cause an explosion. Conflict is a part of life, yes, and a huge part of fighting right is going to be learning how to handle and discuss negative emotions—both our partner's and our own.

Don't Be Afraid of Anger and Conflict

When John first started his Love Lab studies with newlywed couples in the mid-1980s, he wasn't sure what the data was going to show. He believed that he would indeed find patterns in behaviors and interactions between couples that would shed light on how and why some couples stay together and stay happy and why others don't manage it. And he was right. He did. But one fascinating thing about scientific studies is that quite often you go into an experiment with theories about what you're going to find. And half the time or more, you're completely wrong. In the Love Lab, John found he was wrong about 60 percent of the time! But the amazing thing about science is: you can get just as valuable information out of being wrong as you can about being right.

Here's a couple of things John thought he might find that ended up not being supported by the data:

1. That anger is a dangerous emotion.
2. That a lot of fighting at the beginning of a relationship is a bad sign.

Let's tackle the second one first. Early conflict in a relationship might seem like a predictor of bad outcomes for that couple—but no. In fact, it was exactly the opposite.

When we tracked couples through the years, we found that many of our newlywed couples who displayed higher conflict in those first years of their marriages had stronger and happier relationships as time went on compared to many of their low-conflict counterparts. Why?

It turned out that in these couples (all heterosexual, in this study), the women felt secure enough to bring up issues with their husbands, as opposed to women in some of the other relationships who were afraid to do so. This only went in one direction: from wife to husband. When conflict was driven by the female partner bringing up issues, the relationship turned out to be a stronger and more successful one. Researchers called it the "wife negative effect"—sounds bad, but for the relationship it meant good things later.[8] The no-conflict newlyweds might have looked better initially, but when we interviewed these couples later, it turned out that many of the women were suppressing needs instead of expressing them, leading to a kind of low-conflict facade that masked deeper issues—women who were afraid of a blowup or feared abandonment simply wouldn't bring anything up. The low-conflict relationships were in fact more fragile; what had looked initially like a *positive* indicator was actually a negative.

Which brings us to an aspect of our coding system that led us to a fascinating revelation about *anger.*

The SPAFF coding system requires that everything our researchers (or now, our AI!) observe gets coded as *positive* or *negative.* This was how we uncovered the 5:1 ratio of positive to negative interactions in conflict. But as we analyzed the data we were getting from our studies, we started to gather more and more fine-grained information about the nature of negativity. It became clear: *not all things that were coded negative in the moment were negative in the long term.* For instance: anger. Anger was not negative! Sitting there observing couples in the lab, we'd seen anger and thought, "That's bad."

It turned out that it was the Four Horsemen that were bad. When couples displayed their anger with contempt, with criticism, with defensiveness, with stonewalling, *that* was toxic. It was poison for the relationship. But anger in and of itself was not a bad thing or an indicator of future negative outcomes.[9]

From the lens of modern neuroscience, in fact, *anger* may be more aligned with positive emotions like joy and excitement, because it's what neuroscientist Richard Davidson calls an "approach emotion." Davidson was interested in studying brain processes and emotion between the right and left brain, so he took a group of participants, hooked each person up to one of those funny little caps with electrodes that sit right against the scalp, allowing the researcher to grab a picture of the electrical activity in the brain (an electroencephalogram), and asked them to think about a typical day they'd recently had. He charted the brain activity, looking to see which side of the brain "lit up," and then had participants self-report on what they were experiencing emotionally as they were imagining their day—right or left? We think of "right brain" as having to do with creative and artistic processes, and "left brain" as our linear, logical side. But that's not what Davidson found. He saw that when people were experiencing emotions that led them to withdraw from the world (sadness, fear, disgust), they had a right frontal asymmetry (more activity in that area), and when they were experiencing or processing emotions like interest, curiosity, joy, and anger, they had a left frontal asymmetry.[10] More activity on the left meant they wanted to engage with whatever they were experiencing rather than withdraw. They were excited, curious, or angry—and that's why we now think of anger as an *approach* emotion. It doesn't exactly line up with "positive" versus "negative," and when it comes to the science of love, that's fascinating to us. It means that anger—though not usually pleasant to experience—is driving you to approach your partner: to connect and engage, express something that needs to be expressed.

In many cultures—and especially in American culture today—we tend to believe that we have a certain degree of choice over how we feel. So when we're experiencing emotions that don't feel great (anger, sadness), we can get really impatient with those feelings, with ourselves for having them and with our partners for expressing them. We figure, why would we ever choose to feel angry, or disgusted, or sad? We feel ashamed for being angry. We think of anger as bad. We think of conflict as bad. We want to suggest that neither of those things is true. Anger is in fact useful and should be respected. Anger is a natural emotion, and it comes from a frustrated goal—there's very good, productive information in that, but it's essential that it be expressed without contempt or criticism.

Our SPAFF coding was clear: anger is *not* predictive of negativity or poor relationship outcomes. As long as you don't invite in the Four Horsemen, anger can be a positive thing! It puts the complaint you have "in italics." It may drive you and your partner to have necessary conversations. In our respective practices with couples, we've found that anger has always been the thing that is most shaming to people—their own tendency to be flooded. But there is no shame in feeling anger.

Anger—especially female anger, which has more historically been suppressed—is not to be avoided and can be a path to greater knowledge. Unfortunately, people are terrified of anger. But the more terrified we become, the more polarized we become. Broadly in our culture, men are allowed anger but no vulnerable emotions. Women are allowed the more passive emotions—sadness, fear, worry—but not the ones that are more agentic, like anger. Luckily for John, he married Julie, who is comfortable expressing her anger! He's had no choice but to accept anger as part of the process. We do joke about Julie's passionate nature, but in all seriousness it has been quite wonderful to have a marriage where all emotions are out on the table. You don't have to hide anything. Of course, it does matter how you *speak* the anger and how you *listen* to it.

Conflict Is the "Royal Road" to Understanding

So here are a couple of objectives for all of us, at the beginning of this book. One is to recognize anger as an approach emotion and not think of it as bad. Anger isn't bad, and fighting isn't bad.

But here's the second: we don't want to approach our partners with anger that manifests as contempt, criticism, defensiveness. We're going to try to flip it.

We want to approach each other with *curiosity*.

Conflict has a goal: mutual understanding. Without conflict, without fighting, we would not be able to understand each other fully or love each other fully. We often call conflict the "royal road to understanding." The Royal Road, in antiquity, was a highway built in the fifth century B.C. by the Persian king Darius the Great to more rapidly facilitate communication throughout his large kingdom. This is exactly what our fights can do. Conflict sharpens our ability to love—it's like the whetstone to the blade of love. Emotions are information: *listen to your emotions*. They are there to guide you. All of our emotions give us useful insight—including anger.

So, our first goal, as we embark on this journey to "fight better": understand that anger is okay. Conflict is okay. There is no shame in either—they are normal, natural, necessary threads in the texture of a relationship. And both can be forces for good.

We began this chapter with a basic (yet enormous) question:

Why do we fight? The answer to that is simple. **We fight because we have two brains in a relationship, not one.** For the course of our partnerships, however long they last—for many, the bulk of our adult lives—we will be navigating the tension between the individual and the collective, between the *I* and the *we*. This is perhaps most true with our romantic life partners, but it applies to all of our close and collaborative relationships.

As humans, we all want to have agency and autonomy. This is a deep and enduring need. We've always had to make our own personal decisions in order to survive—it's been this way throughout human evolution. As a species, we've had to face so many challenges to survival, like war, disease, famine. Each individual has these competing instincts: on the one hand, we each think we know best. On the other hand, we have this competing sense that others might know better. So we create systems that are hierarchical, with the idea that everybody has a particular gift or ability to contribute, and everybody has challenges and deficits. If you're in a tribe, trying to survive in the wilderness, you need somebody who's strong, and someone else who understands cooperative hunting, and someone else who is vigilant. The question becomes, How do you coordinate all the individual challenges, individual strengths, and differences in skill levels and knowledge in order to create a harmonious unit that has the best chance of survival? And how do you do that with larger and larger groups?

Survival in some ways used to be pretty simple: you had to eat, you had a spear, you had tools you could use to hunt and prepare your food. Progress has unfolded in recent human history with breathtaking speed, and at this point there are thousands of choices people have to make every single day about every aspect of life— What time should I get up? Who showers first? Who gets the sink first? Who gets the kids up? Who dresses the kids? Who cleans up from breakfast? Who stays home when the baby's sick? Who deals with this bill or that one, this task or that one? Are we conforming to traditional gender roles or pushing back against them? Whose career should be prioritized? And on and on. Count how many decisions you make in a day, multiply that by a dozen (each choice has at least that many suboptions to pick from, like a drop-down menu that keeps nightmarishly expanding), and how can you not have conflict?

A relationship is a constant negotiation of *individual* versus *collective*. Each person has their own individual awareness and consciousness, their own preferences, interests, emotions, intellect, and even spirituality—all these things that compose, fundamentally, who they are. And all these parts of the individual are calling out for expression. Humans have this individual need to express and embody who they are. But the collective—whether it's a tribe, a city, a country, or a couple—demands something very different. It demands cooperation. Collaboration. Cohesion. Compromise. And kindness, compassion, and sensitivity to each other's individual preferences and needs. And it will always be there, this tension: between trying to be true to who you are in your own soul, in your own core, versus being true to the collective. This becomes the long-term work of love, of being partners for the long haul.

So, to address this tension, we need to start with a foundational aspect of who you are that trips up many couples: your "conflict culture," which has huge implications for how you and your partner relate to each other and interpret each other's behaviors during a fight. By "conflict culture," we mean the "rules" of fighting that you each operate within, which are often invisible or unacknowledged, yet deeply held. And for each person in a partnership, those unspoken rules can be very, very different.

WHY WE FIGHT
THE WAY WE FIGHT

Why do you fight the way you do? Where do your beliefs about conflict come from? What's your "fighting style," and how does it mesh (or not) with your partner's? A lot of couples who come to us for help in their relationships arrive without ever having been asked these questions—or asking themselves. They haven't looked closely at the beliefs about conflict they inherited from their parents or the culture in which they were raised. They haven't evaluated the impact of past relationships and how that's shaped the way they approach and respond to conflict.

Take Tyler and Noah. These midthirties, urban professionals share many overlapping interests in art, film, and food. Outside of work, they spend a lot of time together visiting museums and galleries and exploring new restaurants, and recently they had a great experience taking a couples' cooking class. When they're out and about doing something together, everything seems to flow smoothly. But whenever they try to have a simple conversation about an issue that's come up, Tyler quickly defaults to raising his voice when he gets frustrated or even just wants to emphasize a point. In response, Noah shuts down, stops talking, or even bails out completely—overwhelmed by the interaction, he'll just walk out of the room in the middle of the conversation, leaving Tyler stunned and deeply hurt. Clearly, he thinks, Noah doesn't really care about his needs or feelings. His coldness, his selfishness, feels like a slap in the face.

Noah, meanwhile, is feeling fatalistic—it's impossible to communicate with Tyler; there's no way to respond to him that won't result in more yelling. Every fight feels like a room with no doors: there's no way out.

With this couple, there's no one particular issue that's causing strife. Their recent fights have ranged from where to go to dinner to whether they have (or will ever have) the financial bandwidth to have a child via surrogate. It's not about the topic—what's causing a widening rift between Tyler and Noah, who do love each other and want to stay together, is that they have deeply divergent beliefs about conflict—beliefs they take for granted and are barely aware of. They have different *conflict styles*.

The Three Main Conflict Styles: Which Type Are You?

There are three possible "conflict styles" within a healthy (emphasis on *healthy*) partnership:[1] **avoiding, validating,** and **volatile.** These each exist as points on a spectrum rather than absolutes—we are not all 100 percent one of these three but may fall somewhere in between two, trending one direction or another. As you read the traits and tendencies of each, you'll likely be able to place yourself along this spectrum, and figuring out which style you most closely identify with will help you nail down how you tend to behave in conflict and why.

To give you the quick overview of each: Conflict-avoidant couples tend not to have conflictual discussions at all, preferring to "agree to disagree" and keep the peace rather than get mired in a potentially upsetting conversation. Validators fight, but they fight politely, discussing issues collaboratively, and are interested in finding a compromise (though whether they're able to is another story, and something we'll talk about later). And finally, volatile couples erupt into conflict more frequently, burn hotter, and are generally more intense and dramatic.

You might recognize yourself and your partner right off the bat just by those one-sentence descriptions, but let's take a closer look at the tendencies and behaviors of each.

The Conflict-Avoidant Couple

Avoiders shy away from active conflict. They just don't see the point. They tend to focus on what's working well about their relationship and choose not to bring up issues that might threaten that stability and equilibrium. In our studies in the lab, the pattern we saw with conflict-avoidant couples was that it was hard to even get them going on a conflict discussion—they would quickly pivot to emphasizing their areas of common ground and talking about all the good things in their relationship. Avoidant couples tend to say, "We enjoy each other's company, we get along most of the time—so what if we do some things differently? Why rock the boat?"

Within conflict-avoidant couples, though, we see two distinct types. The first type rarely talks at all about points of disagreement. They think, *Okay, we don't agree on this at all, so let's not waste any time talking about it,* and immediately drop the topic. These couples have the most trouble with the "conflict task" in the Love Lab. The instructions for this are pretty simple: We bring a couple in, hook them up to our monitors so we can track their physiology (heart rate, etc.), flip on our recording equipment so we can code everything later, and then give them the instructions: "Choose a recent or recurring conflict in your relationship and discuss it—you have fifteen minutes."

Volatile couples have no trouble doing this. Neither do validators, usually. But this type of avoidant couple really struggles to come up with anything at all. We have to press them to come up with an "area of stress" in order to help them arrive at a topic. Then, even if they do manage to land on a topic, they can't manage to fill the fifteen minutes! We have to butt in, nudge, and prod them to get more specific. And with our prodding, they quickly get uncomfortable and then flooded (physiologically overwhelmed). They aren't used to fighting; it feels very artificial for them.

This type of couple often has a bit more division in their lives— certain rooms or areas in the house become the "territory" of one partner or the other—and they can tend to take on more defined roles domestically, which often (but not always) fall along traditional gender stereotypes: he makes the decisions and she defers; he deals with the finances and she deals with the kids. Julie's parents were a classic example of this type of couple. He was a physician, a cardiologist— he was out all day saving lives. Her mother worked part time but mostly stayed home with the three kids. Each spouse had their separate spheres. When he came home, he'd read the paper and she'd cook dinner. At the table the family would talk animatedly about politics and watch the news; the discussion would swirl around world events like the Vietnam War. Julie never once saw them fight.

They loved each other, but they didn't interact all that much, and tensions went unspoken and unaddressed, hanging in the air like smoke.

This type of avoidant couple can risk becoming lonely and isolated from each other, but they can also lead very stable lives. They tend to be low risk takers, content with what they have.

The second type of avoidant couple presents a bit differently. They're very interested in each other. They spend time together. They *do* talk about feelings. But then . . . they just leave it at that. One person feels one way about a situation, the other feels quite differently; they both express it and then—well, that's it! They move on.

This type of avoidant couple actually tends to be the happiest couples, across all types, that we see in the lab. They aren't quite as stereotyped, in terms of gender roles, as the other type; there's more mixing in terms of household roles. But they still don't really know how to accept influence from each other. If they have big differences, they just live with it.

With avoiders in general, if nothing rocks their boat, they might cruise along on calm waters just fine with no real issues.

The Validating Couple

Validators can look similar to the second type of avoiders above—the difference is, they *do* disagree, and they aren't afraid to get into it. They'll debate. They'll accept each other's influence. They'll work on compromise. They'll try to persuade each other of their own point of view (something avoiders aren't interested in at all). They'll problemsolve and work to come up with a new way forward. They tend to be calmer in conflict, but they aren't content to "agree to disagree." They want to get somewhere.

We have some close friends who are classic validators, and it's fascinating to watch them fight: they'll express *some* emotion, but they're very rational. Both will be brainstorming, midfight, to come up with some kind of logical compromise or solution that considers both points of view. Sometimes they arrive at one; other times they take turns (i.e., *you won the last one, I'll concede this time*). They don't raise their voices. It can get tense, but they quickly bring it back down to a more collaborative approach. Overall, they seem like teammates, not rivals.

Sounds pretty good, but even validators run into issues in conflict and face *escalation:* the moment when the fight starts getting heated. Validators tend to deal with escalation by taking breaks. They don't want to be volatile. Instinctually, they shift to being more positive or *validating* to calm the interaction down. They'll summarize the other person: "So you're saying you want me to plan ahead with my parents instead of making last-minute arrangements . . ." A classic hallmark of validators is that they are willing to abandon their position on something in order to stay out of big, volatile emotions. They'd rather give something up than risk an escalated quarrel. Often, that's because they grew up with a volatile parent or guardian and now want to avoid that dynamic at any cost. So some questions we often have for validating couples include: Are you giving up too much to keep the peace? Is there room for emotion and exploration in your fights?

The Volatile Couple

A volatile couple has no problem expressing emotion—it's completely natural for them. Their fights immediately move into heated debate, with high emotion and raised voices, but often with a lot of humor and positivity as well. The complete opposite of avoidant couples, these couples tend to have plenty of overlap in their roles and responsibilities domestically and within the relationships, and they debate and verbally wrestle over them frequently. They might even seem to enjoy arguing—for volatiles this is, in part, how they connect.

In the very first longitudinal study we ever ran at the Love Lab, we had this particularly charismatic—and *very* volatile—couple we nicknamed "the Duke and Duchess of Windsor." The duke and duchess seemed to relish fighting. They had absolutely no problem with the conflict task: they got an A+ on picking a topic and launching right into heated conflict. They had no trouble addressing conflictual topics head on—in one fight in particular, as they argued over whether or not they'd had a "good" marriage for the thirty years they'd been together, the duke asked his wife, "Would we have had a better marriage without children?"

"How could you say that?" she cried. "Of *course*! Those kids turned me into a drudge!"

He burst out laughing—and then so did she. Then they resumed wrangling over the ups and downs of their marriage, excitedly disagreeing and debating. For a conflict avoider, just watching them interact would have made your heart race.

The duke and duchess were overall a happy couple—their fights could be explosive, but like a lot of successful volatile couples, their conflict was defined by humor, which kept things fairly positive. They understood how to make repairs and stay connected, and they made it for the long haul, reporting high levels of satisfaction on follow-ups.

Volatile couples can do well, but they are at risk for what we call "the Richardson Arms Race" in conflict. Lewis Fry Richardson was

the mathematician who modeled the military escalation that pre-
ceded World War I[2]—in brief, it's a phenomenon where two nations
increase preparations for war in response to a perception that the
other party is increasing their preparation for war, leading to an ex-
ponential buildup of aggression. With a volatile couple who loses
their humor and positivity and escalates negativity and aggression,
they can end up in this "arms race" dynamic—now you have screaming, yelling, flooding from one or both partners; later, the volatile
couple might describe the fight as "out of control." In the case of two
people in a relationship, the "weapons" are metaphorical, but the ex-
ponential buildup into battle is real and can do real damage.

Which Conflict Style Is the Best?

Looking at these conflict profiles, it's natural to conclude that the
"validating" style of conflict is the healthiest and that couples who
tend to be volatile or avoidant are less likely to be successful. And
indeed, in the field of couples therapy, this was long believed to
be true.

Is it?

In the1960s, Harold Raush, a biologist who taught at the University of Massachusetts Amherst, launched the first-ever study on the
transition to parenthood.[3] He recruited ninety-six couples and followed them, using observational research methods, as they became
pregnant and had their first baby. He didn't feel comfortable having
them talk about their own conflict—it felt too intimate, perhaps, and
this type of study had never been done before. Instead, he had them
talk about a simulated conflict. The technique he used was this: Each
couple would get a short written vignette of a couple in conflict. The
husband (these were all heterosexual couples) received one slanted

toward the fictional husband; the wife got one slanted toward the fictional wife. They each read their vignette and then were asked to discuss who was more at fault. Essentially, he was setting them up for conflict by intentionally biasing each toward his or her fictional counterpart. He called it "the Inventory of Marital Conflicts."

When he broke down the conflict conversations that emerged from this exercise, Raush did something that had never been done before: he analyzed *sequences* of conversation. He didn't just look at how frequently people did one particular thing, but how frequently a pattern of two-step sequences would appear. This was before John began his research, and it was the most granular analysis of couples' behavior that had been done to date. What Raush concluded from the data from his ninety-six couples—and he wrote a book about it—was that validators were the only truly successful models for relationships, where they could both stay together for the long haul *and* be satisfied with their union. Avoiders were messed up because they never talked about anything. Volatiles were messed up because they were much too emotional. Validators, he decided, were the "Goldilocks" of relationships: just right.

When John began his own research in the same arena, he considered that Raush might be correct. And John did identify the same three profiles of avoidant, validating, and volatile couples—this all tracked. But when John began analyzing their data using the SPAFF coding system—a more sophisticated system than Raush's groundbreaking two-step pattern identification process—he found that it just wasn't true that validators were the only successful couples. According to John's data, *any* of the three styles had an equal shot at being "masters" of love *if they had the 5:1 ratio of positive to negative interactions in conflict.* It seemed that success or failure in a relationship had more to do with the ratio than it did with conflict style—in direct opposition to Raush's finding.

John's response? He called up Harold Raush. Raush, intrigued, and ever the open-minded scientist, agreed to send over all of his audiotapes from the original study. John reanalyzed Raush's raw data with the new coding system and found that the finding held true for Raush's couples as well. The coding system used in the earlier study had simply not been finely grained enough to pick up a critical truth buried in the data: it had nothing to do with which "style" you were.[4]

It was all about the ratio.

Lessons from the Museum of Fights: The Ratio Is Real!

The Exploratorium, San Francisco's renowned science museum, sits on the edge of a pier overlooking the bay. Inside, it is a huge warehouse-like space, creatively lit and divided into separate, rotating exhibits. One popular exhibit was a kind of "museum of fights" based on a study run by John's research partner, Robert Levenson.[5] The exhibit was interactive, with television screens that showed you, the visitor, half a dozen three-minute recordings of married couples, each having a fight—or, more accurately, having the *beginning* of a fight. Your job was to watch each video and then make an assessment: Would this couple go on to divorce or stay together? And how satisfied was the couple with their union overall? At baseline, making a blind guess, you had a fifty-fifty chance of being right: exactly half of the couples in the Exploratorium exhibit had split, and the other half had remained together and satisfied with their marriage.

What do you think? Could *you* tell?

The answer is, probably not—unless you'd been married very recently . . . or recently divorced.

When Levenson ran the study, we'd already done the SPAFF coding. We knew we could predict, with over 90 percent accuracy, the future of these relationships using our coding system. SPAFF could easily discern who would get divorced and who wouldn't. But how did that compare to therapists, researchers, and couples themselves—could they intuit the future of a relationship just as well?

Not even close! Levenson brought in couples therapists and had them predict, and they were at chance—their guesses were no better than flipping a coin. Then he brought in researchers in the field, and they were no better. Then he brought in couples, and it was the same. But one group was notably better than others at predicting satisfaction: newlyweds and recent divorcees. One theory: Those who had been recently divorced *were more attuned to negative interactions.* They picked up on even the most subtle ones—ones that everybody else missed. We're back to the ratio. People who'd just split up were like a divining rod for that 5:1 ratio—highly sensitive to that tilt into negativity, they zoomed right in on it.[6]

We talked briefly about this "magic ratio" in the last chapter, and how so many of our fights that veer in a bad direction usually do so because they've ended up on the wrong side of this simple math equation. Let's take a closer look at what exactly that means.

The Magic Ratio: The Secret to Success for (Almost) Any Conflict Style

The data has shown repeatedly that there is no one "right" conflict style. Any of the types of couples we profiled here can thrive—as long as they have the correct *conflict math.* If you have that 5:1 ratio of positive to negative interactions, you're probably going to do great, no matter what type of couple you are. What that means, precisely: for every *one* negative interaction you and your partner have during a fight (like a biting comment, an eye roll, a raised voice, a dismissive tone or gesture, a scoff or a mocking laugh), you need *five* positive interactions to balance out that negativity. And this is *within the conflict itself!* Outside of conflict, that ratio swells to 20:1—for every single negative interaction or comment, you need *twenty* positives (appreciation, connection, turning toward, compliments, etc.) to balance out the negativity over time. Of course, positivity is harder during conflict. We're fighting! But the data from the Love Lab is clear: we have to manage it. Couples that failed to meet that 5:1 ratio consistently did not make it in the long term.[7]

Add Positivity to Your Fights!

Positive interactions include:

An apology

A smile

A nod

Empathizing

A reassuring physical touch

Validating something your partner has said

Emphasizing what you and your partner have in common

Owning responsibility for your part in a problem

Saying "Good point" or "Fair enough"

Pointing out what you both do right

Recalling your past successes in conflict

A joke, laughter

The simple truth is that, in conflict, the negative carries a lot more weight than the positive. There's a reason it's 5:1 and not 1:1— these interactions are not equal, and they don't balance out that easily. Negativity packs a big punch. And you don't have to sit down in a research lab and code your fights to know if you and your partner are on the wrong side of that ratio—if it feels to you that your fights have been veering into territory where it's more negative than positive (a common situation for many couples), then you're probably right. Your conflict math is off. So one of the things we're going to be working on in this book as we move through strategies for having successful conflict is *imbuing your fights with more positive interactions.* This is going to be a throughline across all the lab-tested interventions we take you through here, and the conflict strategies we work on here are all, in part, designed to help you ratchet up the positive and spool down the negative, even midfight. It's so important, for both the health of your relationship overall and the success of your fights, to hit the magic ratio, and it is possible from almost any starting point to turn things around and get there.

A note here: we are not suggesting that you whip out a notepad and pencil midfight and start tallying the number of negative and positive interactions! You're *in* the conflict conversation with your partner, not a researcher with a thousand hours of videotape and a "pause" button. Any kind of overt counting is going to take you right out of the conversation. You're not going to know the precise math for each conflict conversation you and your partner have. But what we know about couples is this: you can feel which side of the ratio you're on. Check in with yourself. Even if you're upset about the issue—Do you feel listened to? Have you had moments where you felt relieved, understood? Has there been a laugh, or some lightness, in the conversation?

When things start to tilt negative, you'll know. Conflict doesn't feel great even when it's going well—it can be stressful and upsetting to be in disagreement with your partner, even when the ratio is just right. But when the ratio is off, it starts to feel *really* bad. There's escalation, the Four Horsemen; you may start to feel trapped and hopeless; you may feel enraged or out of control. And when you feel that spike of negativity, you can do something about it. You can make the effort to slow things down, inject some empathy or validation into the conversation, or any of the other ideas in the box on page 51. You can even call it out overtly and say, "I feel like this is going in the wrong direction—Can we reset?" (More on this later.)

Now, in practice, the magic ratio is going to look and feel a bit different depending on your conflict style. If you and your partner tend to be more **conflict avoidant,** it might look initially like you're nailing it. On paper, your ratio looks incredible: you're at 10:1, maybe even 15:1. You're all positive, no negativity at all! Bulletproof, right? Well, no—your ratio looks this great only because you're not bringing up complaints or issues. You're skirting around points of conflict, which could catch up with you later. Avoidant couples can do just fine *until there's a crisis.*

Researchers and professors Rand Conger and Glen Elder did a deep sociological investigation into the dynamics of farming families in America during the farm crisis of the 1980s, when the rural Midwest went into a sudden and steep economic decline. Thousands of farmers lost their farms and businesses, and thriving towns emptied out into hollow shells of what they had been. Conger and Elder examined the effects of these extreme pressures and stresses on individuals and on relationships within families. Many of these couples—rural, midwestern, raised in a particular culture—typified an "avoidant" conflict style. One thing they noted: these couples, who were now forced into high-conflict conversations for maybe the first time ever (as they had to debate what to do when the bank was pulling in an outstanding loan, for instance), would go one of two ways. The ones who were able to maintain that 5:1 ratio in discussions about what to do actually got happier, even during this intense financial crisis. The family pulled together, reaffirmed all the positive factors in their lives, and stayed largely conflict avoidant but weathered the crisis well. The couples who did *not* maintain the ratio, in contrast, really struggled, quickly growing distant and disconnected. In these couples, researchers observed, the husband would actually move farther and farther down the dinner table each night, away from his wife. He *physically drifted* away as the two drifted emotionally as well.[8]

This mirrors what we've seen clinically in the COVID-19 era: couples (of all conflict styles) who went into the pandemic on solid ground, with a good foundation of friendship and fondness, did well, maybe even better than usual. Meanwhile, couples who had some underlying issues really suffered. There was this sharp divergence, where couples in stable relationships pulled together more tightly, and couples who were going through a rough patch were suddenly doing really terribly. Picture that extra bit of pressure on a crack in a stone foundation—that point of weakness, which might have been holding up just fine, is going to shatter.

The danger with avoidant couples is that it's less visible: they don't have explosive (volatile) or tense (validating) fights like other couples, so the emotional drift can happen quietly, without anybody noticing the building crisis. Suddenly, these avoidant couples are in a situation where they don't have the 5:1; they're disconnected, and they don't know what to do about it. They're those couples you see coming into a restaurant and not talking for the whole meal. Even if they want to reconnect, they don't know how.

If you and your partner are trending toward the avoidant style, know this: our data shows that you two can do great. And getting to that magic ratio will probably be relatively easy for you—since negativity is less likely to be expressed, a little bit of intentional positivity goes a long way. But learning to get a bit more comfortable with conflict is really going to help you. It'll allow you to learn more about each other and get closer, which is truly a wonderful thing, and will guard against the drift and disconnect that can threaten avoidant couples in particular. Getting more conflict-savvy will help your relationship be more resilient and float over the rougher waves in life that will inevitably come along.

Validators, meanwhile, will need to make sure that their expressions of affirmation, love, and warmth continue to outpace the tension and negativity that will naturally occur in a fight. Let's face it: conflict has a purpose and can lead to great things, but it's not going to be all rainbows and roses while you're getting there. Validators, who can be quite rational and calm in conflict, can nevertheless get focused on logistics and lose track of the positivity piece. Don't get so fixated on getting to compromise that you forget that *how you get there* is a critical part of the process. Remember to keep positivity high throughout with the suggestions from the box on page 51. It doesn't take much, but it does take intentionality.

What to Watch Out For...

Avoiders: emotional drift and distance; too much focus on positivity to the point that the issue is not addressed

Validators: rising negativity; don't get so focused on a solution you forget about positivity, humor, and connection

Volatiles: don't let your humor go dark, sarcastic, or critical

By contrast, **volatile** partnerships will need a *lot* of positivity to keep the scales tipped in the right direction! We just saw a successful model of this with the Duke and Duchess of Windsor, who had a lot of overt verbal sparring in their relationship—reminiscent of two athletic fencers, in a lot of ways—but also a lot of humor and empathizing. Their fights would boil over into passionate overlapping debate and even shouting, but you also heard outbursts of genuine laughter followed by "That's a good point!" Volatiles do need to keep an eye on their humor, however—when these couples start to become unhappy, the humor can turn dark. If the humor turns mean-spirited, tinged with sarcasm, it is no longer a force for positivity in the interaction. *Contempt,* one of the Four Horsemen, is never going to serve you in conflict, and for volatiles, it can ride in in the guise of humor.

Now, there are two final conflict styles we've identified in studying couples that we did not include in the list of healthy and potentially successful styles above, for the simple reason that these styles can never be successful. They are **hostile** and **hostile-detached.**

Hostile couples look more like validators than like volatiles—they are less expressive, more neutral. But instead of being collaborative, they are highly defensive. Partners repeat their own perspective but don't express curiosity, listen, or problem-solve. There are a lot of "you always" and "you never" accusations. They are frequently contemptuous of each other.

One couple we worked with had drifted far into hostile territory by the time they arrived in our office. This was a man and woman who'd been married for over fifteen years. The guy—we'll call him Bill—was the passive, quiet type. His wife, Bobbi, was more fiery. It was apparent that once, when they'd had a healthier dynamic, she'd been somewhat of the pursuer, seeking out connection and engagement from him—maybe even playfully teasing to get a rise out of him, to spark a little tiff so they could wrangle over something. Now that dynamic had turned mean-spirited and aggressive.

Bobbi would provoke Bill over any little thing, poking and prodding until his anger went through the roof and he suddenly blew up, shattering his calm facade—and then she'd record him with her phone. She had a whole digital library of recordings of him absolutely losing it. She'd come into therapy brandishing these videos, insisting that we watch, that it was proof of how awful he was. One day, they arrived in full-blown crisis. The situation was this: Bill had gotten Bobbi a birthday gift. He had bought her a huge can of very special, gourmet peanuts that he had sourced from a company based halfway around the world that was known to produce the very best peanuts.

Except: she was allergic to peanuts.

They weren't sleeping in the same bedroom at this point, so she went into his room, unmade his bed, spread the peanuts out on the mattress, and made it up again. When he went to bed, he found himself lying down on a crunchy bed of all these fancy peanuts he'd given her. And when he burst into her room, yelling, what did she do?

She pulled out her phone to record.

In the session, he defended himself, claiming that he'd never known she was allergic, that he'd gone to these great lengths to get these very specific nuts that were grown in a far-flung part of the world and beautifully packaged. She was enraged—a major theme with this couple was that from her perspective, he seemed to struggle to remember anything she told him, while at work he was praised for his incredible memory and attention to detail. Did he know she was allergic and had he done it on purpose, or had he truly never paid any attention to her? From her perspective, they were both bad.

This couple was at the point where their conflicts showed all Four Horsemen—criticism, contempt, defensiveness, and stonewalling (from the husband, once he became totally overwhelmed)—and *zero* positivity. Hostile couples can have volatile fights, but the difference between a hostile couple and a volatile couple is that the hostile couple has little to no positivity. The ratio is completely broken. It's not 5:1 positive to negative. It's not even half and half. It's almost completely negative. Their fights may look volatile, but they are in fact devoid of all the qualities that make volatile couples successful: the love, the humor, the connection, the deep engagement with what the other wants and needs.

And it doesn't have to be quite so obvious as peanuts in the sheets. Another couple we worked with had been trapped in a cycle of conflict over the issue of sex for so long that their dynamic had become highly hostile. He was a surgeon who worked long hours and was rarely home, but he wanted more of a sensual, sexual relationship and needed that in order to feel close to her; she was a mom who was on her own with the kids a lot and needed to feel close to him in order to be sexual. This is not an uncommon dynamic between men and women, but it's one that can be successfully navigated with a lot of turning toward and daily connection. This couple, though, had lost the capacity to connect on this issue—or any other.

Neither had had their needs met by the other in a very long time; both were afraid of rejection, neither felt safe, and they responded to those feelings by trying to tear each other down. Their fights were volatile, sure, but they were also incredibly hostile—devoid of any positive interactions and laced through with contempt, criticism, and defensiveness.

Him: You're cold as ice. You don't even have any sexuality anymore. I'm not even sure you're a woman!

Her: How dare you! You're gone all the time while I'm raising your children—you like your patients unconscious, don't you? I bet you'd love it if I were unconscious so you could just fuck me!

The difference, again, is the ratio: these fights are escalating, as can happen with volatile or even validating couples, but they have none of the positivity—the moments of validation, humor, empathy, or repair—that healthy volatile couples display.

So, what does it *feel* like to be in a hostile dynamic versus a healthy volatile one?

Well, with both volatile and validating couples, there's always the risk that the conflict may begin to spiral into predominantly negative interactions. We are human! We get overwhelmed and angry; we do lash out unfairly. The critical difference is that with healthy conflict styles, *repair still functions.* One or both parties slows things down. They intentionally defuse any building hostility with an infusion of positivity—anything from an overt apology, to a simple nod of "Okay, I see your point," to a little inside joke that breaks the rising tension. When couples are in the hostile dynamic, they instead seem to relish the spirals of negativity. They never pull out of it or even try to—there are no repair attempts, not even failed ones.

Healthy volatile couples express a lot of emotion—anger, sadness, frustration. They might be furious at times; they might cry. The volume goes up! This can all be part of the volatile tapestry. Hostile couples are *almost always* using the Four Horsemen: contempt mostly, then criticism and defensiveness. Hostile conflict feels like a boxing match: Who's going to land the knockout punch?

Meanwhile, hostile-detached couples have drifted even further apart. They don't even bother arguing. They'll swipe at each other during conflict, but they are at the point where mostly they just don't care anymore.

A couple in their midfifties came in to see us in a last-ditch effort to save their marriage. They weren't sure if there was anything left to salvage but wanted to explore every possibility before calling it quits. They'd been together a long time. Their children were now grown and off to college; they both worked full time—he was an engineer, she an accountant—and it seemed that their lives had increasingly become more and more separate. As they discussed this in our office, their conversation was barbed and bitter but never escalated into an actual fight—there was not enough passion for that.

"You know what," she said, "even with all the years we've been together, I don't think you know very much about me at all."

Her husband was quiet, withdrawn. He had a habit of touching his mouth while he considered his retort. "I'd say that's true of both of us," he finally replied.

"Do you have any idea how lonely that makes me feel?"

"You think I'm not lonely?" he said. "I've just learned to live with it."

"You're just an unfeeling person," she said, matter-of-factly. "You always have been. I guess that's who I married: the cold-hearted engineer. You only think about yourself. You probably should have just lived alone and never gotten married. Now here we are—married twenty years, with two kids, and it's all coming apart and you don't even care."

"That's true," he replied flatly. "I guess I really don't."

This was how all their conversations went: they were each wrapped up in their own pain, had very little empathy for each other, and didn't even care enough to actually fight. When she tried to provoke him by saying, *You don't care,* he didn't rise to the provocation. He just agreed.

Hostile-detached couples have lost even *conflict* as a bridge to connection—the relationship has become a war of attrition with both sides worn down over time. Now there's a vast no-man's-land between them. They take shots at each other occasionally from across the divide, but there is no healthy conflict here.

Can these couples come back from the brink? Perhaps. In the two examples of "hostile" dynamic couples, the first was unsalvageable, while the second made a lot of progress in therapy with support; the "hostile-detached" couple, above, decided to part ways. But with either dynamic, a more significant intervention is required. Ongoing hostility may have all but destroyed "Marriage #1." The only way to move forward may be to think of that relationship as "over" and do the work to create a new one. You'll need professional support in order to re-create a healthy relationship, based on trust, commitment, and friendship, from the ground up. A well-trained therapist can help you start over and build "Marriage #2" on more solid foundations. (If you need help finding someone, the Gottman Referral Network, at www.gottmanreferralnetwork.com, is a free database that puts you directly in touch with therapists in your area who have been trained in the Gottman Method and use data-informed Gottman relationship-building techniques.)

Regardless of where you are on the healthy "conflict style" spectrum—and some of us are a bit of a mix (validators who trend toward the volatile, or vice versa)—we all need to make it a habit to inject our conflict discussions with kindness and positivity whenever we can. Ultimately, any of the three main conflict styles can be happy and successful, providing they keep that math equation healthy.

Where things can get a bit trickier is when couples have distinct conflict styles—or, to put it more scientifically, when they have a *meta-emotion mismatch.*

The Meta-emotion Mismatch: A Recipe for Misunderstandings

How do you express emotion? How do you deal with your own emotions? How do you think others should deal with theirs?

The term *meta-emotion* basically refers to how we *feel about feelings.* When couples are not aligned on conflict style, they often have what we call a "meta-emotion mismatch," which is different beliefs about how emotions should be expressed and handled. Tyler and Noah, the couple we met earlier in the chapter, are a perfect example: One (Noah, who tends to shut down and stonewall Tyler during a heated argument) believes that negative emotions should be avoided. The other (Tyler, who feels iced out and rejected by his partner's refusal to engage with him on issues that come up) believes they should be expressed and explored. That's a mismatch.

What we have here is a classic example of an avoider with a volatile. To a volatile, an avoider seems detached and uncaring. They interpret the avoider's behavior as "This is not important enough to me to engage." Volatiles like Tyler are looking for passion—they want their partner to become vulnerable, and they want it right away. At the same time, this is *exactly* what the avoider is avoiding. They prefer not talking about things, keeping a distance from conflict.

Across the forty thousand couples in our international study, this was a huge one: 83 percent of all heterosexual couples were experiencing issues due to a meta-emotion mismatch, followed closely behind by gay couples (77 percent) and lesbian couples (73 percent).[9] Most couples coming to us for support were struggling with this. But interestingly, John, working in the Love Lab, didn't see mismatches at quite such a high rate—within the population of study participants (who weren't opting into therapy but simply drawn from the general population), many turned out to be aligned on their conflict style, perhaps part of the reason they fell in love to begin with: sharing an emotional "language." Meanwhile, Julie, working clinically with couples who were seeking therapy, would see mismatches all the time. A likely explanation for this is that couples with a meta-emotion mismatch are self-selecting into therapy, because they've hit a point in the relationship where they're really having trouble getting through to each other. In short: a meta-emotion mismatch may make it harder for two people to communicate in conflict.

But not all mismatches are created equal. Let's take a peek into each.

Avoidant-Validator

An avoidant partner with a validator probably won't run into too many problems due to the mismatch, because these styles are fairly compatible in terms of their "feelings about feelings."

In this couple, Hans was the avoider; Beth was the validator. He had been born and raised in Germany; growing up, his parents never fought in front of him. There was one person in his family, his paternal grandfather, who was volatile: he was a heavy drinker who would scream and yell if the grandkids ever did anything wrong. Hans learned to avoid him, and he learned to avoid conflict too. Into adulthood, marriage, and parenthood, he believed in stepping around points of friction. He was afraid that even the most mild of conflicts might quickly get out of control and blow up. Better not to engage on the topic at all.

Beth had a validating style toward conflict—she was a problem solver. She'd grown up in a family that tended to approach conflicts with a managerial, logistical style: "Let's figure out a way to make everyone happy as efficiently as possible." She navigated discussions calmly—and sure, sometimes a little bit of emotion might seep in. She had noticed over time, however, that Hans would be alarmed by even the tiniest bit of frustration or voice-raising from her during a logistical discussion over, say, choosing a vacation destination; he would quickly disengage, put off the conversation for later. She tried to keep discussions even-keeled and calm, knowing that her husband was more likely to engage productively if she kept emotion out of it.

Generally, things went fairly smoothly—until one of their kids ran into some trouble in school. He'd been distracted, acting out in class. Beth felt the teacher was taking a terrible approach with him— shaming, punishing, and making their child even more rebellious and defiant. But she wasn't sure what to do or how to address it. She didn't relish confrontation and, like her husband, preferred conflict discussions to stay calm. She was afraid that the conversation with this teacher would not go well and that she'd get overwhelmed. But at the same time, she couldn't let it go—their son needed their support.

Hans was completely against any intervention. His attitude was "Let the kid deal with it himself; he'll just have to figure it out." Lurking underneath that facade, though, was a deep-seated fear of confrontation and conflict.

Beth was frustrated. She was intimidated by the teacher too. She needed backup from her husband and co-parent—and he wasn't willing to touch it with a ten-foot pole.

When they came in to see us about this issue, we immediately went into their backgrounds to get to the root of the problem. We explored why he was terrified of rage—how his family experiences early on had turned into conflict avoidance now. This was the first Beth had heard of it—she understood now why he reacted so strongly to her voice rising even one degree. And she talked about her own fear: that if this teacher got really angry at her for trying to manage how she dealt with their kid, she would just shut down or cave in. As a validator, she was easily overwhelmed by high emotion or volatility.

"I just want you to be there with me so that she sees we are a team," Beth explained. "I can do this, but I can't do it alone. Two is better than one."

Swayed by her argument, Hans agreed to go along as backup— Beth would take the lead, and he would echo, a role that he was slightly more comfortable with, though it still made him nervous. As it turned out, the meeting went smoothly with the two presenting a unified front—Beth was diplomatic, the teacher was fairly receptive, the conversation was productive. None of their fears about explosive conflict came to pass.

This couple may have had two different styles, but with a little nudge from us, they were able to stretch toward each other. Avoiders and validators have a good amount of overlap in terms of approach to conflict; with some awareness of each other's style and history with conflict, they can do great.

Validator-Volatile

In the validator-volatile mismatch, the validator may feel overwhelmed and flooded by the volatile's high-emotion style of engagement; meanwhile, the volatile, frustrated at not being able to get through, doubles down, raises the volume, and sometimes turns mean-spirited.

Derek and Tamara, a young couple with a nine-year-old son, had just moved to rural Tennessee from Atlanta. The property had a woodpile out back, where their son loved to play and build forts. One day, he came screaming into the house to Tamara: he'd been bitten by a snake.

Tamara, who tended to be volatile, absolutely hit the roof. She was terrified—even after the doctor cleaned the bite and confirmed that it had not been a poisonous snake. Next time, it *could* be.

"There are probably snakes everywhere out there!" she yelled at her husband practically the minute he walked in the door. "What are you going to do about it? Why didn't you move that woodpile already? It never should have been that close to the house!"

Derek took a rational approach: not avoidant, but logical.

"Honey, it's very unlikely that it's going to happen again," he pointed out. "I understand you're freaked out, but I think it's going to be okay. I'll move the woodpile this weekend, and in the meantime, let's reasonably think of a solution—maybe just don't let him play out there until I get to it?"

"I don't want to be reasonable!" she raged back. "This is our son's *life* we're talking about! Are you willing to have our son face *death*?"

"Tamara, let's not be dramatic—"

"Oh, this is being dramatic? Trying to protect our kid, when you can't make ten minutes in your busy schedule to move some wood? *When* are you going to do it?"

"I'll get to it this weekend, Tamara, Jesus."

"We never should have moved here!"

At this point Derek, overwhelmed and running out of ideas for how to respond to her, begins to disengage.

With some validator-volatile combos, this dynamic can escalate over time. The volatile, not getting the response they desire across a pattern of conflicts, resorts to hostility more frequently and grows increasingly negative, trying to break through; in response, the validator becomes more and more detached; nobody is reaching each other at all anymore. If this goes on, we can see rising contempt and stonewalling; now we're in hostile territory.

This couple, however, had a strong friendship overall, though they were suffering a bit from not having enough time with each other lately—his new job had kept Derek away from home more than usual, and they were feeling the loss of time together. A little less opportunity for turning toward, a little more opportunity for conflict and misunderstanding. And because she was volatile, Tamara wanted immediate high engagement on the issue—when she didn't get that from Derek, who took the approach of trying to defuse the situation, she escalated.

To keep things on track for them, we had to work with Derek on really putting himself in her shoes, what it meant to be a mother and the primary caretaker at home, and what it was like to feel this immense vulnerability and fear. His validating style drove him to try to calm down the fight as his primary objective: he focused less on understanding her perspective and more on calming and facilitating her. He was steady and reassuring, but she needed someone to be worried *with* her so she didn't feel so alone. When he shifted tactics during conflict to be more validating (ironic, but yes, the validator needed to learn how to truly validate!), it was really effective. Tamara still had more of a volatile style and tended to be more high emotion than Derek, but when he acknowledged the concerns she raised, it brought the temperature of the argument way down, into a range where Derek wasn't liable to get so overwhelmed.

The validator-volatile combo has its challenges, but this couple was able to thrive.

Volatile-Avoidant

The volatile-avoidant mismatch is, to be perfectly honest, the toughest. Here the avoidant partner is often initially drawn to the volatile's vivacious energy (see also "Opposites attract"!), but when they get together, the dark side comes out. They don't speak each other's language at all. They usually break up quickly; this combo has a high divorce rate.[10] If they stay together, they are at a high risk of turning hostile.

Dave, for instance, was volatile—a high conflict engager. He was comfortable with conflict, even sought it out. To him, it was its own legitimate form of interaction. He found a bit of conflict fun, exciting, even erotic. His wife, Lila, meanwhile, was more avoidant. Deeply uncomfortable with conflict, she tended to freeze up or feel attacked when he attempted to engage with her in a playfully combative way. When she didn't respond the way he'd hoped, he'd start teasing. He saw it as funny! And another volatile, in a similar circumstance, probably would have agreed and teased right back. For Lila, it did not work at all. She found it insulting, felt cornered and attacked. When she overpaid at a valet parking lot one night, he razzed her on the way home.

"You just let them walk all over you; don't be such a wimp next time!" he said. "Isn't this supposed to be the age of women's liberation? Didn't you tell me you were a feminist? Don't be such a scaredy-cat!"

Her, softly: "Don't say that."

Undeterred, he continued to poke. "Sure you are," he went on. "Like a cute little mouse! You're a scaredy-cat in the bedroom too, you know."

She turned her back and looked out the window. His teasing was an attack to her; her silence, to him, was a cold rejection. What he wanted, as a volatile, was for her to jab back, something like *You come too quickly for us to have any fun!* He might be a little wounded by that remark, but that spark of fight would entice him: *Aha, now we're talking!*

As it was, this mismatch was too difficult—they could not be good partners to each other. She experienced his way of interacting as cruel; he experienced her as cold and shut off.

In short, some meta-emotion mismatches present more of a challenge than others, and it's helpful to think about where you and your partner might fall on the conflict style spectrum. The farther apart two people are in that range of beliefs regarding *how* and *when* and *whether* emotion should be experienced and expressed, the more likely they are to hit rough waters during conflict—simply because on a deep level, they want to communicate so differently and have fundamentally polarized beliefs about what conflict even *is*. To one, conflict is to be avoided at all costs, something that triggers flooding and extreme overwhelm; to the other, conflict is an essential way to workshop issues and get closer. This is a culture clash issue; they are not speaking the same language.

The data shows that usually (unless things have drifted into "hostile" territory, which is a different story) we are not *trying* to hurt each other in conflict. In one of our Love Lab studies, we set out to measure the correlation between *intent* and *impact*. When people were being critical or contemptuous, when they hurt their partners and caused them to feel flooded, did they intend to do so? Were they trying to wound each other?

Overwhelmingly the answer to that was *no*.

We filmed conflict conversations and then asked the participating couple to review the tape of their own fight while sitting at a control board where they could turn a dial to record their assessments of each beat of the fight in the two categories of intent and impact. They had to rate the impact their partner had on them in terms of how positively or negatively that comment or action had affected them; meanwhile the partner was rating his or her intention in that moment. What we found: *intention did not match impact.*[11] People in conflict almost never had a malevolent intent. They were all just trying to be understood.

Divergent feelings about feelings are one of the most core, foundational "culture clashes" you can experience in a romantic partnership. It shapes everything profoundly—including your fights. And all conflict styles diverge in one specific and very influential way: how they approach *persuasion,* one of the three "stages" of a fight.

The Stages of a Fight

Every fight has the same basic structure, and it looks like this:

- First, we **build an agenda:** one or both partners express their concerns.
- Second, we try to **persuade** each other to come over to our side.
- And third, we attempt to reach a **compromise.**

Agenda, persuasion, and *attempt at compromise:* those are the three phases of a fight. Where all of our fighting styles differ is on *persuasion.*

The avoidant fighter wants to skip persuasion entirely—in their mind, there's little point to it. "That's a sinkhole," they think. "I'm not going to convince them; better just move on." The volatile fighter, meanwhile, wants to start with persuasion, skimming over the part where they listen to their partner's point of view. Validators go more methodically through the phases but will frequently get into persuasion a little too soon and may be too worried about keeping things nice to go deep enough. They're able to postpone persuasion a bit longer than volatile couples but quite often can't manage to hold off long enough to actually explore the issues.

Let's take one classic scenario: a fight about money. He's been spending more than she's comfortable with, and she's getting stressed.

If they're validators, here's what that might look like:

THE ANATOMY OF A FIGHT

Her: I was looking through the checking account last night, and I see a lot of extra expenses coming out. Looks like we're going to be tight again this month. Did we really have to buy this camping gear?	*Building an agenda*
Him: Well yeah, we made plans with the Davises to do that weekend trip, remember? The kids all needed sleeping bags.	
Her: I know, it just seems like there's always something. We keep saying we're going to save, and then we never do.	
Him: Come on, are we really spending all that much? I know we need to save a little, but what are we going to do—never have any fun?	
Her: I would love it if we could save a *little*, but honey, we're not really saving anything at all.	
Him: Have I ever told you about my uncle Brody? Nobody knew he was a multimillionaire. Brody, he just saved and saved. He was aloof from the family. He'd be at gatherings, but he was this quiet guy, just fading into the wallpaper. Finally, he retired at age fifty, but suddenly had a heart attack and died! Turned out, he'd saved five million dollars and never spent a dime on himself. Lived in a studio apartment, never traveled. He had this great job with Microsoft, lots of stock. Never got to enjoy it!	*Persuasion*
Her: Okay, well, what about my mom and dad? They'd spend on frivolous stuff, and then when we really needed something—like that time our car engine melted down and we needed to fix it—we couldn't afford it. We were always behind and never had enough. It was so stressful. I can't live like that. I don't need to be like your uncle Brody, but I want to save for travel and adventure.	
Him: Well, now you contradicted yourself—are we saving for the future or saving for travel and adventure? I hate thinking about money all day long and pinching pennies. I don't want to live like *that*.	

Her: Okay, okay, I hear you, but you can't just spend whatever you want whenever you want to. We have more on the credit card this month than we can pay off—that's a high interest rate, don't you know that? We're going to be paying for your morning lattes until we're dead. We have to come up with a spending plan we can stick to. **Him:** I'll try, but it can't be "Spend zero dollars this week." That's not reasonable. **Her:** What if we agree on an amount and take it out in cash at the beginning of the week—and when you run out, you stop spending. Can you do that?	*Attempt to reach compromise*

Notice that these validators have some tension, but they stay fairly calm. They each lay out their concerns, but then in the persuasion phase they don't take a lot of time to explore the deeper emotions they're each having about money, security, and what matters in life. They are interested in progressing to a solution. But because they're not talking about the underlying issues, this solution that they've arrived at fairly peacefully may not stick. They may find themselves having this exact same conversation next month, when the checking account is short again.

Now, how might other couples on the conflict style spectrum handle this?

- **With an avoidant couple** . . . this same fight would simply stop after the agenda-building box. They'll never progress to persuasion. Instead, they'll focus on the positives in their life and reassure each other that they really don't need to worry about this:

    Him: We aren't saving a lot right now, but look, we're both doing well at work, we're bound to get

promotions soon. We'll probably be able to start
saving next year.

Her: Yeah, that's true. We're doing okay. We do
own the house, even if we have a ways to go on the
mortgage, and paying a mortgage is kind of like a
savings account.

Him: The kids are looking forward to that camping
trip. I think it was an okay expense.

- **A volatile couple**... will barely spare the breath to build
an agenda—they *start* with persuasion!

   Her: I see you bought camping stuff even though I
   told you we were tight this month—when are we
   going to start saving? We agreed that we would put
   money aside every month! If we don't save now,
   we're going to die poor.

   Him: Hey, let me tell you about my uncle Brody!
   (tells story)

   Her: Sounds like Brody was an idiot! Just because
   he was dumb with his millions, we shouldn't save
   at all? That's nuts.

Volatiles go for immediate engagement and debate. For them,
persuasion is the only part of the fight that matters.

Two important points to make here:

Number one, most people across conflict styles (except for avoiders, who skip it) tend to rush to persuasion. They either leap right
into it (volatiles) or move quickly into attempts to persuade after the
issues have been laid out (validators). And yet, between building an
agenda and persuading each other, there needs to be a *lot* more ex-

ploration of each other's inner world—and that is something most of us do not know how to do within conflict.

The Three Conflict Styles and Persuasion

Avoiders: No attempt to persuade; "agree to disagree"

Validators: Will lay out the issues first ("building an agenda") but move too quickly to persuasion

Volatiles: Begin with persuasion; want immediate engagement and debate from partner

And number two: you can see how these different approaches to persuasion are likely to cause miscommunications and strife. While a more avoidant person will see *any* attempt at persuasion as an attack, a more volatile partner may interpret a refusal to respond to persuasion as a rejection or an intentional, cold turning away.

A Mismatch Is Not a Deal-breaker!

If this is sounding grim, we want to pause here and reassure you: if you suspect that you and your partner have a meta-emotion mismatch, *you are not doomed.* Always remember that we are humans— not labels. You may have one clear, strong conflict style, or you may be something of a blend of two, a gradient. The same goes for your partner. We offer these generalized profiles not to suggest that if you have a meta-emotion mismatch it's the end of the road, but instead so that you are informed, so that you can reflect on your own beliefs about emotions and your own approach to conflict and think about how that's allowing you to connect meaningfully with your partner or keeping you from doing so. Take Tyler and Noah—a couple who were indeed able to reach each other across the gulf of their different conflict cultures once they realized that gulf was there. Imagine if two people sat down to play a board game and were handed two completely different sets of rules.

So where do these beliefs about emotion come from?

With Tyler and Noah, if you took a peek into their pasts, here's what you'd see. Tyler, the volatile half of this couple, had grown up in a family that could be volatile during conflict but would quickly repair. The house he shared with his parents and siblings had frequent spats and explosions throughout the day, but each little storm passed quickly. In Tyler's family culture, conflict was normal—even *sought out* as a form of connection.

In Noah's family, people tended to avoid bringing up issues, preferring to just accept things the way they were rather than have to start a conversation that might be tense or unpredictable. His parents fought rarely, but when they did, it was bad. It escalated fast, and truly hurtful things were said—things that were hard to take back. It almost always ended with one of them storming out of the house. Once, his mother was gone for days, having left no word of where she was going or when she'd be back. He'd learned a firm and clear lesson: that conflict was to be avoided at all costs because the consequences of disagreement were simply too high.

Now, there's not a clear formula for exactly *why* we each end up as a volatile, validating, or avoidant fighter—we are each a unique mix of our neurology and our lifetime of experiences, and we each will react differently to the forces that shaped us. If someone grew up with parents who yelled when they fought, for instance, they might mimic that and become volatile as well, or they might go the other direction and become avoidant.

All of this prompts the question . . .

Can You Change Your Conflict Style?

The short answer: Yes! It takes a lot of work, but if a conflict style mismatch is really causing a lot of issues for you and your partner, it can be done. We can learn to stretch into other styles to meet our partners where they are.

However, you don't have to change your conflict style—the main thing for now is that you *understand* your current conflict style and your partner's, especially if it's different from yours. As you work toward understanding your partner's style, think of it as learning their language. And to understand your own, consider this: the way we were each raised has created deep tracks in our brain, sort of like ruts in wet cement. Given the right circumstances, our wheels will just fall right back into those old ruts. To change our conflict style, we have to carve out a new road, an alternate route to compromise.

Let's say we're very volatile, but we would like to become more of a validator. That's going to take learning how to pause and take a breath before speaking, then thinking hard about what we want to say and its impact on our partner, and deciding how to say what we need to say in a kinder way. Mindfulness and meditation are great tools that can teach us how to slow things down. When our responses have been downshifted to first gear, we'll have time to consider them carefully before blurting out the wrong words. It takes practice, but it's doable!

At the same time, there are all sorts of outside forces—cultural, societal, familial—that are going to be influencing our conflict styles over time. We see couples frequently who start out strongly one way (avoidant, validating, or volatile) and learn to stretch to include some of the qualities of another style. They are able to add a bit of "range" to their conflict style. There's a cultural context to this: for instance, with feminist advances, women have started to become more assertive and are allowing themselves to express anger, an emotion that has traditionally been reserved only for men. Women who were perhaps in the past socialized away from ever developing a volatile style are allowing themselves to embody those tendencies more fully.

The bottom line: when we see people in therapy, it's not because they're one conflict style or another. It's because they're not *happy* avoiders, validators, or volatiles. Conflict isn't working well. They've hit a wall, fights feel really, really bad, and they don't know how to fix it. Every couple is unique and their specific dynamic unrepeatable, but on a basic level there's usually one simple thing going wrong: *they're not listening to each other.* In contrast, when couples have at least the 5:1 ratio or more, they tend to be curious, open, and interested. But if positivity drops away, all that curiosity shuts down. They're attacking or defending, talking past each other. What it looks like is collective monologuing. There is a pervasive feeling on both sides of not getting through, like you're talking into a walkie-talkie and never getting anything back—no recognition, no understanding, nothing. And that feels really bad. So what we're going to do as we move through the five fights in this book is open up that iron curtain so that we *are* getting through to each other—no matter what our default "style" may be.

Take the two of us. We started out volatile. We're still fairly volatile. We have perhaps learned to be more validating over time—we both use validating strategies in conflict, and we find that it serves us well. But even after all these years, our *default* tends to be volatile—that's just where our wheels land.

If we look at why that's the case, it's a swirl of factors. Both of us are Jewish, and there's a saying, "Argument is Jewish love!" It comes from our cultural origins of valuing debate as a way to understand the meaning of our holy scriptures. There's no dogma to tell us what to think: we argue and debate all the time to work out core beliefs and interpretations of the text. It's woven into our heritage. Basically, we have a four-thousand-year history of being arguers.

In the early years of our marriage, our volatility led to some less-than-ideal outcomes: we'd fight, we'd shout, Julie would get flooded, blast out the door, and hit the streets (an old pattern from childhood), and John would be left frustrated, pacing the house. We both had these strong tendencies toward big emotions, leaping to persuasion, *winning the debate.* John had grown up in a family where the fiery debate had been fundamentally loving, but in Julie's that was less true—dinner table debate prioritized the men's opinions, and the women were told to shut up. And in everyday interactions, including conflict, Julie had an influential parent (her mother) who was often contemptuous and critical. That was the model of communication she'd grown up with.

One weekend, when we were just married, Julie had gone down to Portland for the weekend to visit her mother. This was before we had our daughter, Moriah, and Julie had recently experienced a miscarriage. She made the misstep of sharing this news with her mother, who immediately attacked her, suggesting the miscarriage was her fault. Julie drove back to Seattle seething and feeling stupid for having gone down there—she felt obligated and compelled to visit, but always came back from seeing her mother with this awful energy inside.

We'd agreed to meet up for dinner after the long weekend apart at a fancy seafood restaurant right on the shores of Lake Washington. It was a popular spot, crammed with tables, and that night, every single one was full. We were elbow to elbow with the other diners.

Right away, as if she were channeling her mother, Julie started criticizing John for having terrible table manners and picking up food with his fingers. John went defensive; a nasty fight—right there in the middle of the restaurant—was brewing. "Your manners are *awful*," Julie said, verging dangerously on contempt—all that bad feeling from the weekend with her mother leaking out into this moment. "I'm embarrassed to be with you in public."

John—facing a critical moment of decision—suddenly remembered this arcade he used to go to, long ago, when he was in college. One of the coin-operated arcade games had you draw a fake pistol against Wyatt Earp. If you drew faster than Wyatt, he'd say this particular line in his tinny robotic voice, which now flew into John's head, and so he stood up in the middle of the busy restaurant, theatrically grabbed his chest, said, "Nice shootin', partner! Ya got me!" and fell to the ground.

The entire restaurant went silent, shocked. A waiter rushed over, thinking John had had a heart attack.

Julie, meanwhile, was laughing so hard she was in tears.

And that was the end of that fight—over before it had begun.

We have always used humor to recover in fights—but the worse ones early on would end with Julie running (she was faster than he was), with doors slamming, with both of us being very critical and contemptuous, not realizing how damaging that is and how much more repair it takes. Thank goodness for John's research! It really has helped us, and we personally use all of the interventions we'll be walking you through in the "Fights" section of this book. We are still a volatile couple, but over the years we have become better, kinder volatiles. And ultimately, that's the goal—not to change your conflict style (unless you really want to) but to do it better. With more compassion toward each other's enduring vulnerabilities, as John was able to do for Julie that night, understanding where she'd just come from and how it was shaping her reactions to him.

So, to wrap up: your style may certainly evolve over time. You can learn to stretch to reach your partner. But it is important to recognize that we all have these deeply carved starting styles that we will always default to—especially under pressure. So, whether you're matched up with someone who shares a style with you or you suspect you have a mismatch . . . talk about it!

Take a few moments now to discuss with your partner:

- What was my formative conflict culture? What did I learn about conflict from my family of origin? What beliefs about conflict do I carry from that?
- Which of the three styles is my personal conflict style? What's my "meta-emotion mode"—how do I feel about feelings? Are some feelings easier for me to express than others?
- How do our conflict styles interact? Do we have the same style or different? How does this affect our conflict discussions?

Building an awareness of these critical factors that shape how we fight allows us to navigate all our conflicts better going forward. Understanding your own style and your partner's style builds empathy and compassion, which means that even a fight can become a safe enough space for you to really explore your issues together and do something crucial: figure out what you're actually fighting about, deep down.

WHAT WE FIGHT ABOUT

A recent client came to us with a history of divorce. Her first marriage had ended, and now she was on her second marriage—one she'd gone into with all the confidence in the world that it would work out for the long haul. And yet, things seemed to be once again going down the same agonizing path as before. This time, she wanted a different outcome. She loved her husband. She wanted to stay together. But no matter how hard they tried, things just seemed to be getting worse. She wondered why the pattern seemed to be repeating itself.

"It's always so wonderful in the beginning," she told us. "For months, even years, it just feels easy, and good, and right. And then this cycle starts up—we're just clashing about everything. I mean, it feels like a negative superpower we have, we can fight about *anything*. We could fight about the grocery list. We can fight about something we already agree on!"

Just the other night, she said, she and her husband had stopped in the middle of a nasty, name-calling fight and realized that what had sparked their conflict was . . . whether to put the forks in the dishwasher pointing up or pointing down.

They stared at each other, horrified. They needed help.

She summarized it this way: "It seems like relationships start out great and then get to this point where nobody can say anything without starting a fight. It's like . . . going from ecstasy to eggshells."

A question we get all the time is: What's the #1 thing couples fight about?

We've been asked this by patients and study participants. By TV show hosts. On the radio. By friends and new acquaintances. It's usually one of the first things people ask when they hear about our work. Maybe people think that if they can avoid that one hot topic that gets most couples fired up for a fight, they can better maintain their own relationship; maybe they figure if they know what the big issue most couples struggle with is, they can put a little more focus on that arena and make sure it doesn't become a problem. We'd love to give you an answer, but we can't, because the #1 thing couples fight about is *nothing*.

From Ecstasy to Eggshells: What Are We Fighting About?

Scene: Matt and Sophie, a couple in their late thirties, bustle around their messy kitchen, trying to feed their three loud, hungry kids while Matt gets ready to go to a late meeting. Pizza is for dinner; it's been dropped off by the delivery man, and Sophie has popped the boxes into the oven to keep warm while she gets out plates, forks, napkins. The kids swirl underfoot. She looks up and spots Matt, leaning against the counter, already eating a slice. Okay fine, she thinks, he has to blow out the door any second and this is his only chance to eat. But sitting behind him on the counter: the pizza boxes she was trying to keep warm. He does this all the time: serves himself first, and then leaves the food out to get cold.

"Is there a reason for those pizza boxes to be out on the counter?" she says.

Matt notes her sarcastic tone and matches it. "I don't know. I guess because I happen to be eating it?"

"Well, nobody else is ready yet."

"So in what square foot do you want the pizza boxes? Please enlighten me."

"Hmm, that's a tough question. How about in the oven, which has obviously been preheating?"

Even the kids are picking up on the sarcasm, which is dripping from every word. The pizza is not the only thing in the room rapidly cooling—the interaction is positively chilly, every comment sharp as an icicle.

Is this a fight about pizza?

Scene: Nina and Rohan, newlyweds, have just purchased their first house and are deciding where to plant a blueberry bush. Nina wants to keep it in a pot so it can be relocated more easily; Rohan wants to plant it in the yard.

"It's not going to do well in the pot," Rohan says, already starting to dig. "Blueberries need tons of water and drainage."

"How do you know that?" Nina says, suddenly irritated. "Are you a farmer all of a sudden? Stop digging! I didn't agree to this!"

"Whoa, whoa," Rohan says. "It's just a plant."

"It's just a plant, it's just a house, it's just all of our savings and a huge loan we might never pay off—nothing is a big deal to you I guess! There's never anything to worry about; everything will just magically turn out fine?"

She bursts into tears and runs inside, leaving Rohan standing baffled with his shovel.

Is this a fight about a plant?

Scene: Brandon and Todd have been dating for six months and are getting serious. It feels like the right time to meet each other's families. A few weeks ago, they had dinner with Todd's parents and sisters, and it was a blast—they are a loving and raucous family, and they accepted Brandon immediately. He's not sure the dinner at his parents' place will be as smooth. His parents have been standoffish and stiff with his past boyfriends.

On the way to dinner, they stop at the grocery store to pick up some flowers and a bottle of wine. Todd picks out a bottle.

"My mom doesn't like chardonnay," Brandon says, and snatches the bottle out of Todd's hand.

"Okay," says Todd agreeably. "How about a rosé?"

Brandon inspects the label. "This looks cheap."

"It's good. I've had it before."

"I don't care if *you* think it's good. I want to bring something *she* thinks is good!"

Brandon is subdued, visibly hurt. "Well, I don't think we need to spend a lot of money to make a nice gesture."

"You're not listening to me."

"Of course I am. But what the hell are you even saying? Pick whatever wine you want. I'll pay for it."

Brandon slams the bottle back on the shelf and storms out of the wine section, calling over his shoulder, "Forget it. Let's just not even go."

Is this a fight about wine?

When we say the number one thing we fight about is *nothing*, what we mean is that just about *anything* can spur conflict between partners if the conditions are right. Pizza, a plant, a bottle of wine—these were certainly the topics that sparked the fights above, but there are quite clearly deeper issues at play in all of these examples.

When you see two partners locked in a heated argument over something that seems trivial, usually it's not trivial at all. Our conflicts have subterranean fuel, stuff below the surface that's driving that fight about how to divide domestic labor, or what to spend money on, or what to do with our free time this weekend. More deeply, we are often fighting about:

- **Values**: What is love? What is a home? What does it mean to be a family?
- **Unrecognized needs**: There are many, but some big ones are the needs for play, connection, and romance— 80 percent of couples starting therapy say there's "no romance" anymore.
- **Hidden dreams**: What are my hopes and dreams, both now and for the future? What is my life purpose, my reason for being here?

A big part of satisfying long-term love is developing the capacity to realize when what we're actually fighting about is not cold pizza but a longing for efforts to be appreciated; not a plant but the pressures of new commitment and not having had the space to talk about it; not the price of a bottle of wine but a deep fear of parental rejection.

But the truth is: this is hard to do! And that's because, typically, we don't sit down together at the table and calmly say, "So, honey, what do you want to fight about today?" Instead, it flares in moments like the above: in the busyness of life, in the moments we planned to be *good* moments, under pressure, and "out of nowhere," as so many couples say.

One major reason for that is *failed bids for connection*.

Bids for Connection: A Key Piece of the Conflict Puzzle

A "bid for connection" is, simply put, anything you do or your partner does to try to get the other person's attention and connection with them. This can be a comment or a gesture. It can be subtle or overt. It can be positive or negative. Saying to your partner, "Look at this funny meme!" while holding out your phone is an obvious bid for connection. Sighing sadly might be a more subtle one. The main thing to note, though, is that we're not talking here about big, deep chats or "We have to talk" type summits. These are the small, fleeting moments throughout the day—the minor asides and interactions that can be easy to miss if you're busy or stressed. But what we saw in the Love Lab, with our three thousand couples, is that they mattered—a *lot*. When we observed couples, we saw that, routinely, there are three possible ways that partners tend to respond to each other's bids for connection:

1. They **turn toward,** meaning they respond positively to their partner's bid. So for the examples above, that would look like this: You say to your partner, "Look at this funny meme!" and they look, laugh, and maybe comment, "Oh yeah, I saw that one, it's perfect." Or in the other example: Your partner sighs sadly. You say, "What's wrong, honey?"

2. They **turn away,** meaning they ignore their partner's bid. You hold out your phone, but they're too busy to look. "One sec," they murmur and keep typing an email. Or: Your partner sighs, but you don't respond at all. You pretend you didn't hear their sigh—they're always upset about something, and you don't want to open a can of worms right now.

3. They **turn against,** meaning they respond negatively or harshly to the bid: You hold out your phone and your partner snaps, "Didn't I just ask you to stop interrupting me? I'm trying to finish this work email!" Or: your partner sighs and you slam your laptop shut in frustration: "What is it *now?*"

When couples in high conflict come to see us, one of the first things we try to find out is: Has there been a pattern of turning toward? Or has life together been defined by turning away or even turning against? For a couple struggling with constant or intense conflict, the answer to that can be incredibly illuminating.

In the seven longitudinal studies we conducted through the Love Lab, following couples for as long as two decades, we found that bids for connection—these small, ordinary, fleeting moments that fill up our days—were one of the biggest predictors of the future health of that relationship: happy couples turned toward their partners a lot, while unhappy couples tended not to. And when six years later we followed up with our couples who had stayed twenty-four hours in our apartment lab and analyzed our data, we found a sharp divergence: the "masters" of love—the couples who stayed together and stayed happy and stable—had turned toward each other's bids for connection 86 percent of the time. In troubled couples, it was only 33 percent of the time.[1]

Why did it matter so much? Because bids for connection that are turned toward become money in the bank for a relationship. We started calling partners' responses to each other "the emotion bank account." Every time partners notice and turn toward a bid—even the subtle ones, and especially the negative ones—it's like dropping a coin into that metaphorical piggy bank. Couples that turn toward a lot have a deep, full well of goodwill, connection, and affection to draw on when they find themselves in moments of friction over anything from dinner, potted plants, or cheap wine, to issues of caretaking and fairness, home and permanence, acceptance and respect. Meanwhile, couples who show a pattern of turning away or turning against will already be in the red. That means when they arrive at a conflict moment, there's little or no goodwill and affection to draw on to buffer the conflict from becoming harsh.

Any fight can turn into a nasty one when partners are disconnected—when bids have been routinely missed or ignored. We're more likely to misinterpret each other and assume the worst. We're predisposed to have a negative lens on our partner or our partner's actions instead of the capacity to give each other the benefit of the doubt. We are more likely to resort to the Four Horsemen (criticism, contempt, defensiveness, and stonewalling) when the emotion bank account is drained.

If increased or worse conflict has been an issue for you and your partner lately, it's worth asking yourselves:

- How have your recent bids for connection toward your partner been received?
- How have you responded to your partner's bids for connection?
- Has there been a pattern lately of turning away or even turning against?
- How "full" is your emotional bank account right now? To evaluate, ask yourself how true the following statements feel:
  - I'm looking forward to spending time with my partner today.
  - There's shared humor between us—when we spend time together, we have fun.
  - I have a sense of what's going on with my partner this week—what they're stressed about or feeling proud of.
  - When I look at my partner, I feel grateful for their presence and for what they contribute to our relationship and our home.
  - I wake up in the morning with a sense of "we-ness"; even if my partner and I have a busy day, I feel supported and feel that they have my back. I don't wake up feeling alone.
- If you answered "not really" to any of the above, then your emotional bank account may be a little low; if none of the above felt very true, then it may be seriously in the red. Which brings us back to the beginning of this list:

bids for connection. It may be time to make an
intentional effort to turn toward each other a lot more, in
small ways, every day, to build that account back up.

If you're not getting an A+ on bids for connection in your own
self-assessment right now, know that you're not alone. Please don't
beat yourself up. Let's look at the odds against you. What do you
think the chances are that both you *and* your partner are going to be
emotionally available to connect in the same moment—in other
words, that one of you will make a bid and the other one will be open
and available to receive it? Spoiler alert: the math is not in our favor
here. Even if you are emotionally available to connect with your
partner roughly 50 percent of the time and your partner is available
to connect with you about the same amount, the chances of both
your availability overlapping is .50 times .50 or .25. So the odds that
your availability overlaps is only *25 percent.*[2] That means, 75 percent
of the time, you and your partner's availability will be mismatched.
So if you're leaving it to chance and not intentionally turning toward
each other, the odds of your magically finding each other in a moment of openness and availability at the same time are pretty darn
slim.

So before we get into the specific conflict strategies starting in the
next section of the book, your first mission is just this: *turn toward.*
Our lives are not always set up to make this easy. We have so many
pressures—work demands, kids, extended families, urgent tasks, all
those never-ending logistics of life—and those pressures are real. In
a groundbreaking observational study run by the Sloan Center at
UCLA, researchers found that dual-income couples with children
spoke to each other, one on one, for an average of only *thirty-five
minutes per week.*[3] That is not a lot of time! We need to be intentional

about this: to put down the phone, close the email window, put away the book or the urgent briefing we're reading, pause the dishes or the laundry. A lot of things seem, in the moment, so much more urgent than chatting with your partner about the bird they just spotted out the window or pausing to ask them why they look stressed. But in the long term, they aren't. Decades of data backs this up: these fleeting opportunities for connection that are sprinkled throughout every day have an enormous power to affect the future unfolding of our relationship.[4] Not only do they keep us connected, but they build trust. And in conflict, we are always asking, *Can I trust you?*

- Can I trust you to have my best interests at heart?
- Can I trust you to be kind to me right now?
- Can I trust you to treat me with respect during this conversation?
- Can I trust you to be a team with me even though we're disagreeing?

The answers to these questions matter, regardless of whether the conflict we're in is *solvable* or *perpetual.*

The Two Types of Fights: Solvable Versus Perpetual

As we mentioned in the introduction to this book, all our fights fall into one of two categories: solvable or perpetual. Our solvable fights have solutions. They can be resolved. This doesn't mean they're always *easy* to resolve—more on this in a moment. But fundamentally, these are problems with solutions, and once fixed, they aren't likely to come up again.

Our perpetual problems, meanwhile, aren't going anywhere. These are the conflicts we will never resolve but will have to live with and manage for the duration of our partnerships. While the specific points of perpetual conflict will be different for each couple, every couple has them. And for every couple, they represent the vast majority of conflicts.

When we brought couples into the Love Lab to observe their interactions and their conflict discussions, and then followed up with them every few years over the course of up to two decades, we saw that couples were coming into the lab year after year and *fighting about the same stuff*[5] over and over. We would observe a couple in the lab arguing about, say, their social life and how often to go out with friends versus stay home. One partner loved to see friends and felt happy and energized when connected to community; the other missed quiet time with their partner and felt ignored and awkward at parties. When we brought the couple back in, it was still a point of contention! Six years later, they were still fighting about whether to go to a party on a Friday night. The only things that had changed were their clothes and hairstyles.

Why is this a perpetual problem for this couple? Because swirling under the question of whether to accept or decline a simple party invite is a whole lot of other stuff that has to do with this couple's personality differences (an extrovert and an introvert), their differing needs within the relationship, and priorities surrounding how they want to spend their time. Is this conflict destined to break them apart? Absolutely not. But this is an area where they differ significantly, and so they're going to need to figure out ways, over and over again through the course of their lives, to address the conflict, express their needs, create compromise, and, to a certain extent, be accepting of each other's differences.

Remember that 69 percent of our conflicts fall into the "perpetual" category—that's a lot of conflict to live with! But here's what the masters of love understand: perpetual conflict is inevitable in any relationship. When we choose someone for life, in addition to choosing someone to love, we're choosing a set of forever conflicts, points of friction that will always heat up from time to time and sometimes maybe start a little fire. There is no magical, conflict-free relationship out there—it simply doesn't exist. The goal then is to live *well* with these points of conflict—to accept that they are there and to approach them with compassion and curiosity rather than defensiveness and criticism.

So, what kinds of conflicts tend to be solvable, and which are perpetual?

It depends. For any given couple, any given topic—from finances to housework to parenting to how to load the dishwasher—might be solvable or it might be perpetual. The question is, is the problem limited to this one scenario? Or does it link to a deeper conflict, one that is echoed in other fights and that connects to an underlying, core difference between the two of you in your personalities, your values and priorities, your beliefs about "how things should be"?

Sometimes a fight about how to put the forks in the dishwasher is just a fight about forks! You're both irritable, you haven't connected much lately, and something dumb blows up. It happens. But if you find yourselves screaming at each other over the open racks of cups and plates and silverware ("You *never* listen to me! It's always your way or the highway!"), then you might need to have a conversation about control and influence in the relationship. If you're fighting about which car model you should buy next, this might be a solvable problem with an easy decision to reach . . . or it can start World War III, with differences in class backgrounds causing clashes about how you want to present yourselves to the world now (e.g.,what car you're seen driving).

Now—think of the last fight (or two, or three) you and your partner had.

Which category did those conflicts fall into?

If they were perpetual: What do you think the underlying issue or issues might be? Is it something that has surfaced, in one form or another, in other conflicts? Maybe there are unmet needs or frustrated goals lurking under there for you; maybe there's a way you feel life should be approached that you and your partner aren't aligned with at this time. (Don't worry about discussing the topics with your partner right now—we don't want you fighting before we've given you new tools to help you calmly discuss your issue.)

And if they were in the "solvable" category: How did those fights feel? Even solvable fights can feel pretty bad, especially when we're making some common conflict mistakes. Were you and your partner able to arrive at a solution or compromise, or did you get stuck? It's okay if you did! This is common.

Ultimately, though, regardless of whether your fight is solvable or perpetual, there's still *one* unifying factor in whether that conflict becomes damaging.

The Common Denominator in Fights That Go Wrong

All fights that go wrong typically have one major thing in common: **dismissing our partner's negative emotions.**

Our knee-jerk reaction to strong emotions directed at us is often to minimize, invalidate, dismiss. But if we don't have the ability to listen to our partner's emotions without defensiveness, the fight is going to escalate—no matter if the problem is solvable or perpetual. When negative emotions aren't listened to, they intensify, because we can't get our partner's attention. So we escalate. We get flooded. The Four Horsemen appear. We end up in a conflict that is difficult to repair and heal from.

What Causes Escalation?

Negative emotion is expressed ("I'm really upset you forgot my birthday")

Partner responds by minimizing or dismissing ("We celebrated last week; it's not a big deal")

Emotion intensifies

Flooding likely

Four Horsemen enter (defensiveness, criticism, contempt, stonewalling)

Escalation

Damage

Here's the thing about solvable versus perpetual: when it comes to *how to fight right*, it doesn't matter much which type of fight you're having. Perpetual problems will have this existential quality and can feel much "bigger," but solvable problems still need our best conflict management skills to be successfully solved. We're going to use the same strategies to ensure that we fight with kindness and that everyone is heard. However, being able to ID which type of fight it is will help you clarify your goal. Are you working toward a solution to an isolated problem? Or are you working to understand each other better and manage a long-term point of conflict between the two of you? One of the biggest misconceptions about conflict that we see among couples is this persistent and pervasive belief that *all conflicts should be resolved,* or there's something wrong with the relationship. That's pure myth! Let it go. Most of your conflicts will never be fully resolved, and that's okay. It's good, in fact—normal and healthy!

When the underlying causes are not addressed, however, perpetual problems can become a wedge of discord between couples. If our fights over perpetual problems become so repetitive and unproductive that we can no longer open up to each other at all or make any headway toward resolution or compromise, we can end up in *gridlock,* which is not a happy place to be.

Gridlock: What Is It, and How Do We Get Out?

Here's what gridlock looks like:

The same fight, over and over—and it feels awful. Affection, warmth, and humor have disappeared; the Four Horsemen show up more and more.

You are each deeply entrenched in your positions. You can't seem to make any progress toward compromise or resolution. You feel like you *can't* compromise: if you give an inch, your partner will take a mile. (Your partner probably feels the same.)

You end up hurt and frustrated every time you and your partner discuss this issue.

You're becoming more and more polarized—the more your partner fights you on this, the more aggressively you feel you have to defend your own position (and vice versa). As with one of those ever-tightening finger-trap toys, the harder you each pull, the more stuck you become.

You feel rejected by your partner.

You're becoming more and more disconnected.

In gridlock, we become completely shut down to each other. There's no listening, no opening up to each other, no collaborating, no understanding. We may become so worn down by the repetitive conflict that we don't even show much emotion anymore. After having the same fight a dozen, a hundred, a million (it feels like!) times, all the emotion—the warmth, the passion, even the anger—has been wrung out. We've vilified each other in our minds: *You're so selfish. So stubborn. There's no getting around you. We'll never figure this out.* Gridlocked conflict discussions might end with one partner saying, hopelessly, "I don't want to talk about this anymore." We've been through this so many times, we want to give up. When we talk about *gridlock,* we are generally talking about one particular problem area—in that way, it's different from the "hostile" conflict style. In a hostile dynamic, that hostility has taken over all of a couple's conflictual interactions: any time there is friction or disagreement, the hostility comes out. But any of the conflict styles can become gridlocked around a specific topic. So what hot topics do we tend to get gridlocked about?

Absolutely *anything.*

We can end up in gridlock over issues that, to an outsider, might look trivial, even childish. Observing two people in a gridlocked conflict conversation, you might think, *Well I can think of half a dozen potential solutions to their problem—why can't they just work together and figure out something to try?* But inside gridlock, this feels impossible. And that's because, as with all perpetual problems, gridlocked conflict is about something much deeper than the topic at hand.

Here's what we've found: almost all gridlocked conflict is actually about *unfulfilled dreams.*

We all have hopes and dreams for how we want our lives to unfold. Sometimes we've articulated those dreams to our partners—but a lot of the time we haven't. Maybe we haven't even articulated them to ourselves. Maybe they've taken a more latent form—a drive, an ache, a desire, a feeling of missing something important.

Take Amy and Matthew, an Asian American couple living near San Francisco. They have two little kids and have outgrown the tiny two-bedroom bungalow they've been renting since before they were married. They've long wanted to buy a house with more space for the kids, but the area is expensive, and so far they haven't been able to afford it. They talk a lot about how to advance in their respective careers—Amy is currently working part-time as a grant writer for a local nonprofit; Matthew is a UX designer for a certain large social media company. Amy, who shifted to part-time work when the kids were born, is interested in something more full-time, while Matthew has been trying to advance internally to become a project manager. They both worry about money: being able to pay off their student loans, afford a house, afford college for the kids. So when a great job opportunity comes along for Matthew that offers a 30 percent pay increase and the exact role bump he's looking for, it seems like a no-brainer. There's only one problem: the job is with a tech company in Seattle, so the family would have to move, and soon. They give him two weeks to make the decision.

The conversation between Amy and Matt about whether or not to take the job starts out fine—then quickly devolves. They began by running the numbers in a spreadsheet: cost of living, cost of moving, how far the salary increase will go both immediately and then over time. But the financial picture isn't clear-cut: moving is a huge expense, and the cost of living in Seattle isn't any better than it is where they are. They still won't be able to afford to buy.

"But *eventually* we will, if I take the job," Matt insists. "Sure, the first year, my raise is going to get swallowed up by moving expenses. But after that we'll start making progress."

"Is that really worth it, though? To go through all the stress of moving, ripping the kids out of school, just to struggle as much financially as we do here?"

"I'm telling you, it'll be worth it in the long run."

"Well, what if it's not? What if we put another ten grand on a credit card to move and rent a new place and we never pay it off, like everything else we say we're going to pay off? We can't keep doing this."

"Amy, the way we get out of debt is *making more money.*" Matt is getting more adamant. "This is not advanced algebra."

"You know what, if you were better at math, maybe we wouldn't be in this situation!"

By now, Amy is in tears.

The problem is: they are trying to hash this out as if it's a money issue. It's about a whole lot more than that, and neither of them is admitting—or even realizing—that fact.

Underneath her protests about how much moving will cost, Amy is terrified to lose the community they've built in their current neighborhood—friends, schools, support networks. With their youngest about to turn three and more independent, she's been able to have a little more freedom, going out with friends and reconnecting. She's feeling like she's *just* getting her life back—and now Matt wants her to give it up and go forge a whole new one. She had a vision of a life *here.* Is giving up that life worth it for a job?

Matt, meanwhile, has spent the last couple of years getting passed over for promotions. It feels like nobody at his current job sees the value he brings. Recently, his supervisor discouraged him from even applying to a project manager job that was opening up in his department. The place has felt like a dead end—and it has really been getting to him, making *him* feel like a dead end. When he went to interview for the new job, the team was excited about bringing him on board. They saw his skill and experience. It felt amazing to be valued and for his potential to be seen. Matt had a vision of a career where he could move forward, grow, do work that brings him joy. Is it worth passing on this rare opportunity to stay in an expensive city where they continue to struggle? But these deeper issues are invisible. Meanwhile, their fight about "finances" recycles daily, getting more and more acrimonious as the deadline for Matt's decision closes in.

Can they get out of gridlock? *Yes.* Even the most entrenched gridlock can be overcome. But we have to be able to explore the deeper issues coursing under the surface of that gridlocked fight. We have to be able to share those very personal, very significant life dreams with each other. Only then can we start to look for a way forward that honors *both* of those dreams. When it comes to the couple above, they might end up moving for this job, or they might end up staying put while Matt looks for exciting opportunities locally. There is no right answer. But the answer that's right for *them* will emerge only when they actually start talking about the vision they each have for the life they want and how that's showing up in this conflict.

When we see couples in gridlock, we go right to dreams as quickly as we can. What is the core need that is not being met? The dream that is unrequited? And why is it so central to your sense of self?

If you asked us, "What do we fight about?" this is the single answer that could wrap up just about all our perpetual fights into one single bundle: *dreams*. And that's why all of our blueprints for conflict are going to take us through "dreams within conflict" before we move toward any kind of resolution or compromise—we have to do this first.

When Gridlock Means the End of the Road

The majority of couples who've come to our workshops—even the most distressed ones—are able to make major breakthroughs using the conflict blueprint this book lays out. But sometimes one person's dream is another person's nightmare—like when one person wants kids and the other really doesn't. In such a situation, you might find yourself facing the end of a relationship. But even in that painful circumstance, going through the conflict process can be clarifying and healing for both partners—at least you understand why you're breaking up, and nobody is to blame.

Long before he met Julie, John was married once before. In his earlier marriage, his dream was to be a father. This wife also had a dream: to never be a mother. But it was a dream she hadn't fully realized, even within herself. They were trying to have a baby and dealing with infertility for quite a long time. Finally, they went to a fertility expert who identified the problem—endometriosis, which is often treatable—and said, "I can have you pregnant in six months!"

John left the appointment absolutely elated.

She left deeply depressed.

After some fierce sparring over how, if, and when to move forward with treatment, they finally had a conversation about their respective visions for their lives, and it all came out: John deeply wanted to be a parent, and she deeply didn't. She had other goals for her life, a different vision of the future, and having a baby would mean giving those up. For a little while, John tried to accommodate her dream—he tried thinking, *Maybe we don't need kids to be happy.*

But he in fact did. For this conflict, there was no resolution or compromise possible, and it was nobody's fault.

If you feel that your dreams and your partner's may be in opposition, know this: most times, both dreams can be accommodated, even if it doesn't seem possible right now. If you are at the beginning of your conflict journey, then be open to the possibility that as you move through the coming chapters, new paths forward may very well open up to you and your partner—ones you can't even see right now from where you currently sit. And if you do progress through our conflict blueprint and find that you are indeed in a situation like John's above, then we hope that by following this road map, you'll be able to come to the end of this relationship with compassion and understanding instead of hurt and vitriol.

In our long history of working with couples, we've found only three "deal-breakers" in this department that couples cannot (or should not) overcome:

DEAL-BREAKER #1

Abuse

Abuse by one partner toward the other is a deal-breaker. However, up to 50 percent of couples seeking therapy have experienced some degree of violence during conflict, and that's not always a deal-breaker. Let's look at the difference.

Research (both ours and others') has identified two types of domestic violence: *situational* and *characterological*. Situational DV occurs when a fight spins out of control: you see escalation, followed by the Four Horsemen, culminating in mild violence like slaps or shoves. Both parties participate; both feel horrible after; both want to stop. In the United States, the vast majority of DV—80 percent[6]—is situational: confined to specific incidents that spiral out of control rather than representing a pattern of domination or control by one partner over the other. Situational DV can be overcome *with training and support*: in a twenty-week study with mild DV couples,[7] we found that teaching conflict management techniques, self-soothing for flooding with the support of a biofeedback device, and strategies for increasing friendship and intimacy *eliminated* situational DV. Even at an eighteen-month follow-up, the couples from the study continued to approach conflict more calmly, with no recurrence of DV. If situational violence is something that you and your partner have experienced, reach out to a trained professional for guidance and support: Gottman Referral Network, at www.gottmanreferralnetwork.com.

Characterological violence is a different story. With this type of DV, one partner is the perpetrator; the other is the victim. Eighty-five percent of the time, the victim is a woman. Our research identified two types of perpetrators with characterological DV: "pit bulls" and "cobras." Pit bulls are jealous and possessive, fear abandonment, and tend to isolate their partners from friends and family. Cobras, meanwhile, are unpredictable, erratic, and explosive, and strike out of nowhere. Neither type of perpetrator will truly take responsibility for the violence, instead blaming the victim for causing it through her (or his) behavior.[8]

There is no effective treatment for characterological DV. If you are experiencing this, get out of the relationship. National Domestic Violence Hotline: 1-800-799-7233.

DEAL-BREAKER #2

Refusal to Seek Help for Addiction

According to the U.S. Department of Health and Human Services, some forty million individuals in the United States alone struggle with a substance abuse disorder.[9] And it is a disorder—not a moral failing. Recovery is absolutely possible, and there are many trained therapists in our network who focus on helping couples through the recovery process. Recovery can be a long road; partners of those working to overcome addiction will need support in taking care of themselves, healing from the trauma and betrayal of the effects of addiction, and reconnecting and rebuilding trust. We often focus on creating new rituals of connection for couples who are working to overcome addiction issues, as old rituals of connection (like holidays or going out to eat, just for example) can cause relapses.

Unfortunately, many people never seek treatment. In a survey,[10] the reasons people gave for this included difficulty finding the specific treatment they needed, difficulty affording treatment, and worry about what others (their family, neighbors, and coworkers) might think. But the number one reason was that they did not think they needed it. If addiction is causing suffering for you in your relationship and your partner cannot or will not recognize that and seek help, there may not be a path forward.

Addiction is not a deal-breaker—many struggle with this at some point or another. But a refusal to address it may very well be.

DEAL-BREAKER #3

Differences Surrounding Having Children

The decision to have a child or not shapes a couple's life in every way. When one person's dream is a child-free life and the other dreams of becoming a parent, the best thing may be to part ways, even when there's a lot of love. Couples can make a lot of creative compromises to accommodate dreams that might seem in opposition at first—more on this later. But the dream of becoming a parent (or not) may not be something you can give up.

If this has been a point of friction in your relationship, the "dreams within conflict" discussion we'll take you through in the next section of the book can hopefully help you get clearer on whether there is a way forward or if the life you need to live in order to feel fulfilled is very different from the one your partner needs.

Know that, for most couples, it's not going to be the case that the "dreams within conflict" conversation spells the end of the relationship. We've seen that 87 percent of the time, even couples in the most entrenched gridlock can achieve major breakthroughs using the conflict blueprint we'll lay out in the next section of the book, in large part because it allows us to uncover and make space for both partners' core needs and dreams.[11] If you and your partner have come to this book with a goal to fight better, then no matter what your starting point is, we're willing to bet that this isn't the end of the road but perhaps a turn onto a new one.

The Top Ten Myths About Conflict

In this first part of the book, we've covered "Conflict 101." We've gone over the basics of why we fight as much as we do with the ones we love, where our styles of fighting come from and how that shapes our fights, and what we're really fighting about when we fight. Now we move to a more advanced class: how to fight right.

If you and your partner were coming in to see one of us in a clinical setting, we'd start the way we often start: by dispelling some of the most common misconceptions about love and conflict that can trip up even the most solid of couples. Some of these are recaps of important concepts we've already covered here, and some are new.

Myth #1: Once we find a solution to the big fight we're having right now, we'll be all set—no more fighting!

Reality: Most conflicts are perpetual. We need to learn to approach conflict differently, at a fundamental level, not how to solve one particular fight.

Myth #2: If conflict exists in our relationship, we're not supposed to be together.

We are bombarded with fairy-tale versions of romance: *And they lived happily ever after.* None of the stories that pervade our culture, from children's books to rom-coms, end with *And they lived happily ever after, fighting over whose turn it was to take out the garbage every Monday for the rest of their lives.* If they did, maybe we'd all be better off!

Reality: Conflict is unavoidable, even for the happiest of couples.

Myth #3: A conflict is a problem to be solved.

Our urge to solve problems is so powerful. And yes—a third of our conflicts generally have a solution! But most don't.

Reality: We manage most of our conflicts through continuing dialogue—we don't resolve them.

Myth #4: One of us is right, and one of us is wrong.

Reality: Both partners' experiences and points of view are valid. Both of their realities are true. What matters is how we each see things, how we feel, what we need, and if we can hear and validate each other. This is always more important than who is "right."

Myth #5: Men are more logical than women; women are more emotional than men.

This fallacy persists to this day, and the stereotype is damaging, limiting, and simply untrue. An international study examined what made people emotional over the course of a typical day and found that there was absolutely no difference based on gender identity—people were emotional about the same stuff with the same frequency.[12]

Reality: Logic and emotion do not have genders. Men have emotions and need to express them, and women need to be listened to and believed when they describe their reality.

Myth #6: The best conflict management is logical, rational, and unemotional.

This is a more common view among conflict-avoidant couples, but it shows up across the board and often becomes an issue with meta-emotion mismatches, where one partner thinks the goal is logic and the other thinks the goal is connection or expression.

Reality: Neuropsychological research has shown that emotions and logical thinking are intertwined when it comes to problem-solving. One can't problem-solve well without information derived from one's emotions.[13] So the best conflict management allows us to *understand each other better through listening to each other's feelings and ideas.*

Myth #7: Negative emotions are bad and should be avoided.

We believe we can "think our way out" of negative emotions, which makes us impatient with our partner's negative emotions as well as our own. We think anger is bad and should be avoided.

Reality: There is nothing wrong with anger. What matters is how anger is expressed. We should never express anger by aiming contempt or criticism at our partner.

Myth #8: Nobody can hurt you unless you let them.

This emerged from New Age philosophy, and a lot of people believe it: that you have (or should have) 100 percent control over your own emotions. You "choose" to feel hurt by that comment. You "choose" to feel betrayed by that action. The appeal is the belief that your emotions can be controlled and changed, especially the negative ones, and that if you choose to not feel hurt, then no one can hurt you. The flipside is that you are also relieved of any responsibility toward your partner. If you say something that they say hurts them, that's their problem not yours. But this is not how we humans work! Emotions are as instinctive and primal to us as feeling hungry when we haven't eaten for many hours or tired when we haven't slept well. Emotions are hard-wired into our brains, and given the right conditions, varying emotions will surface accordingly. If someone says something contemptuous to us, we're likely to feel hurt and angry. If anniversaries mean a lot to us, and our partner forgets ours, we'll probably feel hurt. But we can heal those hurts if we want to.

Reality: We can and do hurt each other. All couples do this, no matter how great a relationship they have. The difference between "master" couples and the "disasters" is that the master couples *process* what happened and *repair* it. Later on, we'll show you exactly how.

Myth #9: You have to love yourself before you can love somebody else.

Nobody loves themselves all the time in every way. We all have self-doubts and moments when we're self-critical and not self-loving. If we had to be perfectly good at loving ourselves before having a relationship, most of us *wouldn't* have relationships!

The fallout from this belief is that if your relationship fails, no matter what's happened, it's all your fault because you haven't been self-loving enough—the responsibility for anything going wrong is on you. Not true! In most cases, that old maxim "It takes two to tango" applies to our relationships and our fighting too. What may be wrong is that we're attempting to fight with the wrong tools rather than the right tools that can help us fight calmly and kindly.

Reality: We all have enduring vulnerabilities—triggers, traumas, wounds that may never fully heal—and these vulnerabilities may lead us to not perfectly love ourselves. We can still have a lifelong relationship. Our work as life partners is to care for each other, even in conflict, and to love our partners, even when they can't love themselves.

Myth #10: To be "allowed" to have needs, we have to justify or explain them.

So much of dysfunctional conflict has to do with this deeply ingrained belief that we're not entitled to our needs. Many of us have grown up in a culture where "need" is a dirty word. We're supposed to be independent, stand on our own two feet, and not need anything from anyone, including our partner. If we do have a need, the only way we can justify it is to prove how bad our partner has been to us, thus opening up this need in us—it's their fault that we have a need.

Reality: Human beings are pack animals. For eons we've survived by grouping together and communicating with each other in order to nurture each other and ward off danger. In other words, we are built to have needs, as our needs bind us together and help us thrive ... *together.* You can have needs and should have needs—*without* justification! But your responsibility is to *communicate them.* One of the big reasons conflicts escalate is that we don't ask for what we need. Instead, we expect our partners to read our minds and magically fulfill our need. We haven't met any mind readers lately, and until we do, all of us should be voicing our needs loud and clear.

No More Myths or Big Mistakes: How to Fight *Right*

We make a lot of mistakes in conflict—because of the persistent myths above, because of our different conflict cultures, and because "fighting right" is not something we talk about a lot or teach people how to do. But conflict doesn't have to mean pain and suffering—while it may never be "fun," it can become simply one of the many threads in our nuanced and richly textured lives, something we accept as an inevitable part of loving and living with someone for the long haul, and something we know how to use for *good.* But to use our points of friction to actually *know each other better,* we have to stop making the same mistakes over and over again and utilize some basic yet powerful pivots.

So the next section of this book is going to walk you through the anatomy of a fight from beginning to end. We're going to go step by step, from the moment a fight flares up, through the murky middle, and all the way to the aftermath. We'll point out every fork in the road where we typically go *wrong* and show you how to pivot to take a better path. The following fights will take you through each major point in a conflict where you have the power to shape the way your next fight goes and, in doing so, to alter the course your relationship takes moving forward.

We'll answer the burning questions most couples have:

- How do we bring up an issue without starting World War III?
- When the conversation is headed in the wrong direction, how do we get it back on track?
- How can we be collaborative during a conflict when tensions and emotions are running high?
- How can we set aside defensiveness and combativeness and explore the deeper issues at play?
- How do we reach a compromise in which nobody feels like they're sacrificing too much?
- How do we process and repair things when a conflict goes badly and make sure we don't repeat the same patterns again?

Each fight we take you through here will present data from the lab and from our recent research, including an international study with forty thousand couples who opened up to us about their conflicts. Each chapter will offer a kind of "X-ray" of a fight, showing the underlying causes at play that are not immediately visible—even to the people fighting. Each will reveal several key interventions that you have the power to enact immediately with your partner. And each will feature a real example of a couple we've worked with or one who generously shared their stories with us, who were able to flip their fights from destructive to productive, from gridlock to openness and greater closeness.

Some of the fights we show you in this next section get pretty intense—including one of our own. These are stories about real humans. They make mistakes; they say hurtful things, just like the rest of us. But we're going to give you one spoiler alert: all of these couples are success stories.

Now let's dive in, starting at the moment a fight begins.

part 2

The Five Fights Everybody Has

FIGHT #1:
THE BOMB DROP

Mistake: Starting Off Wrong

Kristen and Steve are on the edge of a cliff.

This is not a metaphor.

This is Sedona, Arizona. It's hot, dry, and absolutely beautiful. The desert sky is a cornflower blue. The rocky path under their feet, as they hike along, is an impossible color of red. The cliffs, sheer rock faces that plummet below them and rise high above, are striated, as though the colors of the desert sunrise have been baked into the rock. Kristen is taking it all in, delighted—it feels amazing to be here, just she and Steve, out in nature, on an adventure, *finally*. It's the first "adults only" vacation they've taken in a long, long time. Probably since they had kids. And their oldest has just turned ten! This trip is long overdue.

The trail is getting steeper, but Kristen feels great to be pushing herself physically. Usually they have to do things at the kids' speed. She checks behind her to make sure her husband is keeping up. He is fifteen years older than she, after all, but he's always been active and fit, which was one of the things that first attracted her to him, back when he was her cardiologist—her *heart doctor*, something they joked about a lot once they succumbed to all the subtle flirting and finally started seeing each other. She scrambles up a slippery segment of the narrow path, loose pebbles scattering under her boots. She's eager to get to the top. The guidebook said there'd be an incredible view from up there.

Steve, meanwhile, is nervous. Very nervous. They haven't seen anyone else on this trail since they took that left fork a while back, and on the one hand, it's a good thing they haven't—it's narrow enough that it would be hard to pass anyone else coming down. On the other hand, maybe nobody else on this trail means they're the only ones crazy enough to be on it. One wrong step, and you'd be over that cliff edge and down a very long way. When Kristen showed him the map of this trail this morning, there'd been no topography information to suggest that they'd be hiking inches away from certain death the entire time. He isn't much for hiking to begin with, but she was so excited about it, he figured he'd give it a shot. But this is *not* what he'd had in mind. And now the trail is narrowing even more, curving up steeply around a sheer rock wall. Kristen scrambles up, a shower of rocks clattering down after her, and Steve stops. His whole body has frozen up—this is a terrible idea. Continuing up this path is lunacy.

"Honey," he says.

She turns and looks at him, and immediately her face darkens. She knows exactly what he's going to say.

"I don't think this is such a good idea."

"Steve, come on." Her tone is tense, brittle. "We're almost there. Don't be silly." She turns to keep hiking.

Don't be silly. He bristles. "I'm not going any farther," he says, trying to keep his own tone even and calm—rational. "And I don't want you to either. This trail is too dangerous—this was a terrible idea. We're heading back down."

Kristen looks at her husband—stopped there on the trail with his walking stick and big floppy hat, his daypack full of water bottles and snacks. The anger and frustration she feels are like a pressure building in her chest—she feels like she's going to explode.

"Of *course* you won't go," she says. She is seething. "I should have known you'd be too much of a pussy to go on a hike with me. It's always the same story with you—reasons we can't do this, reasons we can't do that. And so condescending! You treat me like a child. Well, guess what, I'm going to the summit. Are you coming with me, or are you going to act like a coward like always?"

He stares at her, shocked and angry, unable to respond.

"Are you going to grow some balls, Steve? Or just f—ing stand there?"

He locks eyes with his wife—a long, scorching moment passes. Then he turns and stalks back down the slippery path, thinking, *If I fall off this cliff, she'll feel pretty bad.*

Kristen watches him go. He disappears around a bend, leaving her alone on the high red ledge. She can't believe he just turned his back and abandoned her here.

She thinks, *If I fall off this cliff, he'll feel pretty bad.*

Steve has stormed off, so there's a brief lull—but neither of them is able to calm down. Both are hurt, humiliated, and furious.

Kristen heads down the path after her husband. She has plenty more to say to him about this ruined vacation—one she had waited so long for and had so looked forward to after doing everything, as always, every single day, for Steve and the kids, never anything for herself, and he can't do this *one* small thing for her? He can't push himself an inch out of his precious little safety zone? It's pathetic, and she's about to tell him so. When he hears her footsteps behind him, he whirls around—he has plenty to say to his wife about her reck-lessness, her selfishness, and her nasty accusations. What kind of a wife treats her husband like that? What kind of mother behaves that way in front of her children? Because she has—this isn't the first time she's lashed out at him. He never should have married someone so young and immature, and he's about to tell her so.

The conversation that Kristen and Steve have on the trail, on the edge of a thousand-foot cliff, does not go well. This fight started hot, and it never cools down—not even a little.

They scream over each other.

He threatens divorce.

She cries.

It ends when they are both so flooded and overwhelmed, they can't continue.

They make it down and ride back to the hotel in their rental car in icy silence.

A Narrow—and Critical—Window of Opportunity

180 seconds: that's how long we have to get off on the right foot. After that three-minute mark, the tone and trajectory of the fight is pretty much set. The odds we'll be able to turn things around after starting like Kristen did—we call it a "harsh start-up"—are slim to nil.

Here's how we know. When we brought couples into the Love Lab and asked them to perform the "conflict task"—where we asked them to choose an area of continuing disagreement to discuss—we coded their words, gestures, and emotions from the millisecond that discussion began. At the end of fifteen minutes, we'd stop them. We noticed right away that the conflict discussions that started out negative tended to end that way, and that was true regardless of conflict style. (Remember, it's not about volatility—it's about that ratio of positive to negative interactions.) But the nuance in the data was even more fascinating.

We mapped the fights, creating a "cumulative sum graph"—essentially, a Dow Jones chart, but for a couple's conflict instead of for the stock market.[1] This was a visual summary of the couple's conversation, where the rising and falling line represented the changing levels of positivity and negativity over the course of that fight. We expected to see that with the fights that were really negative and ended badly, the partners simply had a lot of negativity (like the Four Horsemen) all the way through their conflict task. But that wasn't necessarily the case. Even those who started harshly—with a big negative valley in their graph at the very beginning—would often try to inject positivity into their conflict discussion by making repair attempts of various types, just like the couples who did better overall and ended more positively. But on the graph, you could see that their fight would never really recover. Those moments of positivity midfight could not make up for the rough start. When we plotted the cumulative sum across all the conversations we observed, we found that *96 percent of the time*, how the fight went over the course of the first three minutes determined not only the fight's trajectory but how the rest of the relationship would go six years down the line.[2]

The data was clear: if you start negative, it's really hard to turn it around. Imagine a pinball machine that gets jammed: you slam those buttons too hard and the flippers get stuck. Now you're not getting any balls through—nobody's going to be able to communicate anything. You can keep trying, but this round is already broken.

And further, the ripple effects of a harsh start don't stop when this particular fight does—they extend far into the future.

We followed the couples whose conflict task discussions we observed and coded for years after their initial Love Lab visit to see how they fared as time went on. We found as we mentioned above that the couples who started their fights harshly, with negative words, gestures, and emotions, were much more likely to have divorced six years later. When we used the SPAFF coding to predict whether the couples we studied would stay together or divorce, we discovered that we could also make that prediction, with 90 percent accuracy, by using only the first three minutes. In other words, if you came into the Love Lab and started a fight with your partner, we could stop you right there—after just the beginning of your fight—and tell you whether you'd be happy together six years later or split up. And nine times out of ten, we'd be right.

Now, an important point: these predictions we made based on data were not prophecies. If we look at a couple's patterns of behavior and predict a negative outcome, that couple is not doomed! *Behaviors can be changed.* The fact that these first three minutes of a conflict conversation are so critical to the outcome of that conversation (and eventually, the relationship itself) is actually good news: it offers us a powerful point of intervention. So let's look at the first major conflict mistake most couples tend to make and how we can flip it.

Conflict Mistake #1: The Harsh Start-Up

We weren't on that trail in Sedona with Kristen and Steve, of course, observing and coding them, as we would be with a couple in the lab—they recounted this fight to us in a comfortable office, safe on a couch, far from any thousand-foot drops. But they were still on a kind of ledge—or at least their marriage was. Even months later, as they described this fight, you could see that emotionally they were plunging right back into it. They might as well have been still standing on that cliff, hurling verbal grenades at each other, starting with that first one: Kristen had raised an issue with Steve, something that had been bothering her for a long time. But she didn't just raise the issue—she dropped a bomb.

Take a look at a few more examples of classic "bomb drops" and see if any of these look familiar:

- You come downstairs after putting the kids to bed, ready to finally relax, and see your partner lounging on the couch, reading something on their phone, while the sink sits piled with dirty dinner dishes. Your blood pressure goes through the roof: "*Excuse me,* were you ever going to get up and clean the kitchen like I asked you to? Or did you think these dishes were going to magically wash themselves? Like everything else around here just 'magically' gets done?"
- You're late coming home from having a drink with your friends, and your phone died an hour ago. You walk in the door ready to apologize, but your partner is waiting: "Where the hell have you been? I guess it wouldn't occur to you that I'd be worried, since you don't seem to think about anybody but yourself."
- You're invited to a work conference and are excited to go—but your partner says they can't cover the kids, as they have a big deadline and work commitments too. You: "You always think your work is so much more important than mine. What do you think this is, a

hobby? I have a career too, you know. Well, I'm going, and you can deal with it."

- Your partner comes out of the bedroom, upset. "I see you forgot to pay the water bill again. What is wrong with you? Do you have any idea how much your disorganization is costing us?"

The harsh start-up is a very common problem. Our recent international study of forty thousand couples found that 90 percent of all couples starting therapy, whether heterosexual, gay, or lesbian, were experiencing issues with a harsh start-up and the problems that ripple from it. It was rare to see a couple that was *not* struggling with this issue.[3]

Harsh start-ups tend to share a couple of key traits:

1. We begin with criticism.
2. We describe the other person instead of ourselves.
3. We pile on other resentments we've been hoarding—we call this *kitchen sinking*. ("You never pick up your socks, you probably forgot to pick up the dry cleaning, you haven't even asked me how *my* day was, and you know what else, you're terrible in bed!")

Let's look at those three basic qualities of a harsh start-up and why they're so bad for your fight.

Harsh Start-Up Problem #1: You Criticize

Criticism is never productive. What distinguishes criticism from a productive complaint is that it takes the form of an attack on your partner's core character or personality. You're not pointing out a problem with the situation at hand; you're pointing out a problem with *who they are* as a person.

Here's the difference:

Criticism:	"Why do you have to be such a slob? Can't you clean up after yourself for once?"
Complaint:	"There's a bunch of dirty laundry on the floor. Would you mind picking it up before we go up to bed?"

We've said this before and we'll say it again: there is no such thing as "constructive criticism." Criticism is always destructive.

Harsh Start-Up Problem #2: You Describe Your Partner Instead of Yourself

Often and especially when we're upset, we launch into a fight by *describing the other person* and everything they're doing wrong. We tend to start conversations about stuff that's bothering us from a baseline assumption of *everything I'm doing makes sense, and everything you're doing is wrong!* "You always" and "you never" are classic criticisms here because they *imply* a personality flaw in your partner.

Describing your partner:	"You always leave your clothes strewn all over the bedroom. Why can't you just put your clothes in the hamper? It takes ten seconds."
Describing yourself:	"It really stresses me out when the bedroom is messy. Could you try to remember to toss stuff in the hamper instead?"

Harsh Start-Up Problem #3: "Kitchen Sinking"

We call it *kitchen sinking* because we don't just address the one issue; we pile in a whole bunch of other stuff that's been bothering us. We figure, *Hey, as long as we're having a fight, I have a couple more bones to pick!* A lot of times we do this because we want to feel "justified" in our anger, and the current, instigating problem feels "too small." We may also habitually not bring up smaller issues until they all add up and make us want to explode. But kitchen sinking never leads to effective conflict resolution. Now, instead of one problem to solve or one dish to wash, we've got a whole pile of them, and where do we even start? It's overwhelming.

Kitchen sinking:	"I see there are clothes all over the bedroom again—it's a total mess in there. The car is trashed and you didn't clean up the garage last weekend like you said you would. And you even forgot Valentine's Day! You never think about me at all!"
Just take care of the one dish!	(And save the rest for later.)

The moral of the story here is: don't store up complaints and resentments. Tackle them as they arise. Sitting on them is one of the reasons we end up starting harshly.

Why the Harsh Start-Up Is Such a Common Mistake

If we asked you right now, "What's the best way to raise an issue with your partner?" you wouldn't reply, "Burst into the room slinging accusations!" Yet this is exactly how we behave. In a nutshell, we're cranky and resentful, and we start in an inauspicious place. But let's go through a few of the big factors that fuel our harsh starts.

Stress

We're human, we're all carrying a lot, and certainly during periods of high stress, we see more harsh starts and the ripple effects of that. The pandemic was a perfect example of this. The early years of COVID were a time of extreme uncertainty and volatility for everyone, and we saw a *lot* more harsh start-ups. With quarantines, people's homes had turned into pressure cookers with no release valve, and fights were more explosive. Couples often felt anxious, frightened, and helpless; and unintentionally they would take out their anxiety, fear, frustration, and feelings of being out of control of their lives on each other and on their families. Times of high stress ratchet up the outpouring of cortisol and adrenaline in our bodies, and when we're cognitively overloaded with worries, that quickly sucks up all our mental bandwidth, leaving us cognitively depleted and less capable of good emotional regulation. We snap when that "last straw" lands—whatever it may be. What might have been "I've done the dinner dishes every night this week—could you take over tonight?" suddenly becomes "Why can't you ever clean up the damn kitchen? You're such a slob!"

Resentment

We pile up resentment over a series of incidents that we keep inside until finally, when we do bring it up, we're so angry and pent up that it comes out with bitterness or sarcasm. We haven't been asking for what we need, believing our partners should already know what it is and are *choosing* not to fulfill it. Resentment builds and builds until we burst. Take Kristen—she had about a metric ton of resentment stored up by the time she lashed out at Steve on the hike. She'd been constantly putting her own desires on the backburner in order to prioritize the kids' needs or her husband's boundaries. The day of the hike the dam broke and it all came out. She hadn't been telling Steve what she needed, and when needs are bottled up for too long, they go bitter and sour and turn into resentment.

Turning Away

Alternatively, sometimes we *have* asked for what we need, and our partner has been nonresponsive, turning away or even turning against. Here again our patterns surrounding bids for connection come into play. We may use a harsh start because we've been reaching out more gently over and over with no response, and now we're trying to get our partner's attention—with a mallet. We feel like we have to bang them over the head to get a response—and at this point, *any* response, even an angry one, is better than being ignored or brushed off.

We Don't Know Any Better

Finally, some of us have never learned another way to begin a conflict discussion. **The harsh start-up is the only start we know.** This is how we learned to raise an issue, and it's become an ingrained habit that we don't know how to break; sometimes we don't even know that it needs to be changed. Julie thinks of her mother as an example of someone who never learned how to bring up an issue without harshness, criticism, contempt, and accusation. It was how she'd learned to interact with others, and it was so ingrained, she never changed. The very first time she met John, we'd invited her to dinner at our place, and Julie—always nervous about living up to her mother's impossible standards—was racing around doing some last-minute cleaning while John was taking a break in his favorite chair after spending all morning chopping vegetables. When Julie's mother walked up, Julie was standing on a stool outside, sweeping the awning of the porch. Her mother, who hadn't even been introduced to her daughter's new boyfriend yet, marched into the kitchen and said to John, "You lazy rat, why aren't you out there helping my daughter clean?"

It was a classic harsh start-up. And even John—a researcher studying the science of relationships—immediately got defensive, leaping up to gesture at the dinner-in-progress. "I'm making *you* dinner!" he shot back. "What the heck does it look like?"

The point is, **it's hard to respond to a harsh start-up any other way but defensively.** When you start harshly, you leave your partner very little room to do anything else.

Opening Up the Conversation

We have to give our partners space to engage with us on the issues we bring to them instead of narrowing their options to one response only: *defend yourself.* From a position of attack/defend, there's no communication. No connection. No understanding. No forward motion. And usually, no positivity, which, as we know now, we really need in conflict.

But how do we do it in the heat of the moment, when we're upset, when we've reached our last straw, when a promise has been broken or a commitment forgotten, when we're feeling put upon or neglected or overwhelmed or angry? When we realized during our research that the fights that started harshly rarely recovered and that over time these harsh start-ups mostly led to unhealthy relationships, we knew we had to create a practical intervention to change harsh start-ups into "softened start-ups." We had to give couples a clear guide through the first minutes of a fight so they could give themselves the best possible shot at a positive outcome for their conflicts—and their futures together.

We turned to the research of Anatol Rapoport, a Russian American scholar who earned a PhD in mathematics and then a second PhD in social psychology. Through this lens of math-meets-human behavior, Rapoport turned his research focus onto an urgent and always relevant question: How do nations make peace? This was an urgent question for us too—How can couples make peace, but in their homes instead of on a world stage? As it turns out, there are a lot of parallels between nations and couples and how they could best communicate.

Rapoport studied international diplomats and looked specifically at how the most successful diplomats operated. How were they managing to communicate and collaborate with other nations—especially when those other nations had different cultural mores, opposing goals and viewpoints, or even hostility toward the other country? Rapoport observed and analyzed the masters of diplomacy the way John would later examine the "masters of love" in the lab. And what he discovered was that the most successful negotiators brought up an issue or complaint in a very specific way:

- Without blame
- Without criticism
- Without contempt

By doing so, they neutralized the other party's defensiveness. Their messages were better received, and their success rate for getting a positive outcome out of the interaction was much higher.[4]

When we went back to the lab, we saw that the most successful couples did *exactly* the same thing as the successful diplomats: they introduced concerns without blame, criticism, or contempt. How? Instead of launching into the conflict discussion by describing their partners and everything they were doing wrong—an easy default approach when we're upset—they flipped it. They raised an issue by talking about *themselves* and their own feelings—not by talking about their partner's bad behavior and character flaws. Then they described the problem or situation factually and neutrally, without assigning blame. And finally, they stated what they needed in positive terms in order for the situation to get better. That was it: the basic formula for a successful start to a fight.

I feel x.

The problem is y.

I need z.

Pretty simple but also highly effective—both in international summits and across kitchen tables. Or across scorching hiking trails in the Arizona desert.

We're going to take you through the steps of the softened start-up in more detail at the end of the chapter so you know exactly what to do—for now, let's come back to Kristen and Steve.

Getting Off on the Right Foot: A Whole New Trajectory

For Kristen and Steve, that day on the cliff in Sedona was the moment they realized: we need help. When they came to see us for a therapy intensive, we started by getting their backstory so we could more fully understand what was going on and where each was coming from.

When Kristen and Steve met, they were married—to other people. Their marriages were both in rocky phases that they weren't sure they could ever pull out of. Both felt lonely and disconnected from their partners, and even though they weren't out there looking for a new relationship, they felt the zing of connection and attraction when they met. Steve was a cardiologist. Kristen was his patient. When they first exchanged phone numbers, it was in a professional capacity—he often gave his phone number to patients so they could reach out with urgent questions. He was a dedicated physician and wanted people to feel taken care of. At first, their texts back and forth focused on Kristen's health. Then they morphed into something more. Something flirtatious.

He'd ask her if she was taking good care of her heart.

She'd text back and suggest that maybe she needed to schedule an appointment soon to get it checked out.

Long story short: they fell in love. Divorced their spouses. Married each other.

Kristen, fifteen years younger than her husband, brought three young children into the marriage; Steve brought a deep dedication to his career and a work ethic that often kept him at his clinic and away from his family. In the following years, they had two children of their own. Life was hectic and busy, and out of necessity, it seemed, they fell into very separate roles: Kristen, the caretaker at home, Steve, the dedicated doctor working long hours. The fights started long before the vacation to Sedona, and they always seemed to start horribly, with pent-up frustration from Kristen exploding at Steve out of nowhere (at least from his perspective). Feeling ambushed, he'd get flooded and shut down the conversation—it seemed like there was no other way to deal with Kristen.

From Kristen's perspective, she didn't really know any other way to express herself during a fight. She'd grown up the only child of a single mom who tended to be contemptuous and critical of her daughter, so to a certain extent, that kind of approach with someone she was intimate with had been normalized. Kristen also described her mother as highly melodramatic—everything was a big deal, everything elicited a huge, overblown reaction, and she would go to great lengths to get her daughter to respond and pay attention to her. She was constantly saying, "I could die, and then you'll be sorry!" Once, Kristen had come home from school and found her mother lying on the floor, blood everywhere, apparently dead. *But it was ketchup, not blood.* Her mother sat up from the kitchen floor and said, "Maybe now you'll realize how important I am to you!"

At this point in her life, Kristen was highly reactive to anything that smacked of melodrama or overreaction. And that's exactly the filter through which she heard her husband the day of the hike. She assumed he was being melodramatic, creating an issue out of nothing. And his refusal to go with her—*for no good reason,* in her view—tapped into a deep well of feelings of abandonment and thwarted dreams. She'd always envisioned her husband as someone who would go out adventuring with her—a partner in exploring the world. When he refused to take her hand and join her in that, it felt like a crushing rejection.

Steve explained to her that in that moment on the trail, he was being anything but performative—he really had felt terrified. Part of why he'd gone into cardiology was to save lives. He told this story: When he was a teenager, he'd seen a kid fall off a boat and drown, right in front of him. Nobody could save the boy, even though many tried. Later on in his medical career, he'd seen many patients suddenly suffer a heart attack, a deadly one from which there was no recovery. All of these had been shocking and traumatic experiences, especially the first one he'd witnessed as a teenager. His experiences had instilled in him the sense that life was extraordinarily fragile and could be so easily snuffed out. He felt deeply the mortality and vulnerability of himself and those he loved and constantly worried about the innocuous moment that could turn into a tragedy. He'd learned to be cautious and vigilant and to weigh risk versus reward seriously. He felt a huge responsibility, too, to his wife and kids—*If something happens to me,* he was always thinking, *they'll be all alone, with no financial or family support.*

Okay—so there's a lot going on here! Are we going to solve all of this in three minutes? Of course not! But the wonderful thing is, *we don't have to.*

Remember: we're not here to "fix" our perpetual problems, and for this couple, this is a perpetual problem. Kristen will always have a need for adventure that involves taking risks, and Steve will always be a cautious person who tends to be more risk averse. Our goal is not to solve their differences—it's to get Kristen and Steve to openly share their hopes and fears and these triggers from their pasts that underlie these differences. Once they understand each other better, they'll be able to find a way to be partners in exploration and adventure—there are a lot of creative ways to have adventures that don't involve thousand-foot drops. But all of that hinges on how they start their discussion.

With Kristen and Steve, the very first thing we worked on was this: When you're disappointed and unhappy and are feeling something very negative, how do you say it?

We went back to what he'd felt on the trail. What she'd felt on the trail. We talked about how important it was to listen and *be listened to*—but if we use criticism and contempt to express our needs, it sabotages us getting listened to. Kristen had a deeply ingrained habit of using criticism to start a discussion; essentially, criticism was her language. We had to replace that learned language with a new language. We asked the two of them to reenact their cliffside fight and to remember exactly what they had been thinking and feeling—the fear from him, the resentment and rage from her—but this time, even with all those powerful swirling emotions, to raise the issue *without* contempt or criticism instead by focusing on their own feelings and needs.

Kristen took a deep breath.

"I'm so disappointed you don't want to go up this trail with me," she said to her husband. "I was so excited to see what's around the next corner—*with you.* I want us to go on adventures together! This was really important to me . . ."

It wasn't all smooth sailing from there, but *wow* did that softened start-up make a big difference. It gave Steve the option of responding to his wife with curiosity instead of defensiveness.

Okay, So We Started Soft—Now What?

Let's hit pause on Kristen and Steve for just a moment and come back to Rapoport's diplomats.

Rapoport found that once one party brought up an issue, there was a critical role for the person on the receiving end too. And that was to listen *without bringing up their own point of view.* And in the Love Lab, the masters of love did exactly that.

As we said earlier, most people—regardless of conflict style—fall into the trap of rushing into the persuasion phase of a fight. But the most successful diplomats, and the most successful couples, postpone persuasion and instead focus on understanding the other person's complaint or problem. This was actually Rapoport's biggest finding with the diplomats. It wasn't just that one party raised an issue gently—the listening party also had to put off any attempt to argue, debate, or discuss their own point of view until they showed that they understood the speaker's position first. Instead, they listened closely, asked questions if there was anything they didn't understand, and then summarized the speaker's viewpoint back to the speaker to ensure that they had understood the issue.

Well, of course, you might be thinking, *these are diplomats—it's their job to be diplomatic!* As it turned out, we saw the exact same pattern of behavior among the couples in the Love Lab who had satisfying relationships over the long haul. In the lab's conflict task, once one partner brought up an issue, the person on the receiving end would do these specific things:

1. Listen closely, without bringing in their own perspective, sometimes even repeating back parts of the story the partner was telling (Example: "Okay, so you were really disappointed when I texted to say I had to stay at work instead of meeting you at the party . . .").
2. Ask clarifying or open-ended questions to understand the issue better ("Why do you think you felt sad about this tonight in particular? Other times it hasn't seemed to bother you").
3. Summarize the problem to their partner's satisfaction—in other words, if their summary was not correct, they'd go back to asking questions to clarify ("What I'm hearing

is that you feel you're not a priority for me because I've been so busy at work—is that right?").

4. And finally, they would offer some words of validation by stepping into their partner's shoes and showing that they understood and empathized with their partner's point of view—*even if they didn't agree with their partner's position on the issue.* Validation is not the same thing as agreement. They'd say words like "Yeah, I can understand how you'd feel that way—I have had to cancel a lot of stuff lately. That makes sense."

In the above example, this couple might go on to discuss how to balance family and work and expectations surrounding financial responsibilities, time together, career goals, and more. The point is this conversation is now poised to be productive and *go somewhere.*

So, regardless of who's bringing up the issue, both of you have a role. Partner 1's role is to bring up the issue gently. Partner 2's role is to listen fully. After Partner 2 has demonstrated that they understand Partner 1's viewpoint, the two can switch roles. Partner 2 can now voice their own position while Partner 1 listens and in turn demonstrates understanding Partner 2's position. Remember that across all conflict styles, we all tend to make the mistake of rushing to persuasion before we've fully understood the problem. Don't make this mistake. Remember that it's best to understand each other's point of view first. At this stage the only goal is understanding. Persuasion comes afterwards.

The Power of Postponing Persuasion

With Kristen and Steve, we worked on these roles during a marathon couples intensive, three consecutive days of therapy, working five to six hours a day. With Kristen, the goal was to use a softened start-up when she brought up an issue. And for Steve, it was not to react defensively when she raised an issue, which was his pattern. Instead, he needed to try to follow Kristen's train of thought as if she were an engine on a railroad track: following closely what she was saying instead of planning his own rebuttals. Kristen was a fast talker and a fast thinker who often slipped into criticisms—Julie would have to interrupt her over and over again to remind her to soften her start-ups. It really was like learning a new language for both of them.

That's why a softened start-up can be hard, as simple as it seems—learning a new language is always hard! It takes practice. The only way you can do it is by repetition and by *having it reinforced*. If you use that new language, you'll likely see the immediate result that your partner is really listening instead of getting defensive. Our next piece of work with Kristen and Steve was to focus on building fondness and admiration. We used our positive adjectives checklist and asked them to choose three qualities off the list that they thought described their partner.

Kristen looked over the list:

Loving / sensitive / brave / intelligent / thoughtful / generous / loyal / truthful / strong / energetic / sexy / decisive / creative / imaginative / fun / attractive / interesting / supportive / funny / considerate / affectionate / organized / resourceful / athletic / cheerful / coordinated / graceful / playful / caring / a great friend / exciting / thrifty / shy /

committed / involved / expressive / active / careful /
reserved / adventurous / receptive / reliable / responsible /
dependable / nurturing / warm / virile / kind / gentle /
practical / lusty / witty / relaxed / beautiful / handsome /
calm / lively / a great partner / a great parent / assertive /
protective / sweet / tender / powerful / flexible /
understanding / totally silly / vulnerable / (fill in your own!)

Then she read aloud to Steve the things she admired about him: *loyal, supportive, trustworthy.*

Steve picked out three for Kristen: *vivacious, energetic, quick-witted.*

These qualities that they adored about each other were, of course, deeply entwined with the ways they were different and currently in conflict over their approach to life. But in conflict, it can help immensely to simply remember this: "We're clashing because of our differences, but these differences are also why I love you."

Kristen struggled with this activity—ever since childhood, she wasn't used to receiving compliments. They were foreign territory and made her anxious. So when Steve read out the positive qualities he saw in her, she handled her anxiety with a knee-jerk response that effectively pushed Steve away: she called him a liar.

Julie reminded her, "That sounds like a criticism, Kristen, your old language. Why don't you try a softened start-up here instead?"

Kristen had to dig a little deeper to describe herself instead of describing Steve. "It's so hard for me to hear that and believe you," she said. "My mother never said anything nice about me unless she wanted to manipulate me. So it's really hard for me to trust that your compliments are real."

Steve had initially responded harshly to Kristen's remark with a counterattack, a form of defensiveness: "Oh, and you expect me to believe you?" he snapped back, sarcastic. "If I'm so 'supportive,' why do you treat me like shit?"

We asked Steve to notice that he felt defensive and rather than *going* defensive to say instead, "I'm *feeling* defensive—can you say that another way?" It was better to make a repair like this one and to give Kristen another chance than to escalate into an attack/defend battle.

And Kristen's job, if she realized she'd blurted out something harsh, was to acknowledge she had done so and to try again.

Her repair might sound like this:

"Oh no, I said that the wrong way. Can I start again?"

We're all human; we're going to make mistakes. Even when we fight right, it can get messy and emotional. The point is not to be perfect but to own those inevitable slip-ups, make a quick repair, and get right back on track. The two of us still make mistakes like these in our fights too, even after all this research! And when we do, we try our best to give each other a little grace and the opportunity to start again.

Script for the Softened Start-Up

Let's go into more detail about softened start-ups. When couples practice softened start-ups to raise a complaint, it really makes a huge difference. Remember: 96 percent of the time, the way you start a fight predicts the way you end the fight as well as how your relationship will go years into the future.[5] Over time, positive start-ups will help you create more success and stability for your relationship.

Here's the basic script for using a softened start-up. You're going to customize this to your own situation but still stay within this essential formula:

"I feel (emotion) about (situation / problem) and I need (your *positive* need)."

Let's take a look at a few examples of this formula in action.

Harsh start-up: "You overspent again! When are you going to stop being so irresponsible with our money?"

Softened start-up: "I feel really stressed *(the feeling)* about our budget this month—it looks like we're going to be short again *(the situation)*. Can we sit down together and plan how to cut some of our expenses *(the need)*?"

Harsh start-up: "You're going out *again*? Great. I'll just sit home alone, again." *(Sarcastically)* "How fun for me!"

Softened start-up: "Hey, listen. I need to talk to you about something. I keep thinking about last week, when you went out with friends instead of coming home for dinner. I know I said it was okay, but for some reason it's still bothering me. I just felt kind of rejected and lonely *(the feeling)*. Maybe it's because we haven't had much one-on-one time together lately *(the situation)*. Could you come home right after work tonight? I miss you *(the need)*."

Harsh start-up: "I can't *believe* you agreed to spend Christmas at your mom's again. You just cave in to whatever she wants. I guess we're never going to spend a holiday at my parents'. Because the only family that matters is yours."

Softened start-up: "Babe, I'm sorry, but I'm still so frustrated *(the feeling)*. Your mom pressured us into spending Christmas with her again *(the situation)*. I miss spending holidays with my family *(more feeling)*. Can you please go back to her and bow out for this year so we can go to my parents' instead? That would make me feel like you really have my back *(the need)*."

You can see in the examples above that although the content, style, and phrasing can vary, the basic rules of the softened start-up remain constant:

1. Describe yourself and *your* feelings.
2. Describe the problem without criticizing or blaming your partner for it. You're talking about the *situation* not about your partner.
3. State your *positive* need—identify what your partner can do to help this situation get better. You're not fixating on the negative or listing the ways they've failed. You're telling them specifically how they can shine for you.

These are the three pieces of a successful softened start-up. And the final thing to remember is this: *don't pile on.* **No kitchen-sinking!** Meaning, don't tell your partner to sit down and then lay fourteen problems in their lap. Focus on *this situation* only, even if the issue is a pattern that repeats itself. No "you always" or "you never." That language sounds like criticism too. It will never get you anywhere in conflict.

Now remember the listener's role:

To be a great listener:
Postpone bringing up your perspective and just listen.
If you don't understand something, ask questions, but only ones to help increase your understanding.

Summarize your partner's feelings, the problem, and their needs to your partner's satisfaction.

Offer some genuine words of validation.

The bottom line: couples who use softened start-ups have a much greater chance of success in their relationship. And remember that "success" in this context means not just staying together but also experiencing high levels of happiness and satisfaction. We said we could predict, with 90 percent accuracy, which couples would divorce after observing a short interaction—but note, that prediction rate forecasts who the relationship masters will be too. Softened start-up is a powerful indicator that a couple is going to be successful in the long term.

A universal quality of masters of love: they start with kindness even when they're upset.

Troubleshooting Softened Start-Ups

Will a softened start-up look different across the different conflict styles?

Sure, but the basic principles remain the same. The formula doesn't change—it's still *I feel x about y situation, and z here's what I need*—but the intensity of speaking will look different, depending on which conflict style the partner is comfortable with. A volatile person is going to have more intensity and more passion. Avoidant partners are going to understate and speak more tentatively. And validators might shift into problem-solving mode faster (sometimes not the best idea—more on this in the next chapter). So:

- **Volatile**

  Instead of: "What the hell? You still haven't paid this? I can't believe I married the most irresponsible person on the planet!"

  The volatile softened start-up: "I'm feeling absolutely hopeless about our money situation. We have overdue bills again. I desperately need you to pay the bills on time like we agreed! What can we do?"

- **Avoidant**

  Instead of: "Hmm, here are the bills again." Or saying nothing at all, while feeling stressed and worried.

  The avoidant softened start-up: "I'm a little nervous that the bills are still sitting here. I'd be happy to pay them if you want . . . or maybe you could?"

- **Validating**

  Instead of: "I see you haven't paid these bills again. You realize you're wrecking our credit rating, right?"

  The validating softened start-up: "I'm frustrated that the bills haven't been paid on time again—it could affect our credit rating. The last time we talked about this, we agreed that you'd take care of these bills and I'd make the doctor appointments, remember? Why don't I do bedtime with the kids so you can deal with these tonight, okay?"

In the case of a **conflict style mismatch,** there's a higher chance of missed signals. An avoidant partner might perceive the volatile's start-up as harsh even if it's softened, because of the intensity of emotion being expressed, even if the softened start-up rules are being followed pretty much to the letter. So the key here, no matter what conflict style you and your partner prefer, is to look closely if you feel defensive or attacked and see: Is there really contempt, blame, or criticism there? You or your partner may tend to use more emotional language, but if you're careful to avoid criticism and blame, your softened start-up can still work.

A final note: Those who are really used to approaching their partners with a harsh start-up will sometimes justify that approach by claiming that they are "just being honest" or "authentic." Our response: We're not saying you shouldn't be honest. We're asking you to be *even more honest* by focusing on *your* feelings instead of describing what your partner's doing wrong. Don't shore up your position with a list of grievances. Don't look for a reason why your partner is inherently wrong. And don't focus on all the character flaws your partner possesses.

And if you're thinking, "But how will my partner improve if I don't tell them what's wrong?"

The answer? It's not your job to improve your partner. That's solely your partner's job. Your job is to be the best version of yourself that *you* can be. And if you are kinder even during conflicts, your partner will likely cooperate more too. It's a win/win.

Make It Softer!

Now it's your turn to see if you can come up with a softer version of a harsh start-up. We're going to give you some vignettes for practicing softened start-ups. There are many right answers to these! We've seen people come up with all kinds of creative gentle alternatives—and keep in mind that a dash of humor can go a long way, as long as it's genuine and not sarcastic. In one of our workshops, we asked the assembled couples how they'd change this harsh start-up from a spouse who really wants to have sex but is feeling rejected by his partner: He says, "You never want to touch me anymore! I guess you're a cold fish just like your mother."

One fellow in the workshop raised his hand and offered this suggestion: "I'm feeling horny right now. I think I'm gonna go upstairs and have sex. You wanna come along?"

Okay, your turn. Your job is to soften the harsh start-ups below. We'll describe a situation and then give you the "devil on your shoulder" version of how you might raise this issue with your partner, especially if you go with the first impulsive thing that leaps to mind. But this time, you'll have a chance to hit pause, think it through, and revise your thoughts into a softened start-up. How would you rephrase these?

Scene: Your partner pulls into the driveway. Immediately you notice that there is a new dent in the front bumper and a long scrape along the door. Your blood pressure goes through the roof—just two weeks ago, you and your partner were pulled over for speeding in a school zone and the ticket was huge.

Harsh start-up: "What the hell is this? *Again?* Do you have any idea how much your reckless driving is going to cost us?"

Reflection: How is your partner likely to reply to this?

Your softened start-up:

_____

_____

_____

Scene: Your partner is helping the kids with their homework while you make dinner. You overhear them working on a math assignment—it isn't going well. Your daughter is in tears, and your partner is frustrated and snaps at her that if she doesn't focus, the homework help session is over, and she can flunk for all they care.

Harsh start-up: "Geez, you sound just like your awful father. Do you want to mess her up the way your parents messed you up?"

Reflection: How is your partner likely to respond to this?

Your softened start-up:

_____

_____

_____

Scene: Your partner has a horrible day at the office and comes home very grumpy. All evening they get angry at you every other minute over trivial things, like leaving the refrigerator door open too long.

Harsh start-up: "Why are you being so mean to me? You're a total monster tonight!"

Reflection: How is your partner likely to respond to this?

Your softened start-up:

_____

_____

_____

Do this with your partner, if possible, and discuss your answers—both your guesses about your partner's reactions to the harsh start-ups for each example and your softened start-up alternatives. If you have trouble thinking of effective ways to phrase feelings and needs, use the two columns below for inspiration, and choose or modify something from the _feelings_ column and something from the _needs_ column to fit each situation—or use the format and list to introduce a real issue you'd like to discuss with your partner. A more extensive version of these lists is available in our free Gottman Card Decks app.

I FEEL . . .	I NEED . . .
• Abandoned	• ...to know what you're thinking
• Afraid	• ...to have a conversation with you
• Alarmed	• ...you to ask me about my day
• Angry	• ...our reunions to be warm and affectionate
• Ashamed	• ...you to put down your phone when I need to talk
• Belittled	
• Betrayed	• ...you to tell me I look nice
• Competitive	• ...to know that you feel proud of me
• Conflicted	• ...some quiet time when I first get home
• Confused	• ...you to listen to me when I'm upset
• Crushed	• ...you to listen to me when I'm sad and not blame me
• Defeated	
• Desperate	• ...to have a weekly date
• Disgusted	• ...you to do more of the housework
• Distant from you	• ...you to speak calmly to me when you are upset
• Distrustful	
• Embarrassed	• ...you to say you appreciate my hard work
• Enraged	• ...to know you think I'm sexy
• Frantic	• ...you to touch me affectionately more often
• Frustrated	
• Furious	• ...you to answer my texts
• Hurt	• ...to talk more about our kids
• I am not sure how I feel	• ...you to listen and not try to give advice
	• ...to hear more compliments from you
• Outraged	• ...you to take my side when your family criticizes me
• Shocked	
• Stressed	• ...to hear you say, "I love you"
• Surprised	
• Tense	
• Upset	
• Worried	
• Unaccepted	

FIGHT #2:
THE FLOOD

Mistake: Attacking,
Defending, Withdrawing

Picture this common scenario: A conversation with your partner starts to get prickly. Maybe it's about someone overdrawing the checking account. Maybe it's about what to have for dinner. Maybe it's whether to move to the suburbs of Timbuktu. Whatever the topic—and perhaps even if you started softly—it's getting contentious. Now you feel attacked, misunderstood, wronged, angry, trapped, or all of the above.

You feel a hot flash; your palms go sweaty.

Your heart starts to beat faster, louder in your ears.

Your chest feels tight.

Your brain feels fuzzy and frantic; you can't even focus on what your partner is saying anymore. Instead, you're thinking, *I can't deal with this. How do I get out of here? I am so done with this conversation.*

Maybe you lash out and say something harsh—meet fire with fire.

Maybe you dig into your position, focusing on blocking the blows that are coming in from your partner. You barely have a second to think and figure out what you want to say, much less the best way to say it. You're in a defensive crouch.

Or maybe you shut down completely. What's the point of saying anything? It'll just make things worse. You go silent, curl inward or turn away, refuse to respond to anything your partner is saying or doing, and you act as if they're not even there—you need this interaction to end! You're *stonewalling*: becoming like a stone wall to shield yourself from your partner's attack. It feels like the only option.

In all of the above responses, there is one universal constant: *flooding*.

What Is Flooding?

Flooding happens when we get overwhelmed in conflict, hijacked by our own nervous system in response to negativity from our partners. The physiological effects are immediate. Our heart rate rockets from a normal resting heart rate range of about 76 bpm (women) or 82 bpm (men) up to over 100 beats per minute, and even as high as 195. Our adrenal gland, alerted to prepare for a survival situation, releases stress hormones into the blood. Like animals being hunted, we go into fight, flight, or freeze mode; now we are more controlled by the racing of our heart and the dump of cortisol and adrenaline into our bloodstream than we are by rational or empathetic mental processes. The body is in a full-on fear response: it's rapidly priming our system to outrun a tiger *not* to have a calm and compassionate conversation with the partner right in front of us.

When we see a pattern of flooding in a couple in the Love Lab, we know that without intervention, they're headed for a split.[1] Because when you're flooded, you are incapable of fighting right. It simply isn't possible. As we get flooded, we begin to rapidly lose the capacity to process information. It's harder to pay attention. We can't hear or understand what the other person is saying. We respond reflexively and use the first three Horsemen (i.e., we're likely to be critical, contemptuous, or defensive), which often results in the fourth Horseman (stonewalling) coming from our partners.

Starting softly, as we worked on in the previous chapter, is important. But as a conflict unfolds, we are presented with decision points at almost every moment: whether to listen or speak, whether to describe ourselves or our partners, what tone to use, and more. A harsh start-up at the beginning of a conversation will have negative ripple effects for sure—but criticism and contempt can creep in at any point during a conflict conversation. And when they do, we tend to retreat to a couple of classic fallback positions.

1. We default to an attack-and-defend dynamic: our partner becomes an enemy.
2. We shut down and withdraw: our partner becomes a stranger.

From these polarized positions, we are no longer able to reach each other. There's no listening, no learning, no capacity to explore the underlying cause of the conflict—nothing. Even when one partner makes an overture or a concession—a "repair attempt"—the other partner won't be able to see it or accept it.

Repair, both during and after fights, is powerful. It's one of the main things that separate the masters of love from the disasters.[2] Remember: the masters fight just as much as any couple out there—

but they also understand how to make repairs along the way. But making a repair in the midst of conflict means admitting that you've stepped off the track of a healthy and compassionate exchange, and flooding makes it really difficult to own your own mistakes.

A *lot* of couples are affected by flooding. Our recent international study found that a whopping 97 percent of all couples, regardless of sexual orientation, listed flooding as a major challenge.[3] Mind you, having this emotional and physiological response during a fight is completely normal—we're human, the issues we fight about matter deeply to us, and this is one of the natural ways that our minds and bodies react when we're fighting about something that really matters to us. But if we want to be able to stay collaborative, stay positive, stave off the Four Horsemen, and fight right, we do need to learn how to cope with those overwhelming moments in conflict so we can be our better selves.

We've talked about how to start off on the right track in conflict. Now let's talk about how to *stay* on the right track.

Enemies and Strangers

We'd like to give you a glimpse here into the fights of two different couples. The issues they're dealing with are worlds apart. One couple is facing a catastrophic relationship crisis that's causing them to question whether their marriage is going to survive. The second couple has a hurtful and surprising fight erupt over something quite minor and routine. But flooding affects both.

Couple #1: Stan and Susan

Stan and Susan seem to have all their ducks in a row. Stan is a high-level tennis pro at the top of his game. Susan, who supported him when he was an emerging athlete just trying to break into the tennis circuit, is proud of how far they've come. They moved around a fair amount when Stan was proving himself as an athlete and working his way up to pro, but now finally they're settled in a house and community she loves. They don't have to worry about money—Stan is practically a household name. And after trying to get pregnant for many years, they did IVF and got pregnant on the first round: *twins.*

The babies are toddlers now, and they are a handful! Life is a whirlwind. Stan travels a lot for matches, all over the world, disappearing for weeks at a time; meanwhile, Susan wrangles the kids with the help of their wonderful nanny who's starting to feel more like her co-parent than Stan does. She and the kids are always looking forward to Stan coming home, but when he finally does, it can feel even more chaotic, with the toddlers clamoring for their dad's attention and acting out. When they go out on dates, Susan fills Stan in on everything that's going on in their babies' lives, feeling sorry that he's missing so much.

One day the landline rings at the house. When Susan answers, a woman's voice asks if Stan is home.

"No," Susan says, "he's at the match in Tampa, but he should be available by cell. Who is this?"

The woman says her name, and it does ring a bell—maybe there's someone by that name on Stan's team. He has a small rotating staff of people who work for him—a manager, an assistant, a social media person. The woman on the phone says something vague about not being able to reach him on the cell, which seems odd.

"Do you work with him?" Susan asks, confused.

The woman hangs up.

When Susan tells Stan about the odd phone call, she sees, immediately, that something flickers across his face: fear, guilt. She confronts him. He denies doing anything wrong. But when she presses, he breaks down and admits it: he's been having an affair. It's been going on for almost a year. He met her through friends at a match; she flew to the next one, showed up at an afterparty, and it just happened. He hadn't meant to do it. It didn't mean anything. It was just sex.

The wind goes out of her like she's been punched. She is astonished—at him, that he was capable of such a thing; at herself, for being so stupid. It's absolutely surreal: this is something that happens to other people, to characters on television, not to her and Stan! Stan, who followed her from house party to house party at college in an attempt to casually meet her, acting surprised when he "accidentally" ran into her again and again on the dance floor. Stan, who held their newborn twins and cried. Everything she thought she knew, it turns out, is a lie. Her whole world is crumbling.

She has one question: How could you do this to us?

Stan is already feeling it: the regret. The shame. But he doesn't like that. He's rationalized his actions: *She never has time for me. We're more like people running a business together these days than like lovers. She'll never know. People do it all the time. It's not a big deal. I deserve this.*

He gets very defensive. She comes at him even harder, shocked that he doesn't see how wrong he is. He defends harder, digging in:

she isn't warm to him. They never have sex anymore. She shuts him down all the time—she's not even interested, so why does she care so much? She only pays attention to the kids—it's like he's invisible.

At this point: He's flooded. She's flooded. Both hearts are hammering hard; adrenaline is zinging through their veins. Stan's physiological response has ratcheted up and overwhelmed him even faster than Susan's, and he'll take a lot longer to come down from it.

Here's why: For evolutionary reasons having to do with protecting the tribe and hunting dangerous animals for food, our prehistoric male ancestors gained a survival advantage by being able to quickly mount and sustain an adrenaline-packed response to danger. Those with this rapid response were better able to fight off enemies and to hunt for food, and because they were better survivors, their genes were more likely to get passed down and eventually inherited by our men today. That kind of enduring fight-or-flight response might have helped Stan's distant ancestors survive, but it isn't doing him any favors now.

"I don't know why I bother coming home at all!" he screams. "You don't even care if I'm here!"

"I wish I had never met you," sobs Susan. "I'd be so much happier."

In the days, weeks, and months that follow, Stan and Susan have fights like they've never had in the history of their marriage. They can't discuss any issue without getting extremely flooded and saying the first, and worst, thing that pops into their heads. Even conversations that start out calmly—like one about how to manage the kids while they try to work things out—rapidly escalate into two nervous systems in extreme overdrive, with the two systems' owners screaming at each other and throwing things in rage. One night, Stan fast-pitches a drinking glass onto the kitchen floor; it shatters so hard a piece of it strikes Susan's leg and cuts her, drawing blood. Horrified, they realize how out of control they are. They decide to seek therapy.

And end up in our office.

The previous story is one they described to Julie, moment by moment, to explain what brought them to her for a therapy intensive. It wasn't easy for them to tell their stories. Both got flooded multiple times. Susan would cry and then get angry; Stan would get angry then shut down. When Julie asked them to check in with each other there in the office, the conversation went like this:

Stan: Check in with her? Okay. I guess. Sure. So . . . hey. How are you doing today?

Susan: *(with an incredulous laugh)* Well, pretty crappy, what do you expect?

Stan: What do you mean, "What do I expect?"

Susan: I mean you've destroyed my life! Of course I'm feeling crappy!

Stan: Hey, this isn't all on me. You're the one who pulled away first. You stopped caring about me. You stopped being a real wife to me.

Susan: I'm a mother to twins. Have *you* ever tried taking care of twins all on your own? No! You haven't! Not even your own *kids*! And don't blame your affair on me. That *is* on you.

Stan: I know! But how many times do I have to tell you? *I'm sorry I'm sorry I'm sorry.* Okay? What is it going to take?

Susan: I know you're sorry, I do. But—

Stan: You're so self-centered. You don't actually want to make this better. You just want me to keep feeling bad. You want to keep me under your thumb and control me.

Susan: Control *you*? Ha! You need to control yourself. You disgust
me. I'm out of here—I don't even want to look at your face.

Can you hear how flooded both partners became in just a few
moments? No wonder. They were both hurling criticism and contempt at one another.

Now let's hear about another couple where flooding also happened but showed up differently in the room.

Couple #2: Nora and Robbie

Nora and Robbie, a dual-income, successful Black couple in their
early forties, were college sweethearts and married young. Their kids
are teenagers, but sometimes (they joke) it seems like the kids need
just as much help with basic daily stuff as they did when they were
toddlers. Mornings especially.

Getting both of them fed and with all their supplies to their respective schools on time (one, high school, one, middle school)
seems to take a Herculean effort. "Are we going to have to call them
at college to tell them to brush their teeth?" Nora whispered to her
husband the other morning, as a surly fourteen-year-old narrowed
her eyes at them across the kitchen. (They shared a quiet laugh.)

On this particular morning, Nora, who's been pushing hard at
work, is sick—really sick. She's corporate counsel for a big tech company and has a major deal to close in less than a week. She feels
awful—pounding headache, body aches, fever. Could be COVID.
She swabs, and the test is negative, but it may just be too early to pop
a positive. Usually she's up before the kids and sets out food for them
to make themselves breakfast: bowls and spoons, instant oatmeal
packets, milk, sliced bananas. But she feels like she's been run over by

a semi. Meanwhile, Robbie isn't sick, but he's exhausted. He spent the whole weekend framing the deck he's adding to the back of their house—he's trying to get it done before the weather turns rainy, and it's been a long slog. He's achy and feels like he didn't get a weekend. But still, when Nora tells him she feels terrible, he says, kindly, "Why don't you sleep in," and goes to get the kids breakfast.

Nora plummets into sleep, waking some time later when Robbie pops his head back in the bedroom.

Robbie: Hey, I'm heading out. Just wanted to let you know that it's already 7:40. The kids'll be late to school if you don't leave in the next five.

Nora: Oh—I thought you were taking the kids?

Robbie: *(with a sigh, clearly irritated)* I can't, baby, I'll be late. Their school's in the opposite direction. I gotta go.

Nora: Honey, I'm really sick. Can't you just deal with this for once?

Robbie: *For once?* Hang on—I just got up early and did *your* job. Now I'm the bad guy? You don't seem that sick. I think you can manage a ten-minute drive.

Nora: How do you know how sick I am? I feel terrible! I think it might be COVID.

Robbie: Okay, well, I assumed it was just a cold, I'm sorry.

Nora: No, it's worse, and why aren't you being nicer to me? I'm always nice to you! I do stuff for you all the time.

Robbie: *(blowing up)* Nora, what the hell do you think I've been doing for the past three weeks while you've been working on this deal? I left work early three times last week alone. I've been picking up *all* the slack around here!

Nora: Oh, God forbid you pick up some slack for a few weeks. Do you know how many *years* I picked up the slack for you?

Robbie: Excuse me?

Nora: You heard me!

Robbie: I can't believe you would say that to me. After everything I do for you and the kids.

Nora: Oh, don't give me that crap. You always act like you're doing me some huge favor just for doing your share. Like you're some hero because you parented your kids or cleaned a toilet! Grow up, Robbie!

Robbie: *(leaves abruptly, slamming the door)*

What Went Wrong?

These conversations started out just fine. We see Stan checking in with his wife to take the temperature of an ongoing source of conflict between the two of them, and that's good. We see Nora asking clearly for something she needs—also good. But pretty soon, both conversations take a sharp turn south. We see a domino effect here, where criticism or contempt from one or both partners leads to defensiveness, flooding, missed repair attempts, and rapid escalation. Both fights end with harsh and painful accusations, meaning they've become "regrettable incidents" where there's been emotional injury to one or both partners. These couples will have to do some work to process and heal from these incidents so they can move past the painful things that were said (more on this in Fight #5).

Look back at the above conversations, and see if you can spot a few of the moments where these fights ratcheted up. You'll notice that with both couples, there are critical or contemptuous comments from both parties and defensiveness from both parties, and where the pace and temperature of the interaction spike, we can infer that one or both partners are beginning to experience the physiological effects of flooding. The big problem here? They fail to address the flooding in any way. Instead, they barrel on with the conversation.

Here's the big thing to understand about flooding: you *have* to stop and deal with it. There is no way to have a productive or positive conflict conversation once you're flooded. This is one of the main reasons that couples don't (or more accurately, can't) put best conflict management practices into play—you might have learned all the "right" ways to fight, but when you're flooded, you can't access your new learning. Your nervous system is yanking you back into a primitive, fight-or-flight response. When you're flooded, those higher forms of cognitive processing are nowhere to be seen. They all go out the window. When you get flooded and keep fighting, damage and hurt are the only results you'll see.

So, when your fight starts softly but then goes off the rails, ask yourself: *Am I flooded? Is my partner flooded?* And *stop.* The number one thing we need to do when a fight takes a nasty turn is stop action and cope with flooding.

How to Stop the Flood

First, learn to identify the signs that you're getting flooded so you can act early. This is *the* most important lesson about flooding that we impart to our clients: to become very aware of the first signs of flooding in their body. These could be any number of things. The signals that your body is flooding will be unique to you, but they will probably resemble other times you've felt emotionally overwhelmed.

Here are some classic signs of flooding:

- Shortness of breath
- Gritted teeth
- Jaw tight or achy
- Heat anywhere in the body
- Face turns red or feels red
- You feel "kicked in the gut"
- Muscles tighten (nobody in flooding is ever relaxed—there is tension somewhere)
- Eyes narrow (think Clint Eastwood's squint when he's sizing up somebody)
- Heartbeat races or pounds (typically over 100 beats per minute)
- Stomach feels queasy
- Mind is "spinning"

Paying attention to your body and knowing your body's flooding signals are super important here, because intervening right away in your own physiological response is how you *avoid* escalating into a regrettable incident with your partner. Flooding shows up differently in all of us in terms of behavior, intensity, and timing. Some people go outward when flooded (lash out, criticize, attack) and others go inward (shut down, stonewall). Some people tend to have a more intense nervous system response and take a long time to "come down" from it back to their baseline (men are more likely to experience this); for others, it's more subtle. Some people get flooded really easily, where it's almost instantaneous after negativity or criticism—half a second, and *wham*, they're in it. Stan was this way. It was just how his nervous system was wired—anything he perceived as an attack would essentially flip a switch in his body. So identifying those "early warning signs" was especially critical for him.

Now, let's imagine for a moment that you're using our AI. The physiology algorithm is extremely sensitive, and it's going to be able to warn you of imminent flooding perhaps even before you notice it yourself. It picks up the most subtle shifts in skin tone and heart rate, alerting you that you're starting to experience physiological arousal. This ability was a big priority for us in developing software to help therapists and couples because this information, about how you are responding *physically* to a conversation with your partner, is so vital to the outcome. But as helpful as an algorithm is, you don't need AI to tell you you're getting flooded. You can be your own highly sensitive AI—as long as you are aware of your own personal physiological "tells" so that, in conflict, your brain can send up a little red flag that says, *Hey, here comes the flood.*

So take a moment now, think about the last time you felt flooded (during partner conflict or any situation), and identify yours—are they on the list above? If they are, circle them, or write them in the chart below, which has a space at the top for each of your names. If your flooding symptoms don't appear, describe them. Your partner should circle and/or add theirs, as well.

WHEN I'M FLOODED, I EXPERIENCE:	WHEN I'M FLOODED, I EXPERIENCE:

The next step, once you've noticed feelings of flooding: Take a break!

The *minute* you sense one of those early physical warning signs, stop the discussion and ask to take a break. Here are the guidelines for that break:

- **Communicate that you need it.** Don't just walk out of the room! Tell your partner you're feeling flooded and need a break, where you're going, and what time you'll be back to continue the conversation. "Sweetie, I'm feeling really overwhelmed and I don't want to say something I don't mean. I'm going to take a walk around the block—I'll be back in about half an hour so we can keep talking about this."

- **Get out of visual range.** If you're flooded, you need to remove yourself from the circle of energy around your partner. Be with yourself and nobody else.

- **Do something soothing that takes your mind off the fight.** You need to take a break not only from being physically with your partner but also from even *thinking* about the fight. The point of the break is not to go off and stew and ruminate! Going over the details of the fight in your mind will only keep your nervous system overly activated. Instead: Take the dog for a walk while listening to music or a podcast. Lie down and read a magazine. Go in the kitchen and cook yourself a snack. Meditate—do some deep breathing or a body scan relaxation exercise. Go for a run or do some other exercise. Work on a piece of art or a home project. Pull weeds in the garden. Answer emails! Anything that occupies your attention and ideally is soothing or stress relieving. (From our experience, we recommend not watching murder mysteries . . .)

- **And finally: Come back!** Flooding is not a reason to indefinitely table the conversation. Return at the time you designated at your departure and try again. Ideally, the break should last at least twenty minutes (that's the minimum amount of time it takes for the stress hormones adrenaline and cortisol to start metabolizing out of the body) but should not last longer than twenty-four hours. And yes—you can go to bed without resolving this conflict. Sometimes it's the best thing to do. But don't let more than a day pass. Longer than that, and it starts to feel like punishment. On average, we've seen that most people tend to take about an hour. But if you catch flooding early, you may not need to take that long.

Those are the basic "do's" of coping with flooding—now, a couple of important "don'ts."

- **Don't** . . . ever say, "Honey, I think *you're* getting flooded. *You* should take a break." (Your partner may feel blamed and condescended to and remind you that you're no mind reader.) Say instead, "Honey, I think *we* need to take a break. Let's come back in an hour and then keep talking."
- **Don't** . . . try to get in the last word before you take a cool-down break. This is not going to help anybody's nervous system and is likely to make this escalated quarrel even worse.

- **Don't**... leave your partner hanging. Come back when
  you told them you'd come back. If the time you asked for
  is up and you're still not calm, come back anyway, ask for
  more time, and designate a later time to reunite. Simply
  tell them: "I need some more time. Can we come back to
  this after dinner / after work / tomorrow morning?" It's
  not fair to just disappear on each other—even when
  we're overwhelmed.
- **Don't**... plan out arguments and rebuttals. We said this
  already, but it bears repeating—we don't want to spend
  this time stewing over how we've been treated unfairly,
  maligned, wronged, accused, et cetera, or planning what
  we want to say when we return. The goal is to come back
  to the conversation calm, open, ready to connect—*not*
  to have your next argument or counterargument
  prepared.

If you feel hesitant to ask for a break midconflict, remember that
making this request is the opposite of selfish. When you take a break
to self-soothe, what you're doing is protecting your relationship
from the additional hurt escalation can cause, like hurling contemptuous insults or even objects at your partner. You're taking an important step to avoid a regrettable incident—one that is bound to happen
if you stay in the fight. The bitter words we say to each other when
flooded usually mean having to do more work later to undo the
damage we've done. When there's flooding, this is the best thing you
can do: allow yourself the break so your mind and body can recalibrate, and give your partner the grace and space to do the same.

Now, depending on your conflict style and your partner's, and
whether or not they're generally aligned or a mismatch (remember,

not a deal-breaker, but something to intentionally navigate!), there are a couple nuances to be aware of. As you might guess, volatile couples are the ones who experience flooding the most. But interestingly, it can take them much longer to get flooded—they're more accustomed to speaking intensely about conflict, so they may not experience raised voices or expressiveness as flooding or as an attack. Someone observing a volatile couple during a fight might assume there's flooding when actually there isn't, so again, our instruction to a couple in conflict is to look and see: Is there criticism, contempt, or defensiveness? When you check in with your bodies, are you experiencing physiological symptoms of flooding, or are you doing okay? When you're volatile, your discussion can be spirited or emotionally intense without automatically leading to flooding.

For validators: they're already in a zone where they negotiate calmly, so flooding is frequently less of a challenge for them. It's still important to know how to cope when it does happen—regrettable incidents can happen to any type of couple. And if validators are at a moment in their relationships where they're facing a particularly painful or challenging issue, they may experience flooding and not be used to it, so it's important that they know the signs and symptoms and how to respond.

Avoidant couples are, unsurprisingly, at the opposite end of the spectrum—they can get flooded *much* earlier in conflict (assuming a conflict discussion happens at all!), and they tend to go from zero to sixty: things get negative, and *whoosh*, they're in full fight or flight. This may be part of the reason that conflict-avoidant people tend to be avoiders: they get flooded so quickly and intensely that they actively work to avoid conflict at all costs. Learning to cope well with flooding can help avoidant couples quite a bit when it comes to addressing their point of conflict in a healthy and productive way.

But regardless of conflict style, the next question is: How do we proceed once we calm down and come back together?

Solving the Moment

During a fight, you don't have to solve the whole conflict. In fact, you shouldn't try. Instead, *solve the moment.*

Remember—our conflicts, when it comes to what they are *really* about, tend to be perpetual. They run deep, down to our core personalities, our philosophies about life, our fears and traumas, and more. What that means is that your goal during a fight cannot be to resolve the issue once and for all—this may never happen. Instead, your job is simply to focus on making *this* interaction a positive one.

We need to recalibrate the goal for a fight:

> The goal is not to win.

> The goal is not to persuade your partner of something.

> The goal is not to come up with a solution to the problem.

> Right now, the goal is not even to find a compromise!
> (This is coming later.)

> The goal is to fight with more positivity than
> negativity.

And yes—this is absolutely possible. And necessary.

Take Susan and Stan. Are they going to be able to work out the issues surrounding Stan's affair and Susan's feelings of betrayal in one fight? Absolutely not. For these two, this is going to be a process, especially because flooding is playing such a major role. Their first mission is to get to the point where they can talk to each other about the affair without getting so flooded. Then they need to be able to have an interaction about this issue that is *more positive than negative*. They need to start feeling *collaborative* again—like they are on the same team, trying to figure out a way forward together rather than polarized into warring camps. There's not going to be any good communication or deeper understanding between the two of them until they can get their conflict conversations on the right side of the Magic Ratio.

Remember: in conflict, we need to have enough positive interactions that they outweigh the negative ones by a ratio of 5:1. Negativity, unfortunately, is *so* much more potent than positivity. It just packs a bigger punch. That means we have to dilute it by making sure that even in a fight, the positive things we say and do outnumber the negative things we say and do by at *least* 5:1. Are we asking you to sit there, in the midst of an emotional fight with your partner, and tally up your negative versus positive interactions so you can whip out your calculator and check your ratio? Of course not! But what we are going to ask is that you follow some guidelines that will naturally carry your fight into positive territory:

1. Self-soothe when you become flooded.
2. Talk about *yourself* and *your* needs (just as with the softened start-up) rather than your partner's qualities.
3. Make, recognize, and accept repair attempts.

When we make the effort to do those three key things, it organically fills our conflict conversation with enough positivity to hit that magic ratio.

We've worked on what to do when we experience flooding. This is step number one in "solving the moment." Remember—nobody's solving anything when flooded!

Now, when we come back together—remembering, as always, to use the softened start-up with each other—we focus on the next part of "solving the moment": expressing needs.

Expressing Needs: Just Do It!

We said this earlier in "What We Fight About": one of the major reasons conflicts escalate into the red zone is that people don't ask for what they need. Instead they assume their partner already knows their needs and is—for whatever reason—refusing to fulfill them. They think, *My partner knows I need (fill in the thing: more help with the kids, more sex, more displays of affection, etc.)—it's perfectly obvious!* One man we worked with said to his wife: "You should know my love language! You're purposely withholding from me!" She was baffled and offended by the accusation, had no idea what he was talking about at that moment, and of course went into a defensive crouch.

It's not easy to ask for what we need. It feels vulnerable. We feel exposed, like a soft little creature without its shell. If you outright ask for something, there's the scary possibility that the other person will reject you and say *no*. Maybe even scorn your need. But when we don't ask—hoping that our partner will simply intuit what we need and fulfill it, or assume that the need is *so obvious* that of course they'll notice and be on the same page—what we end up with is resentment that the need is not being fulfilled, which leads to escalation in conflict. Nora and Robbie, Couple #2, are a classic example of this: both had been overextended in different directions but hadn't been communicating their stresses to each other. Their fight over the relatively minor issue of who was going to drive the kids to school blew up for exactly that reason. Both assumed the other saw that they needed support but was choosing to put themselves first instead. Speaking more clearly about what they needed could have defused this conflict before it became so cataclysmic and "flooded."

The great thing about this issue is that it is so easy to treat! When couples are experiencing this problem with escalating conflict, we can give them tools for expressing needs, and it cools down their fights *so* effectively. Couples that were in the "red zone" (more negativity than positivity) will quickly tip into the "green zone," where they're hitting that ratio much more effortlessly. It's wonderful to see. With the couple we mentioned above—in which the husband assumed his wife was purposely withholding from him—it became quickly clear that, in fact, he had not been asking for what he needed or articulating his feelings, whereas his wife had.

"There's a double standard in our marriage," he said repeatedly in a therapy session. "I'm *always* giving you what you need."

"But I don't know what you need," his wife replied.

"Sure you do!" he would explode, frustrated.

He was a musician and had written his fair share of songs about love. She assumed that if he felt something, he'd tell her. Meanwhile, to him, it seemed he was always doing stuff for her that was never reciprocated; the relationship felt out of balance and unfair, and he resented it. This couple had an interesting history—they'd known each other since they were little kids. They'd been friends for years. But their romance hadn't started until their late twenties, and now they'd been married only a few years. This guy (we'll call him "the musician") felt his wife knew him so well at this point—they'd basically *always* known each other—that he believed she intimately knew his emotions and needs, moment by moment, without him having to actually express them.

It's wonderful to have a long history with someone and to feel known by them. At the same time, we still have to *articulate our needs and feelings.* Our partners are not mind readers, no matter how well and how deeply they know us. The musician wasn't used to articulating his needs or feelings to anyone, and once he was convinced that he had to express them more clearly, he still struggled to put them into words. So we handed him our "Expressing Needs" card deck (you can access this in the free Gottman Card Decks app) and asked him to read through the cards (each one had a need printed on it) until he found something that resonated with his own need. He immediately pulled one card, then another, then finally another . . . three needs. He read each one out loud:

I need a warm greeting from you at the end of the day.

I need more touch. (Not erotic—just affectionate.)

I need more romantic nights away from the kids.

His wife was delighted to hear these. Her response was, "Those all sound wonderful. I want them too."

Moving forward, he continued to use the card decks to help him express needs and feelings, and it helped these two so much both in and out of conflict—his wife felt she was really starting to understand his inner world, and their fights no longer escalated the way they once had. For him, it was hard to mentally crystalize his feelings and needs into a description he could communicate to his partner. Luckily it was much, much easier to flip through the card deck and notice when he felt a tickle of recognition.

Sometimes the things we need in order to feel closer to and more supported by our partners are small and specific, and other times they are bigger, deeper, or more open to interpretation and creativity in terms of how to fulfill them. Here's some more examples from the "Expressing Needs" deck:

I need to go out to dinner and a movie.

I need for us to have an adventure together.

I need some time alone, for myself.

I need you to show interest in how my day went.

I need to talk about how I've changed.

I need to cuddle before we go to sleep.

When I feel down, I need you to listen and empathize with me—not try to solve my problems.

I need to hear that you are still my best friend.

To express our needs and feelings, we of course have to be able to identify them ourselves, and the "Expressing Needs" card deck is designed to do just that—if you or your partner could use some help putting needs into words, try it out! And if you find you also have trouble identifying your own emotions (very common!), try this exercise that Julie developed based on Eugene Gendlin's "focusing" technique.[4]

The Truth Exercise

Think of something you love without mixed feelings. Or something you're grateful for without mixed feelings. This could be anything in your life: a place, a person, a pet, a particular time of day or routine that you have—anything at all. (The musician, for instance, chose a mountain pass where he would go to meditate.) Then, for one minute—which will feel like an enormously long time—tell yourself the lie that you *hate* this thing, repeating over and over to yourself a sentence like "I hate the mountains . . ."

Once one minute is up, stop, and switch back to telling yourself the truth. Repeatedly say the truth to yourself, like "I love the mountains . . ."

Now ask yourself: What felt different in your body from the first minute to the second? And what changed in your body when you switched from telling yourself a lie to telling yourself the truth?

About the first minute, people tend to report things like "My shoulders were tight," "My throat was constricted," "I felt anxious," "There was a pit in my stomach," and so on. After they switched to truth telling, they often reported: "I could breathe," "I felt lighter," "Tension released in my back."

The point of the exercise is to notice the proprioceptive feedback from your body. *Proprioception* refers to your awareness of what's physically happening in your body. The "control center" for proprioception is at the top and front part of your brain, just behind your forehead. The part of our brain that receives information from our senses and nervous system lies behind this center. It in turn is called the homunculus and contains a "map" of what's physically going on and specifically where that is happening in the body. The homunculus helps us to also track our emotions by how our body manifests them. Every individual has unique ways they physically experience their own emotions. For example, if you're angry, your chest might feel hot, and your fist and arm muscles might feel tight. But if someone else is angry, they might sense their anger as a tightening of their jaw.

Even if *you* aren't readily able to put a name to your emotions, your homunculus and other proprioceptive centers know how you feel. In this exercise, when you told yourself a lie about the thing you loved, you activated a particular combination of emotions that your body then experienced in a unique way. These bodily responses were probably mildly uncomfortable for you and signaled to you: *That's not right,* or *That's not my truth.* Then when you flipped the lie and told yourself the truth, those parts of your body most likely relaxed and changed, sending you signals now that something felt right.

The point is, you have this proprioceptive feedback available to you, and you can tap into it when you need to check in with how you're really feeling. When you do this truth exercise, you get better at understanding whether a word you have chosen to describe your emotions is true for you. Sometimes we start out with a really vague feeling of *bad.* But we have to get more specific when we talk to our partners about what we're feeling and experiencing. Are we sad? Frustrated? Lonely? Worried? It matters. When you accurately articulate how you feel, you may realize more specifically what it is you need.

Men in particular can have a tough time identifying their own emotions—for our musician, as clear and poetic as he could be about life and love, he found the terrain a lot murkier when he focused inward on himself. This exercise can help anyone, however, regardless of their gender, to figure out what they want to say before they say it out loud.

We've covered coping with flooding and expressing our own needs—two powerful ways to fight right. Now a final tactic for "solving the moment" and keeping your fight in the "green zone": *repair.*

Small Repairs Prevent Major Damage

In conflict, a *repair attempt* is any comment or action that counteracts the negativity in a fight and prevents a conversation from escalating. Imagine that your discussion is like a train traveling on tracks. If the train begins to slide off the tracks, over a cliff, and down a mountainside, your repairs can prevent a major crash and elevate the conversation back up and onto the tracks again.

A repair can really be anything that shifts the conversation toward the positive. The most basic repair is a straightforward apology: "I'm sorry," or "I'm sorry I said that—let me try again." It can also take the form of empathy or validation: "I understand how you feel," or "That makes sense, when you put it that way." It can be voiced admiration. "You know what I really appreciate about you? How much you care about our kids. We're disagreeing over which school to pick, but I love how much it matters to you that they have a good education."

It can also be something goofy, like pulling an exaggerated "Oops!" face after you've blurted out something you immediately realized was a pretty dumb thing to say; if your partner can see that for what it is (fundamentally, a humorous apology) and laugh with you, the whole tenor of the fight can be reset. A repair can even be a fleeting gesture, like nodding encouragingly or reaching out for your partner's hand—the specific shape the repair takes ultimately doesn't matter. It telegraphs anything from *I love you* to *I hear you* to *Oops, I goofed up!*

In the Love Lab, after studying over three thousand couples, we saw something interesting about repair: what determined the success or failure of a repair attempt was *not* how it was made. In other words, we could not predict whether a repair attempt would work based on how well it was phrased—some of the most elegantly worded apologies failed to get through, whereas many clumsy and inexpert repair attempts landed wonderfully. Why? It came down not to what the repair looked like but to how the partner received and responded to it.[5]

Friendship and connection correspond to a successful repair.[6] How strong is your connection to each other going into this fight? How much quality time have you been able to spend with each other lately? How much have you been turning toward each other's bids for connection? Have you been able to set aside distractions and respond to your partner's attempts to connect, or has life been getting in the way?

One of the saddest reasons we see couples split is when they never quite manage to get aligned on repairs—when one person makes an attempt, the other is closed off to it or misses it completely, and vice versa. Imagine one of those pairs of hotel rooms with a connecting door—each room has its own door that opens and closes. If you were to open your door to the neighboring room and no one was there, you'd just see a closed and locked door. Sometimes our fights can go that way—one partner opens the door to the other, sees a closed door, and closes themselves back up; the other does the same in turn. We're both trying to open up, but nobody meets us there. Flip back to Stan and Susan's fight, and then to Nora and Robbie's. In each fight, there was a repair attempt, when one partner attempted to extend an olive branch—can you spot those? (In the first fight: "I know you're sorry, I do"; in the second: "I assumed it was just a cold, I'm sorry.") Unfortunately, the other partner was too flooded or otherwise not in the headspace to notice or accept that repair.

Repair is about meeting each other in the moment: both doors open at the same time. And for that to happen, what both partners need is the kind of knowledge about each other that only comes from daily, routine *turning toward*. The takeaway: if you and your partner have been suffering from escalation in conflict—if every fight turns into "attack and defend" and repair attempts are not getting through—then look at the flow of your days *outside* of conflict. Can you find more time to just sit with each other and catch up? Can you make it a point to watch out for your partner's bids for connection and turn toward them—*even the ones that take a negative form*? Sometimes bids for connection come out sideways, especially when we're feeling disconnected or neglected. For example, you get off the phone after arranging a meetup with an old friend you haven't seen in a long time; your partner says bitterly, "I guess you have no interest in going out for a drink with *me*."

You might naturally feel a rush of frustration and defensiveness and snap back, "When was the last time you asked *me* out?"

Or, in that moment, you could see that at its core, that comment—wrapped in hurt and criticism as it is—is actually a bid for connection.

"I do want to go out with you—I guess we've gotten out of the habit of asking each other out. I miss that. When should we go?"

That would be *turning toward* the bid, even though it was couched in negativity. And this can make an enormous difference for how your fights will go.

The bottom line is, all couples fight; everyone says things too harshly sometimes. What sets successful couples apart is that they *make repairs during conflict*. And they're able to do so because they walk into that conflict with a good solid understanding of each other. They've been learning about each other's day when they come home from work. They've been connecting over topics large and small. They know what will land with the other person—what will strike them as funny and sweet, what will work as an apology (humorous or otherwise), what they need to hear in order to feel heard and validated. They are experts on each other.

One couple—both lawyers—had this phrase they would say during a fight when things started ramping up because one of them was being stubborn and arguing the finer points of a disagreement ad nauseam—something they both tended to do. They knew this about themselves but still got swept up in it before they could catch themselves. So when one person realized they were going into that pattern again, they would quickly pull out of it by making fun of themselves: "Let the record show," one would announce as if they were in court, "that I was the one this week who cleaned out the garbage disposal on four occasions out of five!" It was funny and had this subtle way of both pointing out the problem or imbalance being discussed but also saying, "Okay, I'm being a little ridiculous about this—I'm sorry for being defensive; we can move on." It became a kind of repair shorthand for them. At a certain point, they wouldn't even have to finish the sentence. They could just theatrically yell, "LET THE RECORD SHOW!" and they'd both laugh, and the attack/defend dynamic that had been building would drain away. They could go back to addressing the issue of conflict feeling like they were on the same side again, teammates trying to problem-solve *together*.

A Do-Over, with Repair

So, what about our two couples from the beginning of this chapter?

Both were adversely affected by flooding; neither was able to clearly express their needs to each other; both missed each other's repair attempts. Practicing solving the moment—that is, prioritizing making the interaction positive and collaborative rather than fixing the whole conflict—was key for these couples. As they learned to self-soothe, take breaks, use more positive language (as we learned in the first fight, with the softened start-up), and *make and accept repairs,* things started to improve. We're happy to report that Nora and Robbie are doing great—when they were no longer overtaken by "the flood," everything else felt a lot easier. As for Stan and Susan, they have a longer road ahead of them, but they're on a much better trajectory. A betrayal like an affair can be a trauma for the other partner and can actually cause symptoms of PTSD. It might not literally be life-threatening, but it *feels* like a mortal threat to the life you had. Stan was going to have to build that life again—and build trust—from the ground up, starting all over. And that meant a *lot* of talking through stuff.

So, with Stan, we worked first on being able to have the conversation at all without automatically getting flooded. That looked like taking breaks—a *lot*—then coming back and starting again. We asked Susan to work on describing her feelings and experience without making attacks on Stan's character or using critical, contemptuous language when expressing her anger, which of course she was allowed to feel. The difference: "You've ruined my life! You're a horrible person!" versus "I feel so hurt and angry, I don't know if I can get over it. I'm worried we won't be able to get past this."

With both, we worked on repair. They were really suffering from missed repair attempts. One would drop the wall for a moment and reach out, but the other wasn't in a place to receive it. Their fights were like a balloon of negativity filling up more and more, with no air ever getting released. But as they got better at coping with flooding, they also got better at seeing and accepting repairs. It didn't magically solve the issue of the affair, which they will continue to process together in therapy, but their conflict conversations look much different without "the flood."

Stan: Hey, how are you feeling today?

Susan: Well, pretty crappy, what do you expect?

Stan: What's making you feel crappy?

Susan: What do you think? You! This whole situation!

Stan *(choice point: he validates instead of defending):* Yeah, I know. You're still really upset with me. I understand that.

Susan *(softens, calmer):* Well . . . I'm glad you do. I'm having nightmares every night.

Stan *(getting a bit defensive):* Wait, so it's my fault what you dream about?

Susan *(choice point: she could say, "It sure is! This is all your fault!" but is not flooded, so takes a different route):* I just meant that I can't stop thinking about it, even when I'm asleep. I know we've talked and talked about this, but I don't feel any better yet. I'm upset all day, and then I'm upset all night.

Stan: That sounds terrible. *(Validating)* What did you dream? *(Curiosity, seeking to understand better)*

Susan: It's all jumbled and hard to remember. But we were in bed together, and then I rolled over and you were gone. And I don't know how, but I knew that you were gone forever. That you were never coming back. When I woke up, I thought it was real, that our life together was over. I can't even tell you how bad it felt—I thought I was going to have a panic attack. I couldn't breathe.

Stan: Honey, I'm here. I know I messed up—bad. But let me tell you, I'm never going to do that again. I know I'll need to tell you a thousand times more until you believe me, but I'm here because this is what I want. You. Us.

Susan: You know it is really hard for me to believe that.

Stan: I know, I think it's just going to take time. *(He holds his hand out, and after a moment of hesitation, she takes it.)*

That day, this was the end of the conversation. Did Stan and Susan resolve anything about the betrayal? Did they arrive at a resolution or "fix"? No. But they had one really solid, positive interaction. They talked about this big, overwhelming conflict with more positives than negatives. And that is a huge win.

Your Mission

We can disagree and still be on each other's side. We don't have to become enemies, even if we start out on "opposite sides" of an issue. In conflict, your mission is to allow yourself to be vulnerable—to turn *attack and defend* into *self-disclosure and openness*. This is what "solving the moment" is all about—reframing the goal at this stage of conflict so that your primary objective is to find out more about what your partner is thinking and feeling and needing, and express that yourself *before* trying to progress to persuasion and compromise. And you make sure you're on the right side of that magic ratio by filling up your fight with moments of positivity.

You do that by:

- Using the softened start-up and *continuing* to use those guidelines throughout the conversation. Introduce topics gently. Ask questions. Avoid critical language.
- Self-soothing when you become flooded, *before* things go off the rails. Take breaks and communicate clearly about them.
- Making, recognizing, and accepting repair attempts. *Repair* is the secret weapon of the masters of love—use it!

This is the language of fighting right. It's a language of repair and collaboration, and anyone can learn it. On page 187, you'll find our Repair Checklist. If a fight starts to heat up and you need a quick reminder on ways to slow down the action, request that your partner rephrase their words so you can be less defensive, or put your own feelings and needs into different words, flip to our Repair Checklist and use it as a midfight cheat sheet. You'll see that we've organized the suggestions into six categories so you can easily navigate to what you need. Here are the categories and what kind of repair they help with:

- **"I Feel"**: When you need help expressing your emotions in the moment
- **"Sorry"**: When you need help phrasing an apology
- **"Get to Yes"**: When you want to validate your partner or meet them partway
- **"I Need to Calm Down"**: When you're starting to feel flooded and/or need a moment of repair
- **"Stop Action"**: When you are flooded and need a break
- **"I Appreciate"**: When you want to make a repair and add positivity

If it feels awkward to whip out a book in the middle of a fight, then here's a little secret: we do this in therapy sessions all the time! We had a couple recently who were disagreeing over a difference in parenting styles, and it started escalating. We interrupted. "Stop," we said. "How are you feeling?" Their answer: "Not great!" We asked: "Is this conversation working for you?" From both, a resounding "No!"

We flipped their workbook open to the Repair Checklist.

"When you feel like a conversation is getting off track and not feeling good, take a look at this list, and find a phrase that fits what you're needing at the moment," we told them. "You can paraphrase it, or you can just read it right off the page."

They both took a look at the list. To the first partner, we pointed out: "You just said to your wife, 'You never set limits for the kids and they really need them.'" Then we turned to her wife and said, "Then you got really defensive. Now, look over the first section, 'I Feel.' Go down to number 9. Rather than going defensive, how about making a repair by saying that phrase, by saying instead, you *feel* defensive?"

And she did. "I'm feeling really defensive," she said, reading verbatim from the Repair Checklist. "Can you rephrase that?"

"Yeah, I'm sorry I said, 'You never,'" the first partner said. "That's not really true." She looked down the list, saw Number 1 under "I Appreciate," and knew it was right for the moment. "I know this isn't your fault," she read, and then continued on her own: "You're on your own with them more, and managing them all day isn't easy. I just think we need to be more consistent. When you say okay to TV before dinner and then I say no because we decided that's a no-screens time, then I'm the bad cop again. I don't want to be the mean mom all the time."

There is absolutely nothing wrong with pulling out the Repair Checklist midfight and reading directly from it. These phrasings are tried-and-true ways for calming down an escalating conflict, pulled from years of observation on thousands of couples—use them! This particular couple, above, had so much success using the Repair Checklist that when they got home, they ripped it out of their workbook and pinned it to the refrigerator. Anytime a discussion started to get heated, they'd go and stand in front of the fridge to continue talking, so they could go down the checklist as they worked through the issue. It was so helpful that it became a habit.

One day, their youngest, a three-year-old boy, was getting dressed for preschool and having a tantrum over something (probably involving the way his socks felt inside his shoes—a typical toddler complaint). He was throwing his shoes, frustrated, and his mom raised her voice as she said, "We're late! We have to get in the car!" He noticed that her voice was angry. So he stood up, took her by the hand, and pulled her into the kitchen. He positioned her in front of the fridge.

"*This* is where we have to talk," he said. He knew the fridge cooled things down.

Discuss the Following Questions with Your Partner:

- In your own family growing up, did you witness your parents or caretakers getting flooded? What would happen then? How did they deal with it?
- Think of a movie or TV show where people got flooded a lot—what did it look like on the screen? How does that compare (similar or different) to your own experience during conflict?
- What happens in your body when you get flooded? Be as specific as you can about physically where you feel it and what it feels like for you.

- What are your flooding "triggers"? And what moments during conflict tend to set off that reaction in your body? Is it when things are moving too fast? When you feel trapped? When there's "kitchen sinking"?
- In conflict, do you get flooded frequently or rarely? Quickly, or does it take a while? What do you think your conflict style (and your partner's) has to do with this?
- When you're just starting to get flooded, is there anything your partner can do to help cool things down? What are the most effective repairs that your partner has made in the past? For instance, some people are calmed by physical connection; others don't want to be touched at all because it makes them more agitated. They may respond better to reassurance, for example.
- Finally, sometimes when you're really flooded, it's hard to communicate calmly and clearly and ask for a break. If you and your partner think this would be helpful, come up with a simple but clear hand signal you can use if you are feeling really overwhelmed and need to pause the conversation. (Don't pick the obvious one that only requires one finger . . .) Choose something that both of you will remember, that can quickly signal, *I need to stop but will continue when I am calmed down.* Your signal could be both hands over your heart, or hands in praying position, or anything you like. If you do choose one, respect it—when your partner signals a need for a break, take one, even if you personally don't need it. If you have more to say, it can be said later; it's much harder to unsay things we've said in conflict that we don't mean.

GOTTMAN REPAIR CHECKLIST

I FEEL

- I'm getting scared.

- Please say that more gently.

- Did I do something wrong?

- That hurt my feelings.

- That felt like an insult.

- I'm feeling sad.

- I feel blamed. Can you rephrase that?

- I'm feeling unappreciated.

- I feel defensive. Can you rephrase that?

- Please don't lecture me.

- I don't feel like you understand me right now.

- Sounds like it's all my fault.

- I feel criticized. Can you rephrase that?

- I'm getting worried.

- Please don't withdraw.

I NEED TO CALM DOWN

- Can you make things safer for me?

- I need things to be calmer right now.

- I need your support right now.

- Just listen to me right now and try to understand.

- Tell me you love me.

- Can I have a kiss?

- Can I take that back?

- Please be gentler with me.

- Please help me calm down.

- Please be quiet and listen to me.

- This is important to me. Please listen.

- I need to finish what I was saying.

- I am starting to feel flooded.

- Can we take a break?

- Can we talk about something else for a while?

SORRY

- My reactions were too extreme. Sorry.
- I really blew that one.
- Let me try again.
- I want to be gentler to you right now and I don't know how.
- Tell me what you hear me saying.
- I can see my part in all this.
- How can I make things better?
- Let's try that one over again.
- What you are saying is…
- Let me start again in a softer way.
- I'm sorry. Please forgive me.

STOP ACTION!

- I might be wrong here.
- Please let's stop for a while.
- Let's take a break.
- Give me a moment. I'll be back.
- I'm feeling flooded.
- Please stop.
- Let's agree to disagree here.
- Let's start all over again.
- Hang in there. Don't withdraw.
- I want to change the topic.
- We are getting off track.

GET TO YES

- You're starting to convince me.
- I agree with part of what you're saying.
- Let's compromise here.
- Let's find our common ground.
- I never thought of things that way.
- This problem is not very serious in the big picture.
- I think your point of view makes sense.
- Let's agree to include both our views in a solution.
- What are your concerns?

I APPRECIATE

- I know this isn't your fault.
- My part of this problem is…
- I see your point.
- Thank you for…
- That's a good point.
- We are both saying…
- I understand.
- I love you.
- I am thankful for…
- One thing I admire about you is…
- I see what you're talking about.
- This is not your problem; it's our problem.

FIGHT #3:
THE SHALLOWS

Mistake: Skimming the Surface

Manuel and Shanae had been having the same fight for years. An interracial married couple (she was Black, he was Pacific Islander), they were in their late thirties, married for almost a decade. By the time they came to us for a couples therapy intensive, they had no problem describing their positions and how the fights went—by that point, they'd done it hundreds of times. There was no dissent between the two of them about what their fights were about: according to them, they were fighting about gift giving and money. They were both clearly in agreement on that. The problem was, they never seemed to be able to fix it. The solutions they came up with never stuck. They relentlessly found themselves, once again, back in the *same* contentious debate, like some kind of Twilight Zone.

Here's how it always went: Shanae deeply wanted Manuel to be more spontaneous, especially surrounding gifts. He rarely showed his appreciation for her in a tangible way, and she felt strongly that he should surprise her once in a while with a token of his affection—

this is what people in relationships did! But she had trouble expressing that to him. Instead of bringing it up directly, she'd try surprising Manuel with a gift to model the kind of dynamic she hoped they could have, but he would get upset: "What are you thinking, spending money on this junk? We can't afford this!"

Manuel, for his part, was frustrated. They were on a tight budget. Money had always been a source of stress for them—in fact, a few years prior, they'd been forced to file for bankruptcy. They had made a clear plan to be more financially responsible and avoid the same thing happening again, and this kind of extra, unnecessary gifting would push them right off the responsible track they'd worked so hard to get into.

They came up with various agreements to solve this conflict. For instance, they would do gift giving only on major holidays. Or they would stick to a price limit for gifts. All the agreements backfired for one reason or another. One Valentine's Day, Manuel presented Shanae with a large, beautifully wrapped box. Thrilled, she tore the wrapping off and found . . . a new blender.

He noted her disappointment. But she said nothing. She thanked him flatly and went back to unpacking her lunch bag from work and cleaning the containers. Manuel was upset. He'd followed the rules they'd agreed on—today was a holiday, he'd gone right up to the price limit (this was a fancy blender, one she'd been wanting), and he hadn't forgotten. He'd done everything right, and she was still not satisfied. *What would it take?* he wondered. Did he have to drain their bank account to make her happy? Build her the Taj Mahal? He followed her as she moved around the kitchen.

"What's the problem?" he demanded, raising his voice. "Shanae? Hmm? What's wrong? You constantly say you want gifts, and I got you a gift. I spent a lot of money on that, you know."

"I know," she said, already on the verge of tears. "It's nice." It *was* nice, of course, but it wasn't a *gift*. It was just something they needed. But if she criticized it, she knew he'd blow up.

"Nice? So what's the matter with it, hmm? What *exactly* was I supposed to get you instead? There's always so many secret rules with you. I can never win."

"Don't yell at me!"

"I'm not yelling!"

He was yelling. Shanae turned and left the room, locked herself in the bathroom, and cried.

So, first: Shanae and Manuel are great examples of people with very different conflict styles. He was volatile, while she was avoidant. She avoided bringing up the problem overtly, trying to model the behavior she wished for instead; when they finally did address it, he'd blow up. When we met with them, Shanae said her husband clearly didn't care about her as much as he cared about money. Meanwhile, Manuel told us that his wife didn't care about their future, or the amount of financial stress he was under. And they had run out of hope that they would solve this conflict, which seemed to be rearing its head over and over and causing nastier and nastier fights. After their last one, Shanae had gone to bed in tears. Manuel, unable to come down from the intense physiological flooding he experienced during their fights, had been up half the night, pacing the house. They came to see us as a last resort. They both wanted to know: "How do we get past this?"

When couples get stuck in cyclical, gridlocked conflict where there is no progress, it's generally a sign that instead of moving on from it, they actually need to pause, slow down, and go deeper.

When we fight, we often try to fix a problem before we understand it. We get stuck in a superficial argument instead of digging down to the deeper source of the conflict. We push toward a solution or resolution before we've actually understood our partner's position and what's beneath it. It's not always easy to see the real cause of conflict—as we see here with Manuel and Shanae, we can quite literally spend *years* having the same fight again and still not know what's truly fueling it.

Manuel and Shanae didn't need to come up with a solution to the surface problem they had surrounding gifts. They'd already tried that! They needed to stop right there, in that hot point of friction between them, and dive *down*.

Signs You Need to Go Deeper

Observing couples in the Love Lab, we initially assumed there would be certain "content areas" that couples tended to get gridlocked about. Well, there weren't. People could get gridlocked over anything at all.

As we discussed earlier in "What We Fight About," we quickly saw that couples could be in cyclical gridlock over every issue under the sun, including the most trivial-seeming topics: Who's going to control the remote? What temperature do we set the thermostat at in winter? Are the kids allowed to have peanut butter and jelly sandwiches for dinner if they don't like what we made? There were no categories! And that's because any point of conflict between two people—no matter how large or small—can have all kinds of stuff under the surface. Our conflicts, in that way, are a little bit like icebergs: sometimes we're only seeing the tippy top. We have no idea yet how far down this obstacle goes or how big it is—until we crash right into it.

Now, we also know that the majority of our conflicts are

perpetual—that we will have to manage them over the course of our lives and that they may never be "solved" once and for all. So, what's the difference between managing perpetual conflict and gridlock?

The answer is, it feels *very* different. You may come back to a particular topic over and over again throughout your lives together—that doesn't mean you're in gridlock. That means you have a difference between you in personality or lifestyle preference. You simply need to learn how to dialogue calmly and constructively with one another when your differences come up. The strategies you've learned so far will definitely be helpful here.

Gridlock is different. Gridlock feels bad—really bad. You're in gridlock if:

- Your conflicts over this topic leave you feeling rejected by your partner.
- You talk and talk about this issue and make zero progress. There's no movement at all toward a solution or compromise.
- Every time you discuss this issue, you feel worse afterward. Your continued conflicts over this issue are causing hurt and emotional damage to one or both of you.

When they came to us, Manuel and Shanae were in gridlock over giving gifts. They were experiencing all of the classic signs above: they felt terrible after their fights; their attempts at compromise and problem-solving had failed; they were getting more and more frustrated with each other and more predisposed to assume the worst. At that point, they were both experiencing **negative sentiment override,** which we also call the negative perspective. It basically means that we've been fighting cyclically so much, we're unable to view our partner's words and actions any way but negatively, even if that's not how they were intended. We stop giving each other the benefit of the doubt—instead, we assume the worst. If we ask our partner a question and they don't respond, instead of thinking, *Oh, he didn't hear me,* we think, *Ignoring me again, as always.* Even neutral situations will be perceived as negative. When we get caught in gridlock, it's hard to stay out of the negative perspective.

Gridlock is a big sign you need to go deeper: it's like a flashing alarm light indicating that it's time to uncover what's really fueling this conflict. But even if you're not yet gridlocked on something, there are other signs that you and your partner need to pump the brakes on this fight and figure out what you're really fighting about before you try to proceed.

Signs you need to slow your fight down:

- You're stumbling over something seemingly trivial— you're thinking, *Why are we fighting about this minor thing?*
- You have actually arrived at compromise—but then it gets undermined by one or both of you. You can't stick to it.
- The same topic keeps popping up in other fights or conversations like an uninvited guest.
- Or it's the reverse: you avoid a particular topic like the plague—it's becoming a kind of elephant in the room that both of you skirt around.
- Your partner has a surprising, outsized-seeming reaction to a discussion that "comes out of nowhere" and takes you off guard.

That last one can be a big tell. You think you're having a routine logistical conversation, and your partner has a big emotional reaction that seems to come out of nowhere. If you get a response that doesn't make sense to you—say, they get flooded or angry over something you thought would be a mundane, unremarkable planning conversation about the calendar or plans for the weekend—that's a clear sign that something's up. You just crashed into an iceberg—something lurking under the surface that you didn't see. So what do you do? You spool down your engines and slow wayyyy down.

Say, "Let's back up. Looks like this might be a deeper issue than I thought."

When we were first married, we had an incident like this one. John was arriving home from work, and Julie was already home, starting dinner in the kitchen. As John walked in the door, he spotted the mail sitting on the foyer table, and it reminded him that we'd had a plumber out a couple of weeks ago, and John couldn't remember if we'd paid the bill. He strolled into the kitchen and said, "Hey, did you pay the plumber?"

Julie dropped the knife she was using to slice onions and whirled around. "I don't know!" she snapped back. "Did *you* pay the plumber?"

She stomped into the bedroom and slammed the door. Hard.

John stood there with the mail in his hand thinking: *Did I marry a lunatic?* He marched into the bedroom and confronted her: "What on earth is the matter with you? I just wanted to know if you paid the plumber!"

"Oh right!" she said. "I'm just the secretary around here. You don't even say hello first! You just move right to the checklist that *I'm* supposed to complete. Well, I *didn't*! So I'm bad!"

John was baffled and defensive, and the conversation didn't go particularly well at first. But finally, we both calmed down. John sat down on the bed and asked Julie more gently now: "Where is this coming from?"

Julie thought about it for a while and finally was able to explain. "When I was a kid growing up," she said, "I'd come home and my mother would always have some criticism for me like, 'Is that what you wore to school? Well, you look fat in it.' When you came in just now, you sounded exactly like her."

Julie's request, in the end, was actually fairly simple: "When I first see you at the end of the day, I really need you to come kiss me and say hello and ask how the day was. *Then* you can ask me if I paid the plumber." We arrived at it because we took a bit of time to go deeper, ask questions, figure out why something that seemed small caused such a big reaction. Reactions like that are a red flag planted in the ground, saying, "Dig here," and asking for your care and attention.

If you're seeing any of the signs that you need to go deeper into an issue, we have a blueprint for that. It's called **dreams within conflict.**

Unlocking Your Fight: Dreams Within Conflict

The story behind this particular intervention is a personal one. This method didn't originate in the Love Lab (though we thoroughly tested it there). It came from our own life and relationship.

Very early in our marriage, before we'd created our marriage theory and interventions, we were trying to solve a gridlocked problem, and we weren't getting anywhere. The problem in a nutshell: We were living in Seattle, a busy city. John loved it. Julie didn't. John had grown up in New York City, and to him, the streams of people, the rush of traffic, the noise and bustle of a city were all familiar and comforting—the sensory experience of *home*. For Julie, who'd grown up in Portland in a house on the edge of one of the biggest wild urban forests in the country, wilderness was home. She sought out the calm and silence of trees. She often sneaked out of her house to sleep in the forest, returning before dawn the next morning. Her parents never knew. Deep, raw nature is what kept her sane.

One weekend, we rented a little cabin up on Orcas Island, in the upper northwest corner of Washington State, a long drive and ferry ride away from the city. Julie immediately fell in love with Orcas. She had always envisioned someday having a little cabin in the forest somewhere, and after we returned to the island over and over again, scrambling for rentals each time, she realized this was the magic spot for her. So one day, she brought it up to John.

"I really want to buy a cabin on Orcas," she said.

"What?" John replied, startled. "Absolutely not."

And just like that, we were off and running. The fight escalated; we both retreated, angry and dissatisfied. And we kept fighting about it, over and over, for *six years*. Julie couldn't let it go—that treasured vision of the cabin in the woods. And John could not get to yes—the whole idea of *buying* a place up there seemed extravagant and un-necessary. He stood his ground. She stood her ground. We were gridlocked.

It became a pretty big deal in the relationship, an obstacle that swelled bigger and bigger every day, that we couldn't help but trip over constantly. Resentment over the issue was leaking into other conversations and seeping into our day-to-day interactions; negativity was taking over. So we went to a couples therapist. (Yes, couples therapists need couples therapists too!) This therapist—referred to us by a friend—really liked John. She found him brilliant, talkative, and charming. She was on his side, and it showed up in therapy. Julie receded into the background. One day, as we sat in her office arguing, trying yet again to find a way forward out of our gridlock, she said, "You know, John, you have every right to just say no, and she has to accept it. You can create boundaries—good relationships are all about boundaries. Just say no!"

Afterward, we walked out to the car together in silence. John was obviously going over the session in his mind—he was deep in thought. At home, he put down the car keys and turned to Julie. "Do I sound like that? Like that therapist? All that 'Just say no' stuff?"

"Yes, actually," Julie said. "You do."

"Well," John said, "that's not the kind of husband I want to be."

We decided to fire the therapist.

Then we sat down right there—in our own living room instead of someone else's office—and had, on our own, what would soon become the model for the "dreams within conflict" exercise. We stopped arguing about whether or not to buy the cabin. We stopped trying to persuade each other of anything. We started asking each other questions and just listening.

We started talking about the past and about the future. Julie told John about how awful it felt to be at home when she was young—how it was a house full of criticism, contempt, and at times physical abuse. She never knew what cutting thing her mother was going to say to her; she never felt she could relax or let her guard down. So she would slip out the back door late at night, when things were tense and heavy in the house, and run out into the wild nature preserve at the heart of Portland. She described how sometimes she'd stay out all night, sleeping under one of the swooping red cedars. In nature, she felt safe. It was where she could go to take in the nurturing beauty of the trees and to spiritually recharge.

"The city drains me," she told him. "The forest revives me."

Then it was John's turn.

He told Julie a story about his parents, a young married couple living in Vienna at the beginning of World War II. One night, they found out that within twenty-four hours, the Gestapo were coming for their block to round people up and send them to concentration camps. They fled, leaving the city that was their home and crossing the border into Switzerland with nothing but the clothes they were wearing and some packets of salt and sugar they had stashed in their pockets. They left everything behind—their jobs, families, studies, friends, their apartment and everything in it, their books and treasured photographs, furniture, and family heirlooms. From Switzerland, they escaped to the Dominican Republic, where John was born in 1942; eventually they arrived in New York as refugees of the Holocaust.

They taught John what they had learned: you don't accumulate stuff or property. You never know when Nazis under another name are going to come after you, and you'll have to leave it all behind. Everything you pour your resources into should be something within you that you can take with you, like education and skills. We already had one house—we didn't need two—and the thought of it made John feel weighed down and afraid when he thought about his parents and their story.

After we exchanged these stories, we both melted. On the other side of this conversation, everything felt different. Compassion filled the air. There was no way we weren't both going to do everything we could to honor each other's dreams.

Fairly quickly after that, we came to a compromise: we'd buy a little place on Orcas. And if, after a few years, John felt it had been a bad investment, we'd reevaluate and see if we should consider selling it. Meanwhile, Julie would keep a traditionally Jewish kosher kitchen—something that John had been deeply wanting.

We found a rustic little place on the north side of the island, up on a bluff called Raccoon Point, where you could catch a peek across the strait to Canada. John loved the place—although he tended to spend his time at the cabin cozied up on the couch reading while Julie laced up her boots and hit the trails—and after a year, he was thrilled they'd bought it.

The process was so successful for us that we thought, "We need to take this to the lab."

Taking Dreams to the Lab

We went back to Lab footage and data and looked more closely at gridlocked conversations. We found that, for couples in gridlock or couples in distress, there was always an underlying dream lurking underneath the discussion that hadn't been unearthed or clearly articulated. Meanwhile, in couples that were navigating their conflicts successfully, those dreams were discussed openly and directly.

As we began to map out all the things that the masters of love did *right,* we found strong, consistent throughlines: they spent time building and expanding their "love maps" for each other, which means asking exploratory questions, being curious about each other, and understanding each other's inner world. They shared genuine fondness and admiration and expressed it daily. They turned toward each other's bids for connection most of the time. They maintained a positive perspective on each other—they were more likely to notice the good things about each other, what the other person was doing *right*, than the negative, or what they were doing wrong or not doing. And when they arrived at a conflict, they almost immediately drilled down to what was essential to them philosophically, historically, and emotionally: their beliefs, their values, their memories, and their dreams.

Our approach that day, when we had the breakthrough in our own gridlocked fight, wasn't unique. And that was great news because that meant this was a repeatable strategy that other couples could access. We'd resolved our biggest conflict exactly the way the masters had done in the lab, and that gave us the confidence to develop this intervention: a series of questions designed to help couples get to the bottom of their conflicts instead of skating around on the surface.

We started out by testing it in our couples workshops. We made sure to set up the scenario clearly. The rules: There would be a speaker and a listener. The speaker's job was to be open and honest, to speak from the heart, and to use the interventions we've covered in this book so far: the softened start-up to introduce their position on the issue, describing only their own needs rather than their partner's flaws. The listener's job, meanwhile, was to make it safe for their partner to be open and share the dream beneath their position on the issue. Their mission was to give their partner the benefit of the doubt and to patiently listen to the speaker's point of view. No judgment. No defensiveness.

Then the listener would read aloud a series of questions and simply listen to the speaker's answers without bringing up their own point of view. After the speaker had answered all the questions one by one, speaker and listener would trade roles—whoever started out as the listener would now be the speaker, and vice versa. We started out with a longer list of questions for the listener to ask, but after testing and honing the exercise, we winnowed it down to these six.

The Dream Catcher's Magic Questions

1. What do you believe about this issue? Do you have some values, ethics, or beliefs that relate to your position on this issue?

2. Does your position relate to your history or childhood in some way?

3. Why is your position on this issue important to you?

4. What are your feelings about this issue?

5. What is your ideal dream here? If you could wave a magic wand and have exactly what you want, what would that look like?

6. Is there some underlying purpose or goal in this for you? What is it?

This exercise works because it *opens up space and time.* It expands the conversation so it can breathe. And it calls for clear roles between partners: one speaker and one listener. It gives both partners a calm, protected space to both figure out what their deeper dream or fear is and to articulate it.

You can't solve anything until you understand your partner's approach to this issue on a deeper level. When you've heard your partner's initial position using a softened start-up, you've still heard only a statement or two. You've barely scratched the surface; there's so much more you need to understand.

What that means is that the *speaker* and *listener* roles are essential to uphold. Make sure each of you takes a full turn. A full turn means the speaker first gives their softened start-up and then answers the "dreams within conflict" questions asked by the listener. Don't cut in on each other. Don't skip any questions! The listener should go down the list and ask the speaker each question one by one. Don't move on until they are answered to the fullest extent possible.

Your goal is to find out everything you can about your partner and this issue: why it's so important to them, where their stance on this comes from, how their personal history interacts with their position on this. You can't always extrapolate from someone's experiences how their beliefs and values will take shape—for instance, especially among some older generations, people were punished physically by their parents when they were kids. Some of those people are going to take from that experience that they turned out fine, it didn't hurt them, it taught them a valuable lesson, and it's fine. Others will think: *That was abusive. I didn't learn anything, I only learned fear; I will never lay a hand on my children.* Background is super important, but we see that the same exact background can create divergent belief systems. We have to delve into this stuff to understand each other's positions on a point of conflict.

Even people who have everything in common (class, race, hometown, family structure, religion) can have two totally different points of view about something, because each person's physical, emotional, spiritual, and intellectual constitution is going to interface differently with that shared environment and produce something unique. Manuel and Shanae, for instance, had a lot in common in terms of their childhoods. They'd both had a rough time, with absent parents, inconsistent caretakers, and a history of deprivation and scarcity. But from those parallel life experiences, they'd formed vastly different belief systems.

Manuel and Shanae: It Wasn't About Money

With Manuel and Shanae, we knew the first step in breaking through their gridlock was setting aside this ongoing conflict over money. Instead, we talked about their pasts. We asked: What was the culture surrounding gift giving in your family growing up? Did your parents or caregivers show love in this way? What meaning did you attach to it because of this?

Their answers were incredibly illuminating. When Shanae was growing up, her parents weren't around. Her father was in jail, and her mom was an addict—she loved Shanae but was incapable of being a reliable parent or providing for her daughter. For a large chunk of her childhood, Shanae lived with her aunt and uncle. At Christmas, they had the habit of giving their own kids tons of presents. For her, they would wrap up a new pair of socks. That was it. Just socks. She saw what gifts symbolized: that you mattered more. Gifts equaled love—and she wasn't getting any.

Meanwhile, Manuel wasn't getting any presents at all. His parents were absent, abusive, and eventually divorced. He essentially raised himself. The only person who ever gave him presents and made him "feel rich," as he described it, was a family friend, his godmother, whom he spent all his holidays and summers with. This felt like the one relationship in his life he could count on. But then, when he was a teenager and started selling drugs to support himself, she told him that she couldn't condone his lifestyle and abruptly stopped seeing him—for good. As a result, he never trusted anyone that completely ever again. When someone gave him a gift, his knee-jerk response was *Why are you giving me this? Probably to manipulate me.*

We asked Manuel if it was possible that he was unable to accept gifts from Shanae because it meant opening himself up to accepting love from her and all the vulnerability that involved—and he admitted that, yes, that was right. Meanwhile, she was starved for demonstrations of love from him. This couple had been coming at this fight—quite literally for years—with the lens of *money.* But it had nothing to do with money. It was actually about all the hidden, underlying meaning of love: how we give it, how we receive it, how we open ourselves up to it.

When they did the dream catcher's questions, the tenor of their conversation was so different. With this format—taking turns, talking about themselves and their childhoods, taking their time to answer each question—they were receptive and really able to listen to each other. Manuel, who tended to be more volatile, was much calmer and less intense when going through the six-question interview, which in turn let Shanae, who was more avoidant, feel safe opening up and sharing her answers too.

When Manuel asked Shanae, "What are all the things you feel about this issue?" and Shanae said, "I just feel like a little kid again, waiting and waiting to be important to somebody," we saw the expression on his face shift as he started to understand. When it was his turn, and she got to the fifth question and asked him, "If you could wave a magic wand and have exactly what you need, what would that look like?" he said, "It would look like everything is easier between us. You know that I love you, no matter what."

Manuel and Shanae didn't stop having conflict over this topic. But the next time conflict flared up over this issue, the conversation went very differently.

Shanae: *(looking into the shopping bags that Manuel has just brought into the house, with a disappointed sigh and an eye roll)* Ah, a box of nails from the hardware store. Exactly what a girl dreams of.

Manuel: I told you I was stopping there. What did you expect me to bring home? A diamond ring?

Shanae: I just thought maybe you'd bring me something today. I've been missing a show of affection from you. You've barely paid any attention to me at all lately.

Manuel: Shanae, I'm trying to finish these repairs so we can sublet this place and look for a bigger apartment. We talked about this. I thought this is what you wanted!

Shanae: I do. I just want you to actually show me you care once in a while. That's what people in relationships do, Manuel. It's normal to want that.

Manuel: *(frustrated sigh)* I just really don't get why little gifts are so important to you. You know I love you. Why isn't that enough?

Shanae: Well . . . I believe that if you love somebody, you want to show them that you do. It's not enough to just say the words. Anybody can just say the words, without any meaning. If you go and get somebody a gift, it means you're thinking about them. It takes effort. It takes time. It takes thought about the person you love.

Manuel: Yeah, but I don't have time!

Shanae: I know, I know.

Manuel: Look, I know this was an issue for you growing up. And I'm trying. But I don't want us losing this apartment because we can't pay rent.

Shanae: Is that the only reason?

Manuel: Well . . . I guess I still do have that same old reaction when you talk about wanting me to give you something—like you're trying to get something out of me. My dad taught me, never trust anybody because they will rip you off. And sure enough, people always have. People only give you something when they want something back. I remember kids used to give me stuff, like candy or a cigarette, and then tell me it was my turn to go try and buy beer, so I'd have to be the one to stick my neck out. I'm so used to being used. I got smart when I was about fourteen, fifteen. I stopped letting people use me and manipulate me.

Shanae: But I don't want to manipulate you! That's not what I'm saying at all.

Manuel: I mean, I know that now, but it still triggers that feeling.

Shanae: *(putting her arms around him, sweetly)* Could I at least manipulate you into bringing me one of those chocolate bars I like the next time you stop in town?

Manuel: *(laughing)* Okay, okay, we can probably afford a chocolate bar without losing the apartment.

This difference in values surrounding money and gifting will remain a perpetual problem for this couple that will show up in different ways throughout their lives. Going forward, Manuel's default tendency to view gift giving as manipulative will still sometimes crash into Shanae's deep-seated belief that gifts equal love. But the "dreams within conflict" conversation completely changed the framework for those conflicts. These two still fight about this issue, but they are no longer in damaging gridlock over it. They are usually able to find some kind of resolution or compromise for that particular fight. They are less likely to feel judged and attacked. They are now operating from a deep understanding of each other, an awareness of these enduring vulnerabilities that they each carry, so while this issue will never be "solved," exactly, it has stopped being a source of pain and misunderstanding.

The Worst Conflicts Are the Greatest Opportunities for Intimacy

This is counterintuitive in a way: when a particular topic is something that you and your partner can't touch without setting off an awful, stressful, high-octane fight whose aftereffects linger for days (or longer), the most natural response would seem to be to avoid that topic. There's a certain logic to figuring, *Okay, this is a perpetual conflict and it hurts too much to touch it, so let's just not.* In gridlock, too, couples can start feeling hopeless: *We've beaten this topic to death; there's no point anymore.* Or: *I married the wrong person—they want me to be someone I'm not. I won't be able to keep this relationship together unless I change my whole personality.*

What we've found in working with couples in workshops in particular, where we take people through the "dreams within conflict" intervention step by step, is that 87 percent of the time, the six questions lead to major breakthroughs in a gridlocked conflict.[1] Sometimes it is the case that we are truly not compatible—we're not going to sit here and tell you that all relationships can or should be saved. The data doesn't back that up, and neither does our clinical work with couples. Sometimes two personalities are too much of a mismatch. Sometimes, dreams are too much in opposition. But almost 90 percent of the time, this is not the case. People just need to understand each other's underlying dreams better, and they can move forward from gridlock and have more productive conflict in general.

One of the great surprises for us as researchers over the years was coming to see how deep people's conflicts ran and how deeply existential they ultimately were. These small mundane issues of daily living that couples tangled over so quickly revealed themselves to be tightly tied to bigger concerns. We brought all kinds of people into the lab—couples from every demographic out there. And what we saw was that no matter your background or your education level, every person is a philosopher. Every person has struggled with the same questions: *Why am I here? What's my purpose? What is my point of being here, of being alive in this world? How do I want to live this one life that I have?*

Human beings are meaning makers. We are storytellers, and we have been for millennia. We've told ourselves origin stories to explain the world. We tell ourselves the story of our own individual lives, shaping our autobiographies. And as we tell ourselves the story of our lives, we search for meaning, for a moral. Because of that, trivial issues—right down to whether or not you pick your husband's clothes off the floor—can be seen as symbolic or connected to some underlying belief or purpose that guides your life. This is why we say that our biggest conflicts can be the greatest opportunity for intimacy: because they can serve as a spotlight, putting something that is deeply important about who we are, something that will help our partners to know us, in a bright circle to be seen and understood.

But sometimes dreams are so subterranean, so buried, that we ourselves aren't aware of them. And yet emotions surrounding them will still surface in our fights. The "dreams within conflict" conversation can be useful, but it may take a little more time to get to the bottom of it.

Making Space for the Dream to Surface

We aren't always aware of our dreams and needs. This is very common—especially in Western culture. We work so much. We spend so much time trying to survive, to get a leg up. We often don't spend enough time reflecting on who we are or on *why* we are the way we are. That means we may run into instances during conflict where we won't be able to answer a question because we haven't ever thought of it that way before. You or your partner may need time to reflect.

This is where a therapist really comes in handy—if you've been seeing them for a while, they may have a broad knowledge of your concerns, day-to-day thoughts, background, et cetera, and often can intuit what will be meaningful to you and what personal history may tie into your position on an issue. They can ask questions, point to potential connections, give you some clues about what might be going on for you. But people can also figure this stuff out for themselves if they give themselves time to do some heart searching and memory searching; to stop and think: *Have I ever been in a situation like this before? Have I had this feeling before?* One couple in conflict, fighting over whether to use their savings to buy a house before interest rates spiked, fighting endlessly over the price of real estate in their city, actually needed to ask themselves two entirely different questions. Partner 1 needed to explore *Why is keeping my life stable and secure so important to me?* Partner 2 needed to explore *Why is it so important to me that I don't put down roots and am free to travel?*

If you are in the middle of a fight, you may not have the answers to questions like these. This couple needed to have many conversations—and breaks in between them to reflect on it all—to talk through their personal histories surrounding *place* and *home* and whether they had a sense of permanence or safety growing up, and how that led to their current position on how to live and what to prioritize. So if you're in the middle of a fight and you find yourself thinking, *Oh wow, I have no idea where this is coming from,* then the number one thing to do is create some space for yourself to reflect.

Say: "I wish I could answer that, but I think I need some time."

Then take the time to think about it!

If you're having trouble going deeper, here are some things that can trigger connections and revelations:

- Looking through old photos, yearbooks, or journals
- Thinking about the nature of your past romantic partnerships or a previous marriage and what that was like
- Reflecting on your relationships with your parents or caretakers or siblings
- Thinking about your early relationships with peers and your early school experiences
- Looking for multigenerational patterns within your family (for example: if you're having a gridlocked conflict around money, it's helpful to ask, "What's my family's legacy around money?")

Finally, come back together and share what you've been thinking about with your partner. You don't have to have all the answers yet. You're not a jigsaw puzzle to be "completed." Share your thought process with them. Describe anything that has popped up that you think is interesting or relevant. For example, in thinking about a family legacy surrounding money: "I grew up in Alaska, in a fishing family, and money was always 'boom or bust.' We'd have nothing, we'd be eating government cheese for dinner, and then all of a sudden the crab came in and we were rich. We'd run out and buy everything we'd been waiting on—furniture, groceries, winter shoes. And then the money was gone again, and we would have to hang on and wait. I guess I still have this urge to *spend* whenever we have a little extra, because otherwise it's just going to vanish again."

The wonderful thing about practicing the "dreams within conflict" conversation is that it becomes a skill you can build. The more you and your partner talk about your respective goals, both big and small, and about your visions for the kind of life you want to have, the less you'll find yourselves in damaging conflicts fueled by unacknowledged or tamped-down dreams. Something that might have once turned into a big fight instead becomes a moment of connection and collaboration where the two of you pull together to face a challenge.

Getting Close to Your Dreams Will Help You in Conflict

One couple from one of our longitudinal studies in the Love Lab showed us how profound and effective this could be. We'll call them George and Marianne. They'd been married just a few years when they participated in the study; for both, this was their second marriage, which they'd each come to with two kids; they were now raising four teenagers together. We began, as always with our participant couples, with the oral history interview, which we conducted in their home.

The oral history interview is an assessment tool we'd honed over time in an effort to get a broad sense of a couple's relationship history *before* they came into the lab to be observed in conflict. John and his research partner at the time, Lowell Krokoff, drew inspiration from the work of Studs Terkel, the Pulitzer Prize–winning radio broadcaster and writer who did groundbreaking work interviewing ordinary Americans about their experiences during the Great Depression, compiling some of the most captivating and profound oral histories of that time ever to be preserved. When we started out with the marital oral history interview, it was loose and wide-ranging, covering every relationship question under the sun, and could last hours to a whole day. Over time, we whittled it down to the most essential questions that got right to the most important beats of a couple's relationship history: How did they meet? What had their courtship been like? How had their relationship unfolded over time? What had been the big ups and downs of their union so far?

One of the big revelations of the oral history interview was that *how a couple told the story of their relationship predicted their future.*[2] Over time, through follow-ups every few years, we saw that marital satisfaction was tightly linked to how that couple described their history—did they speak fondly of their meeting, remember the details? Did they recall and speak fondly of the reasons they fell for their partner? Did they talk about their lives together with a sense of "we-ness" (using *us* or *we* rather than *I*)? How did they describe tough times and past conflicts? Was there a sense that they could and would pull together to overcome challenges?

When we asked George and Marianne to describe a challenging time, they had a story for us right away. It happened right after they'd gotten married and combined households. George was a successful salesperson, and to accommodate their larger blended family they'd just bought a bigger house, going out on a bit of a financial limb. George went into work one day shortly after they married, and his boss pulled him into a meeting. "I'm going to be reorganizing things and I want you to go on the road," his boss said to him. "I'm giving you a great new territory. This could be a huge increase in your salary if you make the most of it. Congratulations!"

Sitting there in his boss's office, George did not feel like he was being congratulated. It did not feel good at all. He knew right away: this isn't what I want. He told his boss he was turning down the promotion. His boss was shocked and told him that this was his new job, so take it or leave it.

"All right, I'll leave it," George said. "I quit."

He went straight home, walked into the house, and said to his wife, "I've quit my job."

Her reaction? She panicked.

"You did *what*?" she cried. They'd been married less than a month. They had kids in school, college to pay for, a bigger mortgage. "Why did you do this? You didn't want to talk to me about it first? George, I can't believe you!"

"Yeah, I did," he replied. "I had to. I just realized: I'm at a point in my life where this is not what I want. I've done the traveling job. I've made the mistake where I put my career above my marriage, and that didn't work out so well. Now I'm married to someone I love that I don't want to be gone from. I don't want to be gone from you, and I don't want to be gone from our kids."

Marianne was still reeling from the news . . . but she got it.

"Well, okay," she said. "We have to tell the kids."

When they sat their kids down and told them the news, George's older son broke in with a suggestion. "Dad, why don't you put your money where your mouth is. You're always volunteering to do motocross stuff. You love it. Why don't you just open your own racetrack?"

George thought about it and said he'd try it if they all pitched in. The kids agreed. And he went for it. He applied for a business loan and opened a motocross shop and a track. They sold bikes, offered lessons, did repairs. The business worked—it was a success. When this couple came into the lab a few years later, George was still running it; the teenagers—now college students—would still work at the shop sometimes. And George and Marianne were a tight couple, really solid. They had a shared sense of humor that popped out right away in the oral history interview: when we asked how they met and what attracted them to each other, George said, "Oh well I was attracted right away . . . to her butt." And Marianne cracked up. He continued: "Then, of course, I got to know her. . . . I knew right away I was going to marry her."

When we asked them to tell us about a time they'd overcome conflict, they told the story above. The funny thing about their story, though, is that there *wasn't* a big fight in there. There could have been—that moment when George came home and announced that he'd unilaterally quit his job without consulting his wife could really have gone another way. But in that moment of crisis, they went *right* to their dreams. George knew what he wanted and what he didn't want, and he expressed it.

During the interview, Marianne turned to him and said, "I still can't believe you did it so suddenly. Weren't you scared?"

"Sure I was scared," he replied. "But I knew it would be okay. I can do anything with you."

What Are the Dreams Within Your Conflict?

With your partner, try the exercise below to get beneath the surface of one of your conflicts. There's a wealth of knowledge we can come to understand about each other, which can truly be relationship-changing—and life-changing—if we can access it.

Choose a gridlocked or perpetual problem to discuss. If you need help brainstorming what to choose, take a look at the list below that we've compiled and see if any of these hit home with both of you. While couples can be gridlocked on anything, and perpetual problems can take various forms, these are some common problem areas that many couples find themselves in conflict over. Choose one, or if you prefer, you can each choose a topic and go through this process twice.

Perpetual problems may stem from differences in . . .

- [ ] neatness and organization in the home
- [ ] the raising of children, including the division of childcare, discipline, strictness versus gentleness, etc.
- [ ] optimal sexual frequency
- [ ] preferred lovemaking style (for instance, one person sees sex as a road to intimacy, while the other requires intimacy as a precondition for sex)
- [ ] dealing with extended family (do you want more independence from family or more closeness?)
- [ ] handling finances (one partner is more conservative and worries if you don't save; the other is more of a free spender who values living for the moment)
- [ ] how to break down domestic labor (for instance, an equal division of labor versus a more traditional arrangement)

☐ socializing and relating to friends and community (extroversion vs. introversion)

☐ relationship fidelity (what does it mean to be loyal to each other?)

☐ the need for excitement and adventure

☐ ambition and the importance of work (one person is more oriented toward work and success in that arena than the other)

☐ religion

☐ the desire for independence (one partner may want more)

☐ core values (are there major differences in what you most value and prioritize in life?)

What's not on the list? Are there differences in personality, ways of living, values or beliefs about how things should be that have shown up in your own conflicts? Add them here:

_____

_____

_____

Next, discuss this problem using the following guidelines:

Your mission: To work on a gridlocked or perpetual problem by helping your partner understand the underlying dreams, history, beliefs, or values in your position on this issue.

Speaker's job: Your task is to honestly talk about your feelings and beliefs about your position on this issue. Explore what this position means to you, what the dream might be behind your position. Tell the story of the source of this dream or this belief: where it comes from and what it symbolizes. You must be clear and honest. What do you *really* want on this issue? Why is it important to you? Try to make your partner understand.

- Don't argue for or try to persuade your partner of your point of view; just explain how you see things. Tell your partner all of your thoughts and feelings that you have about your position on this issue.
- You may want to look over the list on the following page for a sample of dreams that people sometimes have (or have lost) that could underlie the position you've taken on this issue.

Listener's job: Your job here is to make your partner feel *safe* enough to tell you what's behind their position on the issue: their belief, dream, or story. Toward this end, you will *listen* the way a friend would listen. *Ask the questions* that are listed on the next page as sample questions for the "dream catcher" (that's you!), which can help draw out your partner and their point of view. Try to *suspend judgment*—your job is not to evaluate or analyze your partner's story but just to hear it.

- Don't try to arrive at a solution. It is much too soon for that. You first need to end the opposition of dreams and become one another's friend instead of one another's foe. Try to understand the meaning of your partner's dream. Be interested!
- Realize that the goal is not to solve these problems. The goal is to move from gridlock to dialogue and to understand, in depth, your partner's position.
- Do not argue your point of view! Just listen and ask questions.

SAMPLE QUESTIONS For the Dream Catcher (Listener)	SAMPLE DREAMS For the Dream Speaker
• What do you believe about this issue?	• A sense of freedom
• Is there a story behind this for you?	• The experience of peace
	• Unity with nature
• Does this relate to your background in some way?	• Exploring who I am
	• Adventure
• Tell me why this is so important to you.	• A spiritual journey
	• Justice
• Does this relate to some belief or value for you?	• Honor
	• Unity with my past
• Does your background or childhood history relate to your position on this issue?	• Knowing my family
	• Becoming all I can be
• Why is this so important to you?	• Having a sense of power
	• Dealing with my aging
• What are your feelings about this issue?	• Exploring a creative side of myself
• What would be your ideal dream regarding this issue?	• Becoming more powerful
• Is there a deeper purpose or goal in this for you?	• Getting over past hurts

(table continues)

SAMPLE QUESTIONS	SAMPLE DREAMS
For the Dream Catcher (Listener)	**For the Dream Speaker**
	• Becoming more competent
	• Asking God for forgiveness
	• Exploring an old part of myself I have lost
	• Getting over a personal hang-up
	• Having a sense of order
	• Being able to be productive
	• A place and a time to just "be"
	• Being able to truly relax
	• Reflecting on my life
	• Getting my priorities in order
	• Finishing something important
	• Exploring the physical side of myself
	• Being able to compete and win
	• Travel
	• Quietness
	• Atonement
	• Building something important
	• Ending a chapter of my life
	• Saying goodbye to something
	• Love

The bottom line: You don't want to have the kind of relationship in which you win and are influential in the relationship but wind up crushing your partner's dream. You want the kind of relationship in which each of you supports the other's dreams. If your dreams connect, so much the better.

Troubleshooting the Dreams Conversation

A note here about conflict styles and how to successfully manage this conversation depending on your and your partner's conflict styles:

- **Tips for conflict avoiders:** You may feel reluctant to have this conversation at all. It will help enormously if you feel that the listener is not going to react negatively to your answers but instead is absorbing the information and learning from it. You can help a conflict-avoidant individual open up by really taking to heart the instructions for the listener: Listen like a friend. Suspend judgment. Don't jump in and interrupt. As with all conflict styles, but especially for avoiders, *safety* during this discussion is key.

- **Tips for validators:** Validators often have an easier time with this one—they just need to remember to give each other lots of space to answer and not move along to persuasion too quickly. Remember the goal: learning about each other so you can draw closer to each other. We are *not* moving to solutions yet—it is much too soon for that. Remind yourself to stay here, in the exploration phase, until you've gone through the questions thoroughly with both partners. If ideas for solutions or compromises leap to mind, push them away for now.

- **Tips for volatiles:** You may have a harder time not interrupting your partner or bringing up your own point of view in the middle of asking your partner the dream catcher questions. You may have negative emotions triggered by their answers and feel the urge to cut in—

back-and-forth debate may be a familiar way you've had
for exploring emotions, but for this exercise, you need to
flex the muscles of *waiting and listening.* It's tough! But
your work is to resist jumping in and debating or
persuading. You have to wait until both you and your
partner have had a chance to answer those questions in
depth without interruption.

The fact that this is essentially an interview—where you progress
down the list and ask your partner a whole sequence of questions
and don't offer your own thoughts at all—may feel odd at first. But
we think of this as the biggest gift of this exercise. When we're in the
middle of a fight, there's *so* much back-and-forth. There's debate.
There's rebuttal. This format, in contrast, creates a ton of time and
space. People can speak without having to navigate a partner's response. Without having to *fight.*

A great tactic, if you're having trouble staying out of persuasion
and just listening, is to **take notes.** Seriously! Pull out a pen and
paper and write down your partner's answers. It's a simple way to get
your brain to focus just on what your partner is saying and not doing
what human brains tend to do, formulating your own response.

Final Tip: Don't Rush It

You probably noticed that in the instructions for this exercise, we
don't get to solutions or compromise yet. We will! In fact, that's up
next. But what we have seen is that understanding the issue at a
deeper level makes compromise *so* much easier and more successful.
Our motto: *understanding must precede resolution.*

Now—once dreams are out in the open, there is of course still work to do in order to accommodate them. What if we uncover our dreams, and they seem to be in opposition?

Occasionally, yes, dreams in opposition can be deal-breakers, like the example we talked about earlier, where one partner wants children and the other does not. But more often, there's space for both. You don't have to have the same "big life dream" to have a wonderful, fulfilling, and successful relationship. When we first met, Julie's dream was to take a group of women up Mt. Everest, past base camp and up to at least 18,600 feet, and to live an adventurous life with a lot of outdoor exploration. Meanwhile, John's dream was to create nonlinear differential equations of human relationships ideally while sitting on a warm couch with a fire and a giant pile of books nearby—*not* to go sleep on rocks at the top of the world where there's no oxygen. And yet, thirty-five years later, here we are—and we both feel our dreams have been honored. Finding a way forward that makes space for both dreams is up next. But for now, stay here in the exploration phase, and find out everything you can about each other's dreams. The more you know, the better the next stage will go.

FIGHT #4:
THE STANDOFF

Mistake: Competing to Win

In game theory, a "zero-sum outcome" is one where a win by one person represents an equal loss by the other. Poker is a good example of this; however many chips you lose is how many I gain. Some situations are truly "zero sum." There is no other way to play the game. But research has found that many people tend to interpret nuanced and complex situations as "zero sum" even when they are not.[1] They may be predisposed—for whatever reason—to perceive any scenario, even intimate partner relationships, as a win-or-lose gambit. In conflict, we are all especially vulnerable to this pattern of thought.

You want your partner to do the dishes after dinner; they want to respond to some pressing work emails. A fight starts over who does what around the house and how someone's work (their own) always seems to take precedence over domestic tasks; you point out that you've done the dishes every other night this week. Your partner agrees to clean up but is clearly stressed. You win; they lose.

Your partner wants the kids to go to summer camp because they went when they were a kid—you want to save the money for urgent house repairs, and summer camp is a luxury not a necessity. You fight, it escalates, you both yell and interrupt; you get overwhelmed and flooded and give up. Fine, send them. Put it on a credit card. They win, you lose.

You want to talk about moving closer to your family, who live across the country; your partner thinks it's a nonstarter, as there are fewer career opportunities there, and the real estate market is not great—not a good time to sell and relocate. You point out the financial upsides of being close to grandparents who can help with the kids, but your partner says it's "out of the question" and ends the conversation. They win, you lose.

Final score? You're down one, in the red.

Often, we try to "win" because we wholeheartedly believe that our way is the right way or the only way. It seems so obvious to us— of course you should do the dishes when I've been picking up the slack every single night! Of course we should stretch a bit so the kids can go to camp—the experience is priceless, and if I could just ex- plain a little bit more, you'll understand. Of course we can't move right now, in this real estate market. What are you, nuts?

In our minds, we are logical, neutral, correct—our partners just need to be convinced to see the light. Why would we compromise when their position is so clearly incorrect or impossible?

If You Could Just See Things My Way...

Vince and Jenny, a couple in their midsixties, lived in Bellingham, Washington, a sleepy college town north of Seattle, on Puget Sound. They'd been there in the same house on a hill above the downtown for just about their whole adult lives—Vince was a commercial fisherman who frequently traveled up the coast to Alaska to fish crab and halibut; Jenny had been a teacher but quit to raise their kids. Now the kids were grown and off living their own lives, Vince was on the brink of retiring, and both had been dreaming about what they'd do with this next chapter of their lives.

The problem was, they were dreaming *very* different dreams.

Vince had always wanted to travel. He'd loved his life with his family in Bellingham, but now he wanted to see the world. For years, he'd dreamed of retiring, selling the house, and buying a sailboat— not those clunky trawlers he'd spent his life on, hauling cages full of crab onto the deck in the freezing rain. What he wanted was a big gorgeous boat, a thirty footer like a Catalina or an Islander, with living quarters below deck, that he and Jenny could live on and sail around the world.

Jenny, meanwhile, also had a dream for their retirement. She dreamed of selling the house and moving back to her family's farm, to the beautiful old turn-of-the-century farmhouse she'd spent summers in as a child and had always thought of as "home." The farm had been in her family for generations, and while it had sometimes been a working farm and sometimes just a home, it had always been lived in and loved by someone in her family, from her great-great-grandparents down to her own parents, and now—she hoped—she and Vince. And where was this farm?

Iowa.

You can see the problem.

We met Vince and Jenny when they traveled down to Seattle for a weekend workshop. By the time they showed up in our class, they'd been battling over this for more than a year, without any progress toward compromise. How could they compromise? Their dreams were polar opposites, and neither one could give up their vision of how their lives would go. These dreams felt like part of them at this point, a whole life they had planned for, fallen in love with, and couldn't let go of. There was no "middle ground": there was no ocean in Iowa; there was no ancestral farmland in the middle of the Pacific. At this point, they'd both almost entirely given up on their dreams. The resentment and bitterness between them ran deep.

And yet, they couldn't seem to give up on their marriage. They had a lot of good years behind them. In the aggregate, they'd been good partners to each other, kind and supportive. They'd worked hard and they'd poured themselves into raising their kids well. But they were both a bit grief-stricken: all this time, they thought they'd been working toward a similar vision, and it turned out they hadn't been. Now, for the first time in their long relationship, they were fighting all the time, and those fights were tinged with resentment and contempt in a way they had never been before. They'd burned through the stock of goodwill and friendship they'd built up—they were hanging on by a thread. Bitterness leaked into every interaction.

In the workshop, when we asked couples to think of a conflict they were having trouble compromising on, Vince and Jenny had no trouble choosing their topic. And they wasted no time getting right into it—we've found that when couples disagree strongly about something, they can easily shift into heated conflict whether they're at home alone, in a lab with electrodes attached to their bodies and cameras trained on them, or in a conference room with twelve hundred other people.

Jenny: We need to approach this logically.

Vince: *(snorting sarcastically)* Oh, *logically*, right, a top skill of yours.

Jenny: *(ignoring the sarcasm for now)* Yes. You need to just think about this practically. You're talking about going out on a huge limb here. You've never done this kind of sailing. Fishing crab with a whole crew of guys isn't the same thing! You don't know the first thing about sailing on the open ocean. It's a pipe dream, Vince. And you're holding our lives hostage over it.

Vince: A pipe dream! I've been going out on boats for the last *thirty years.* You think I don't know my way around a boat? That I picked this idea out of a hat on a whim?

Jenny: No, but—

Vince: For years I've been talking about doing this, for years. "Sounds nice," you always said. Was that a lie?

Jenny: Vince, it was like someone saying, "Wouldn't it be fun to live on the moon." It's a crazy idea! I never thought you'd actually want to liquidate our whole life and do it!

Vince: But it's okay to liquidate our whole life and move to *Iowa*? You're the one who's not thinking clearly. You have some romantic idea about farming—what are we going to do, grow potatoes? This whole thing is stupid.

Jenny: Oh, I'm stupid. Stupid.

Vince: You're twisting my words.

Jenny: I don't understand it. I don't know why you're being so selfish. This was supposed to be our time, to just settle in, talk to
each other, have some quiet comfort . . .

Vince: The last thing I want right now is quiet comfort. That sounds
like being dead.

Jenny: *(shaking her head)* My God, so dramatic.

Vince: Come on, what the hell am I supposed to do on a farm? I'm
going to be a farmer? Sit in a rocking chair? What am I going
to do all day? I've been working on a fishing boat for forty-
five years and now I want to do something fun!

Jenny: *(bitterly)* Well go ahead then, go do it, if that's what's important to you. Sail away. Sail away from me.

Unlike the couple in the last chapter, there's no mystery here
about what's fueling this fight—the dreams are right out on the table!
But those dreams are so oppositional, they can't find a compromise
that doesn't feel like an enormous loss for one or the other. It appears
to be a clear-cut zero-sum situation: if she gets her dream, he has to
give up his, and vice versa.

As a result, both have locked into their positions, unwilling—
unable, really—to give any ground. To compromise at all would be to
lose everything to the other's advantage: *zero sum.* Neither can
budge.

The Big Problem with a Win-Lose Dynamic

In 2010, John and his frequent research collaborator Robert Levenson were wrapping up a twenty-year longitudinal study on couples
based out of Levenson's lab at the University of California, Berkeley.[2]

The study had a similar format to others we've run: couples came into the lab and were asked to bring up a point of ongoing conflict between the two of them and discuss it. We recorded their interaction for fifteen minutes. Then we sat them down and had *them* watch the tape. As they watched, they sat in front of a control board with a rating dial, turning the dial to rate the interaction moment to moment as positive or negative. Some couples would be, for the most part, aligned—when one spouse thought the interaction was going well, so did the other. But there was another category of couples who had the opposite trend: when one rated the interaction more highly, the other's rating plummeted. At the end of the experiment, their graphs looked like the graph on this page.

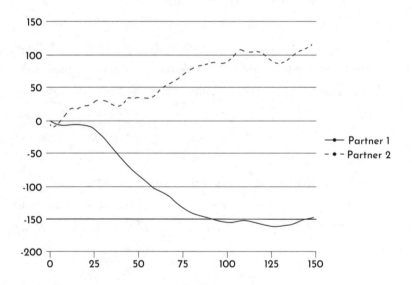

As you can see from this couple's rating dials, any positive gain by one partner was wiped out mathematically by a corresponding negative drop for the other. We started calling these couples our "zero-sum couples": in their interactions, there was always a winner and a loser. One person's gain was always the other person's loss. Of course, this mentality works great in poker, where the point is to win chips. But what we know about relationships is that if one person "wins" and the other "loses," what happens in the end is that *both* partners lose.

We were interested to see what would happen to the zero-sum couples over time. But we had a problem. When we invited couples back to the lab through the years for follow-ups, a lot of the zero-sum couples weren't showing up. Well, we figured, maybe the experience had been too stressful and unpleasant for them, and they were just opting out. But when we reached out to them to find out, we discovered that they hadn't dropped out.

They'd died.

Specifically, the men. Fifty-eight percent of the husbands in the zero-sum couples had passed away over the twenty-year time span of the study, compared with only 20 percent of the more collaborative couples.

Obviously, this got our attention! We launched another study to see why this could be happening. What we found: In couples where there was trust and cooperation, the blood of both spouses flowed slower.[3] Their heart rates stayed lower and steadier—not only during conflict but *all the time*. That's just good for overall health on a very basic level. In the zero-sum couples, spouses experienced a big spike in heart rate and stress hormone levels. That kind of physiological response to your partner takes its toll over time. Our conclusion? A zero-sum approach to conflict discussions was not only hurting their relationship, it was also hurting their health. (Why only the men? Women, we believe, were more protected from the high-stress effects of zero-sum conflict because women's bodies also produce *oxytocin* during moments of closeness and bonding, which can counteract the stress response.)

The takeaway here is that a zero-sum dynamic in conflict is never going to serve you. Unfortunately, it's extremely common: across the forty thousand couples entering therapy whom we assessed, 84 percent of heterosexual couples were struggling with a chronic inability to find compromise, with gay and lesbian couples close behind, at 81 percent and 78 percent, respectively.[4] Zero-sum thinking is a trap that any couple can fall into in the roller coaster of a conflict discussion.

What we ultimately want is to replace that line graph—where any gain by one partner is mirrored by the other's loss—with a different mathematical model of conflict: one that shows *cooperative gain*. In this version of the graph, the ups and downs of conflict are a shared experience. We don't see one partner's rating dial plummet when the other's goes up. We see more of a correlation in the two lines: the "wins" are shared and collaborative. These couples have a better experience of conflict—less physiological arousal and more positivity— and in the long run, that is protective not only of the relationship but also of their physical health.

So how do we get there? How do we arrive at a place of cooperative gain in conflict rather than a toxic zero-sum dynamic?

Lab data shows that the most successful couples, and the ones who do best in conflict, are those who can *accept influence* from each other.[5] A counterintuitive finding from the Love Lab: if you want to "win" in partner conflict, you need to yield some ground.

"Yielding to Win"

There is a core philosophy in aikido, a Japanese martial art often referred to as "the art of peace," called "yielding to win," where you use your sparring partner's energy and movements instead of fighting against them. If you were sparring in aikido and moved toward your partner, you'd encounter no physical blocking or resistance; your partner would instead flow *with* your momentum, joining you in your forward motion and guiding you in the direction they choose to go. They've yielded to you, and in doing so, they're now guiding the action.

This is precisely the energy we want to bring into our fights.

We want to allow our partners to influence us—both in and out of conflict. We want to move *with* them not against them. Aikido teaches that you cannot win if you try to strong-arm your partner—you will only burn energy. The goal is not to overpower your partner but to achieve balance. The same is true in romantic partnerships. It sounds paradoxical, but the more you allow yourself to be influenced by your partner, the more capacity *you* will have to influence them. In aikido, of course, we're talking about *physical* influence—moving together, staying centered. When we talk about accepting influence in a romantic partnership, what we're talking about is a kind of emotional aikido: moving together, staying centered, not trying to strong-arm each other. To be clear, "accepting influence" does not mean simply collapsing into whatever your partner wants. It means being open to your partner's ideas and being willing to change your perspective as you learn more about how they feel and why.

In the Love Lab, our studies found that in heterosexual marriages, the men who allowed their partners to influence them had happier marriages over time and were significantly less likely to divorce than those who resisted their wives' influence.[6] In fact, men who refused to share power and decision-making with their spouses had an 81 percent probability of splitting up. That's high!

The focus is on men here for a reason: because of the way we're socialized and the messages we receive about masculinity and femininity from the minute we're born, men do tend to struggle more with accepting influence than women do. Even today, men who are aware of this cultural gender dynamic and work to make their relationship egalitarian are vulnerable to this deeply embedded social conditioning that to be influenced and give up ground, especially to a woman, is to be "weak." Even if we don't believe that on a conscious level, that cultural messaging is coded in there somewhere, like a stealthy computer program running in the background.

Gender, Sexuality, and Accepting Influence

In gay and lesbian couples, we do see that accepting influence comes more easily. John and his collaborator Robert Levenson ran an observational study with twenty-one same-sex couples for over a decade that came to be known as "the 12 Year Study."[7] They observed that gay and lesbian couples, to begin with, seemed to have a better capacity to laugh at themselves—in conflict, they tended not to take things as personally as heterosexual couples. They also tended to be more positive and upbeat during fights; they were more likely to use humor and affection, even in the midst of conflict. And along with that came lower levels of physiological arousal—less flooding. But perhaps most significantly for this chapter's discussion, they were, by default, more open to their partner's influence. They were far less defensive than heterosexual couples and more likely to entertain the possibility that their partner was right.

Why is that? Well, we puzzled over that for quite a while. According to the latest Gallup poll, only 7.1 percent[8] of the population of the United States identifies as gay, lesbian, or transgender, and many who identify as LGBTQ grow up feeling isolated or alone. Perhaps, we theorized, when they do find love, they're predisposed to be more accepting. Another possibility is that these individuals may have experienced more difficulty and rejection from their family of origin—statistically, much more so than cisgender or heterosexual individuals have. Because of that, they may tend to have more empathy for their partner's pain and a desire to relieve it by accepting their partner's influence.

Whatever the reasons, what the data showed is that the same-sex couples from the 12 Year Study, which wrapped up in 2003, were much more sensitive to *not dominating each other*. We saw this with female partners in particular: most women have experienced misogyny and objectification in this culture, expressed through male domination, suppression, and oppression. Women in relationships with other women don't want to manifest that same dynamic with their partner, so they may bend over backward not to. Working with couples clinically, we've observed that lesbian couples may end up talking in circles because they're trying so hard to not overpower their partner; nobody wants to make a decision and be the more influential one. (Julie had one couple who joked, "Twelve-year study, huh? It'll take us twelve years to figure out where we're going to dinner tonight!")

Some men in heterosexual partnerships will argue: "We split childcare and domestic labor 50/50—accepting influence is not an issue for me." To that we say: the roots of misogyny run deep. They go back to the beginning of recorded time. Some historians will point to cultures that have existed throughout history where women wielded more power or that were more egalitarian; however, they were few and far between, and even where female power existed, misogyny coexisted.[9] Women have historically been enslaved during wars; they have been the victims of sexual violence. Women have been sold as chattel and political pawns. They have been valued as objects or property, evaluated on their perceived fertility and ability to produce heirs. Their voices have been universally silenced. It wasn't until the mid-1970s that a woman could get a credit card without her husband's permission; today, women still hit their heads on the glass ceiling, making 81 cents for every dollar a man makes. And somewhere between one in four to one in three women are the victims of rape—we think probably even more, because many don't report it. The world is simply a more dangerous place for women than it is for men—for a woman, the probability that she'll be assaulted in her lifetime is 40 percent. For men, it's 9 percent.

Women have a special relationship to the emotion of *fear*—over millennia, men have been the protectors and the aggressors, while women have been the ones to maintain vigilance for themselves. We see this play out with our female primate cousins, who care for their babies and eat in a circle so they can maintain a 360-degree view of any approaching danger. For thousands of years, a heightened awareness of threat and danger has been essential to female survival, and this legacy persists. Women, for instance, tend to require a sense of safety in order to feel that a situation is erotic. "Women need a reason for sex," Billy Crystal once said. "Men only need a place." It's a joke, but it has a lot to do with fear: for women, physical safety and emotional safety are tightly braided together.

All this to say: *influence,* and who has it in a relationship, does not exist in a vacuum. There are evolutionary, historical, and cultural pressures that show up in our conflicts, especially when it comes to our capacities to exert influence and accept influence. Girls and women—and it's been this way for thousands of years—perceive, on some level, that they are valued only on the basis of the measurements of their bodies and how they rack up to the standards of the day. That belief lives in the bones of women—they feel it, they know it, even if they don't know exactly where it comes from. It permeates our culture. It's why we ask men in particular to reflect on their capacity to be influenced by their partners. It's why, when we give workshops, John gives the talk about accepting influence and how critical it is. All of this human baggage is still the backdrop of our relationships to this day.

Julie has found, working clinically with couples, that she often faces a challenge with heterosexual couples where the man will be used to having power—he's either had it his whole life or he's been scrappy, fought hard to get to a certain level of influence and power, and doesn't want to lose it. Beneath all that, there's often a lot of insecurity about his own masculinity. So one thing we do is explore *what masculinity means to him.* That means teasing apart the distinction between being a *dominator* and being a *protector.*

A lot of men in our culture have conflated the two things. But what does it really mean to be a "protector"? One of a protector's main jobs, with a woman he loves, is to protect her humanity. What does that look like? How do you protect a woman's humanity in this culture? Well, you don't know what's at the core of her humanity until you ask her: *What dreams do you have? Who do you want to be? How do I protect your pathway toward fulfilling your dream? What obstacles do you face, and how do I help get them out of your way?*

We've had many experiences being interviewed on TV and radio in which the interviewer turned out to be notably biased toward John's authority while dissing Julie's similar expertise. On one show, the interviewer pitched us a question about our clinical work. Julie answered it. With no response whatsoever to Julie, as though she hadn't said anything, the interviewer turned to John and said, "Dr. Gottman, what do you think?" (Note: Both of us are doctors, but John was the only one addressed as such.)

John responded, "I think Julie has answered your question."

John proved to be Julie's loving protector that day. He was protecting her right to be respected as an authority too.

Actually doing this—being the protector a woman needs—can sometimes run contrary to the deeply ingrained ideas we may also have culturally about masculinity. For instance, she wants to go back to school to get her degree. As her protector, you take over more of the childcare so she can do this. You're going to step into the caregiver role, attuning to the needs of the kids, handling the logistics of hair brushing and lunch making. We ask couples struggling with roles: Is that a masculine thing to do or a feminine thing to do? The classic answer is "feminine" because traditionally, this sort of caretaking is coded as such. We say it is equally "masculine," because he's protecting her as a human being in her right to fulfill herself. There's a lot of power in that.

When our daughter was eight, John once again proved himself to be Julie's heroic protector. How did he do this? By learning to braid curly hair.

Since we'd first married, Julie had dreamed of taking a group of women to the base camp of Mt. Everest and higher. John, the consummate indoorsman, was frightened for Julie's safety, but he realized how important the dream was to her. He supported her going. But that also meant taking care of their daughter solo—for four weeks! For the first time, John learned how to braid Moriah's long, curly (and uncooperative) hair. It was a tall order, but he proved to be quite good at it and patiently combed his daughter's hair and wove that braid for her every morning for twenty-eight days.

Another example that's very close to us: that same daughter has now grown up, married, and recently had a baby, our first grandchild. She's nourishing the baby with breast milk, which, as anyone who has breastfed knows, is a lot of work. Because she needs a lot of rest to produce the amount of breast milk this baby needs, her husband has been doing night duty with the baby. He's the one to get up multiple times a night, warm up some fresh breast milk from the fridge, and feed his little son in the rocking chair so that she can sleep. He's done this every night since the baby's first few weeks, which were really rough on her—she wasn't getting enough rest, and her milk supply was dropping. So when she said to him, "I need things to be different," what did he do? He accepted her influence; he shifted his expectation of what his role would be as father; he protected her emotionally and physically by protecting her nighttime rest.

We talk about this—with our daughter and son in-law's permission—because it's hard to push back against cultural and systemic pressures. Deeply coded expectations surrounding gender roles are one form of pressure that can make it hard, especially for men in this society, to accept influence when we should. But any of us can struggle with accepting influence. And ironically, refusal to accept influence is the main way we *give up* our own influence.

Don't Be the Rock!

Here's the bottom line for all people and all couples: when you can't be moved or influenced, you *lose all power* in the relationship. If you're someone who always says "no" to whatever your partner wants or proposes, you become an obstacle. You're a dead end for them. There's no new information there; no inroads to connection, and no collaborative way forward. So they find a way around you. If you're hiking a trail and there's a big rock in the middle of the path, what do you do? Do you try to reason with it, convince it to move out of the way? Of course not—you just find a way around it. When you won't accept influence because you don't want to give up power or control in a situation, you become that rock that your partner is just going around. Now you're powerless. *You* have no influence.

The only way to become powerful in a relationship is to be capable of accepting influence. It's only when there's a true give-and-take that a person has real power. That means you treat the other person—their emotions, needs, and dreams—with honor and respect. You are willing to see things from their point of view. You are willing to be flexible in certain areas to accommodate their needs and dreams. This, then, has enormous implications for how ready *they* will be to listen to your point of view and to bend and flex to accommodate *your* needs and dreams.

How readily are you able to accept influence from your partner?

How would each of you answer the following questions, generally true or generally false?

- I'm interested in getting my partner's opinion on an issue.
- I listen with curiosity to their point of view and ask questions.
- I think my partner has a lot of basic common sense.
- I learn something from my partner even when we disagree.
- I'm willing to try things my partner's way.
- I want my partner to feel influential and respected in this relationship.

The Gottman Island Survival Game

Want to explore the dynamic of influence a bit more? Try the following activity with your partner. It can be fun, and it can also illuminate some common issues surrounding influence, helping us become aware of the conditions that spark us to resist influence and to become rigid and unyielding. We call it "the Gottman Island Survival Game," and the basic rules are simple: you're shipwrecked on an island, and you need to agree on what critical items you most need for survival. We're going to provide you with a list of options; from that list, you and your partner must agree on ten essentials.

If you start this activity and one of you finds yourself quickly becoming critical of your partner or slipping into a domineering attitude (Looks like: "Let me answer this one," "Let me figure it out," "You don't know what you're talking about"), then consider: Do you tend to do this during actual conflict as well? If so, use this exercise as "influence practice." This is an imaginary scenario with low stakes, making it a great opportunity to try out a different mode of being open and willing to go with someone else's energy. Give your partner more space and latitude to make decisions. Seek their input. Say, "What do you think?" If you disagree with one of their choices, go with it anyway! See how it feels. See if it changes how *they* respond to your suggestions. See if you can use this exercise to explore the dynamic of accepting influence and moving together, aikido-style.

Imagine, then, that your cruise ship just sank in the Caribbean, and you awaken to find yourselves alone on a deserted island. Here is the scenario:

- The two of you are the only survivors.
- One of you is injured.

- You have no idea where you are.
- You think there's some chance that people know of the ship's distress, but you're not sure.
- A storm appears to be on the way.
- You decide that you need to prepare to survive on this island for some time and also to make sure that you'll be spotted by a rescue party.
- There is a bunch of stuff from the ship on the beach that could help you, but you can carry only ten items.

Your mission has three steps:

STEP ONE

Each of you circles what you consider the ten most important items to keep from the ship's inventory list below. Then rank-order these items based on their importance to you: give the most crucial item a "1," the next most crucial a "2," and so on. There are no right or wrong answers!

Ship's Inventory:

___ Two changes of clothing

___ AM / FM radio receiver

___ Ten gallons of water

___ Pots and pans

___ Matches

___ Shovel

___ Backpack

___ Toilet paper

___ Two tents

___ Two sleeping bags

___ Knife

___ Small life raft with sail

___ Sunblock lotion

___ Cookstove and lantern

___ Long rope

___ Two walkie-talkies

___ Freeze-dried food for seven days

___ One change of clothing

___ One fifth of whiskey

___ Flares

___ Compass

___ Regional aerial maps

___ Gun with six bullets

___ Fifty packages of condoms

___ First-aid kit with penicillin

___ Oxygen tanks

STEP TWO

Share your list with your partner. Together, come up with a consensus list of ten items. Talk it over and work together as a team to solve the problem. Both of you need to be influential in discussing the problem and in making the final decisions!

Our Consensus List:

1. _____

2. _____

3. _____

4. _____

5. _____

6. _____

7. _____

8. _____

9. _____

10. _____

STEP THREE

When you've finished, evaluate how the game went and, together, answer the questions below.

1. How effective do you think you were at influencing your spouse?

2. How effective was your spouse at influencing you?

3. Did either of you try to dominate the other, or were you competitive with each other?

4. Did you sulk or withdraw?

5. Did your partner sulk or withdraw?

6. Did you have fun?

7. Did you work well as a team?

8. How much irritability or anger did you feel?

9. How much irritability or anger did your partner feel?

10. Did you both feel included?

If you had trouble accepting influence during this game and having fun with it, talk with your partner about how a difficulty with power sharing might be showing up in your conflicts and in your life together. Even being able to acknowledge that this is challenging for one or both of you, and to take responsibility for that tendency, is a major leap forward.

Moving forward: If you catch yourself feeling defensive, rigid, or unwilling to share decision-making with your partner in the future, ask yourself: What would I lose by giving my partner more influence here? What might I gain?

Collaborative Gain: Toward True Compromise

While we were writing this book, we took a long-awaited trip to the northern tip of Norway and then high up inside the Arctic Circle. It was breathtakingly cold and breathtakingly gorgeous. It was John's preference to stay in the cozy cabin on board the ship, enjoying the view of the stark rocks and ice through the portal while practicing Irish tunes on his flute; Julie, as always, was restless to get out into the beautiful natural landscape. She kayaked or hiked on the icy rock every day. But she missed John. So one day, John gathered all his love for Julie and some warm layers, and we both joined a hiking excursion.

As we prepared to begin our hike on land, we saw offshore a small group of kayakers. The group was coupled and paddling tandem kayaks, meaning one person sits in front of the other and is in charge of forward propulsion; the other person sits behind and has more control over steering. We've done lots of kayaking in warmer climes, and we know double kayaking takes a fair amount of collaboration and goodwill (just like a good fight!). We noticed a couple in the closest kayak to shore. They were arguing fiercely.

"You need to paddle faster!" said the woman, who was in the front. "You can't just sit back there like a lump while I do all the work."

"I am paddling," her husband snapped back. "I'm trying to steer around those ice patches. This isn't easy. You try it."

"I'm busy paddling for the both of us."

"You're not giving me any credit! Just paddle straight and calm down."

They disappeared around a rocky outcropping, bickering the whole way, their conversation laced with criticism and put-downs. As we hiked around a rocky shoreline corner, we can't say we were surprised by what we saw: they were stuck, their double kayak jammed up on a shelf of rock and ice.

"I can't go forward. Push off with your paddle."

"That won't work! We'll just get even more stuck."

"It will, it'll rock us loose—just try it. You're the one who got us stuck up here. Just listen to me for once."

"Who steered us right onto this damn iceberg? It wasn't me! Now just grab that rock and pull, we have to go that way."

"You wanna break the kayak? That's a terrible idea."

In the end, the kayak trip leader had to call the whole boat group together, everyone had to maneuver over to where this boat was stuck, and they all had to pitch in to pull this couple's boat off the ice. It worked out fine—eventually. Nobody got hurt. But the couple in question were red-faced, seething, and barely speaking to each other by the time all the hikers and paddlers returned to the ship and headed back to our warm rooms. What was notable about watching them during their struggle was that either one of their ideas would probably have worked—if they'd pushed together with both paddles, they'd have slid off one direction; if they'd helped each other reach out to grab the ledge and pull themselves the other direction, that might have worked too. There wasn't one right way to get themselves unstuck. They could have done it her way or his—they just needed to be more open to each other's influence.

Having influence comes from *being* influenced—and so does cooperative gain. There is no more zero-sum trap, where you both need to win so badly, you stay stuck on the rocks. You get unstuck. Everybody wins.

Now—let's go back to our couple from the beginning of the chapter, Vince and Jenny. When we left off with them, they were locked in a battle over who would get to have their dream play out in retirement: his or hers. Their dreams were in polar opposition, and both individuals were at the point where they felt that if they gave in even a little, they'd be giving up something core to who they were and what they wanted out of life. They couldn't compromise—they stood to lose too much. And so they were stuck—just as stuck as the couple in the tandem kayak. They needed a push off their rock. And so we gave them one in the form of an intervention we call "the Bagel Method."

The Bagel Method is intended to help couples in conflict find a *true* compromise: one that feels good to both partners. It offers a whole new way of approaching the "facts" of a fight. It allows partners to drill down to the core essence of their dream or need or goal and cut away the distracting chaff that's getting in the way. It allows both partners to have influence while not demanding that either partner give up something that's nonnegotiable to them. And most importantly, it illuminates the generous amount of space we may have to accommodate both dreams.

The Intervention: The Bagel Method

During our first three fights, we kept telling you to *postpone persuasion*. Well—not anymore! We're finally here. We have arrived at the persuasion phase.

We named this the Bagel Method because it literally looks like a bagel. Take a look at the image below:

COMPROMISE OVALS

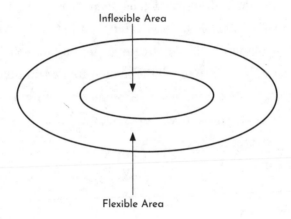

Inflexible Area

Flexible Area

My inflexible area or core need on this issue is:

My more flexible areas on this issue are:

We ask couples to make this simple drawing on a piece of note-book paper. Then we ask them to do two things. First, identify your nonnegotiable aspects of this dream or goal, and write them down inside the inner circle. The inside of the bagel is your area of inflex-ibility, the *core* of your dream or need in terms of your own identity, who you want to be, how you want to live your life. This is the thing you cannot live without in order to be happy and whole and to have a successful relationship. This is your absolute necessity.

Next, think about your areas of flexibility related to this issue. These are often the nitty-gritty details of *how* you fulfill this dream. Identifying what's flexible for you can be hard at first—many of us have been hanging on to our dream so tightly, we feel inflexible about everything—but to break the mental traffic jam here, we ask people to ask themselves questions similar to those a journalist would ask, to get to the facts of a story. Questions such as:

- When?
- Where?
- How much?
- How often?
- How will it start?
- How long should it last?
- What's in the middle?
- What's at the end?

When Vince and Jenny began this exercise, they'd been grid-locked for a long time. Jenny was feeling angry about all the times over the decades of her marriage that her choices had been taken away from her, all the times she'd put her husband and kids first. And now, at age sixty-five, she'd finally decided: Enough. I want to live the way *I* want for once. Meanwhile, Vince had been shocked and taken aback by this attitude from his wife—it was new, and he didn't like it. His instinct had been to dig in—he tried to claw back territory he was afraid he might lose. Historically, he'd taken on the responsibility for finances and decision-making. He'd carried that burden, and it had seemed to him that she was happy to let him. She'd never expressed appreciation for him doing that all these years for their family.

But Jenny was thinking about how *he* hadn't ever expressed appreciation for the work she did. She did everything for the kids. He'd been gone for weeks at a time, out in the Bering Sea, and she was just completely on her own, running the household by herself. She'd let go of some of the career goals she'd once had in order to put the family first. She carried the burden of planning and anticipating and taking care of everyone's needs all these decades.

She hadn't expressed her appreciation; neither had he. They'd both been feeling taken for granted in terms of what they'd given to the family. They both felt they'd already overextended themselves. And this was a huge part of the reason they couldn't compromise: this feeling of *I've already given up so much.*

They came to our workshop believing it was all or nothing: his dream or hers. And yet, once we began moving through the conflict blueprint, things really started to loosen up. In the "dreams within conflict" exercise, they took turns, for the first time, interviewing each other about their dreams. They heard the other person talk about what this vision for the future really meant to them: for him, adventure . . . *with her.* For her, living in a meaningful place, with a profound connection to the past and to her family . . . *with him.* Neither one of them wanted their dream if it meant doing it without the other one. From that vantage point, when they sat down with their blank "bagels," they were able to find so much more flexibility within their dreams than they'd been able to see previously.

Here's what their diagrams looked like, after they completed the exercise:

Jenny's Inner Circle (Inflexibility): "Fulfilling my family's legacy by living on the farm."
Vince's Inner Circle (Inflexibility): "Experience the freedom and adventure of sailing around the world."

But then, this was interesting: they both had identified a lot of the same potential areas of flexibility, summarized here:

- Whether or not we sell the house
- Whose dream goes first
- Where we go
- When dream fulfillment starts / when it ends
- How long it lasts
- Whether we do it part-time or full-time
- How much money we'll spend versus save

Vince and Jenny didn't figure out all the logistics in a single weekend workshop—but with this exercise, they realized that there was way more flexibility than they'd previously been able to see. It wasn't actually a zero-sum situation, where someone had to lose and give up their dream to accommodate the other. There was room for both dreams if both of them were willing to be flexible.

Before the workshop wrapped up, Vince and Jenny came to us and let us know that they'd decided to do both. They were going to move to the farm for a year and be based there; Vince was going to look for an intensive sailing course to take so he could fill in his skill gaps. And then, they'd find a boat to buy and go sailing. Vince had conceded that he probably didn't want to spend the next, say, *thirty years* living on a boat; Jenny admitted that being able to leave the Iowa farm for a few months—maybe in the dead of winter?—sounded pretty appealing. They weren't sure yet if they'd sell their Bellingham house right away or rent it, or where they'd go for their first sailing trip, or exactly how long it would last. Maybe they'd do some shorter trips first and build up to a longer one. The details were still emerging. But for the first time in a long time, they were both excited about the future.

Here are two more brief examples of couples who used this method successfully, so you can see the inner workings of the process.

Couple #1: Public versus Private

The situation: Andrés, a teacher at an innovative private school, wants his son, who is entering sixth grade, to attend the middle school where he teaches. Tuition is quite high, but because he is a teacher there, their family would receive a significant discount. Andrés attended private school as a child, and he wants his kid to have the same opportunity for a hands-on, elite education. Moira, his wife, is not feeling great about this—she went to public school as a kid and feels it's important to support the public school community as a social good. Plus, she's uncomfortable with the high tuition and the bubble of wealth and privilege the school represents. They can't compromise. She wants to keep their son at the local public school, which is just down the hill from their house and which he could walk to; he wants their son to get the best possible education. Plus, he's really been looking forward to having his son as a student and driving to school together every day.

They sit down to do the Bagel Method.

His area of inflexibility: To have my child as a student; for our son to get the benefits of this innovative school where I've poured my creativity and skills into creating a great curriculum.

Her area of inflexibility: To remain connected and involved with our local community and to support public education.

Areas of flexibility: Andrés was flexible on their son's life outside of the school day; Moira realized that she'd be okay with their son attending her husband's school if they could remain involved with their local community in other ways. And they had both listed something along the lines of "Take into account what our son wants to do" as an area of flexibility.

The compromise: They spoke with their son and laid out the options; he was torn but ultimately decided that he most wanted to go to school with his dad. He agreed with his mom about not losing track of his friends and neighborhood community, so they enrolled him in after-school soccer at the school down the hill. After a year, they'd see how things were going and if everyone was happy with the arrangement.

Couple #2: Geneva versus Nigeria

The situation: she lived in Geneva, he lived in Nigeria. She was white, he was Black. They met on a committee at work: he'd flown to Geneva to be on a panel; she was the panelist next to him. They flirted, hit it off, started dating. At first it was light and casual—he managed to get more trips to Geneva, and he called her when he was in town—

but quickly they fell in love. He proposed. She said yes. And then they had the conversation about where to live.

The problem emerged immediately: she'd been expecting him to move to Geneva. He'd assumed she would move to Lagos. And they both had complicating factors: kids.

He had two young children back home in Lagos and an extended family that relied on him—in the culture he came from, adult children took care of their parents. He felt strongly that she should move to Nigeria—she only had one son, and it was just the two of them. But her child was autistic and had special needs, and after a lot of research, she had not been able to find a school in Lagos that could provide him with the support he needed.

She couldn't move to Lagos and be the mother her child needed her to be; he couldn't move to Geneva and be the son his parents needed him to be. They pushed against each other, unable to understand why the other person couldn't give; their fights became more frequent and then constant. Resentment over each partner's perceived stubbornness and selfishness leaked into every facet of life; the negative perspective fell over them like a dark cloud. So they came to us.

Across many therapy sessions, we discussed dreams within conflict and drilled down to the core needs, and they came to understand each other at a truly profound level. He grasped, with deep compassion, her love and commitment to her son, her only child, and finally understood that she couldn't pull him away from the supportive educational community they'd established in Geneva. It would be the biggest betrayal of her mission as a parent: to give him every resource she possibly could. He didn't feel anymore (as he had initially) that she was "choosing her son over him." And she realized the value he placed on honoring his parents and his ancestors. He'd grown up in a small, tightly knit village, and he needed to be sure that, as the oldest son, he was going to be there for them. To move away to another continent would be a huge betrayal of what he believed and where he placed value in his life.

They were able to get down to what was at the core of each other's souls. What fueled them as human beings. Where they found meaning in life.

This couple had a long road to get to this point, and they almost broke up. When they got to that place of understanding, they might have easily decided this relationship was simply not going to work out, even though they loved each other. And maybe that would have been okay. But instead, from that point of deep compassion for each other, they committed to figuring it out. Why not do something nontraditional? They both had jobs that had both a lot of travel and a lot of flexibility—they could use that to their advantage.

His area of inflexibility: to be there for his parents in the tradition of his culture.

Her area of inflexibility: to provide her son with the best possible education.

They decided that she and her son would spend half the year in Lagos with him, with a tutor along to provide educational stability; the other half of the year, the couple would live apart, and he would travel to Geneva as he had when they were dating.

This arrangement wouldn't work for all couples, but these two were fiercely independent, and for both, the relationship was worth the logistical headache and the nontraditional living situation. In the end, they did do one thing the "traditional" way: they got married. And they had two ceremonies: one in Lagos and one in Geneva.

When This Fight Really Does Mean the End

The Bagel Method is really all about accepting influence and getting to compromise. You figure out: What's the beating heart of my dream? What is the core of it? Not all the extra possibilities or logistics I've been imagining, but the most essential version of what I need in order to feel whole, to be myself, and to live my life authentically. And then you try to be flexible surrounding that. You allow your partner's needs and dreams and goals to influence the how, the when, the where, and more of the unfolding of these dreams.

Couples generally find this process extremely helpful, and the vast majority are able to break through gridlock and move forward. But when one person's dream is the other person's nightmare—*and* that dream is core to who you are—then you may have to part.

When you pare down your dream to its essential core and it's *still* in direct opposition with your partner's—when all the flexing in the world isn't going to accommodate both dreams—there's not much you can do. When partners have oppositional dreams on the question of becoming parents, for instance, as in John's experience with his first marriage, there's no compromise possible. You can't have half a child. That's not people being too rigid—that's being true to your soul's needs. But at least you can part knowing that you honored yourself and your partner, and it's nobody's fault.

If you go through this conflict blueprint as we've laid it out in this book so far—from exploring the issues together, really listening and validating, exploring the dreams within conflict, and going through this exercise toward compromise, and it *still* feels impossible, like a huge painful loss, then the question you may be forced to ask yourself is: *How much do I love this person? What does love mean?*

Sometimes it does mean sacrifice. These compromises shouldn't feel like a loss of self, but they will not always be easy. Do I love my partner enough to work less, for example, and forsake or postpone a promotion I might get so my partner can go to school? Do I love them enough to move far from my family for an opportunity that represents their dream? Would they, have they, done the same for me? A whole lifetime with another person is a lifetime of fluctuating sacrifice and gain, of give-and-take, of carrying the heavier load sometimes, or giving something up for the greater good of the unit that the two of you represent together. And often, when partners progress through the conflict blueprint and try this approach to compromise, they are able to gain valuable clarity that this particular sacrifice—whatever it may be—is worth it: that on balance, they gain much more than they lose. They can feel at peace about giving up something they'd been tightly clinging to, because when they zoom out and look at the whole, there is so much more that they have that is valuable.

But sometimes couples go through this process and come to the realization that they do, in fact, have irreconcilable differences in terms of how they want to live their lives. Their dreams are not compatible. The sacrifices are too great. In that instance, the right choice may be to move on so that both parties can have the chance at a partnership where their dreams *can* be honored and accommodated. When it comes to relationships—even long ones—"success" is not always "forever." You can honor each other and what the relationship was even as you realize that your paths must diverge.

From Zero Sum to the Nash Equilibrium

We began this chapter by talking about the zero-sum dynamic that can plague our fights, locking us into a win-lose mindset that makes compromise really tough. In the study of game theory—and specifically, how it played out in politics and economics—it used to be widely accepted that any negotiation in a conflict was going to be a zero-sum situation, where a win by one party would always represent a loss by the other. But in the 1950s, mathematician John Nash put forth another model in which the "game" being played reaches a point of stability where neither player can do any better, given the strategy of their opponent.[10] They have arrived at the ideal outcome of the game for both players, given the game's parameters. It's a mathematical model, but it translates to relationships in the sense that it becomes the point in a conflict where *both* partners win: they've compromised, but they're also satisfied with the outcome. They can't do any better under whatever circumstances life has served them.

A crucial thing to remember, though, is that in relationships, we are not opponents. In the arena of love, we arrive at the Nash Equilibrium not by trying to "win" for ourselves but by *thinking for two*. This is one of the core habits of really successful couples—instead of thinking, *What's best for me in this situation?* they're thinking, *What's best for us?* Their conflicts are pervaded by a sense that both partners ultimately have each other's best interests at heart even though they're disagreeing. Ultimately, this is where our capacity to compromise successfully comes from: *trust*.

Whether we're talking about who does the evening dishes, where to spend our hard-earned money, if we should consider a big move, or whether to move to a farm in Iowa or sail around the world, that conversation is going to unfold *very* differently based on our "trust metric." Do I fundamentally trust you to be thinking about what's good for me while thinking about what's good for you? Do I trust you to consider my point of view and give it equal weight? Do I trust that you're someone who can and will change their position when the situation calls for it? Do I trust you to care about my goals and dreams and to try to make them happen? When the answer to those questions is *yes*, it's so much easier to be flexible and to find a compromise that feels like the best thing for *both* of you.

None of these strategies will work without trust and commitment. So with couples where trust has been degraded, this is where we begin: with rebuilding both.

In couples where commitment has dipped, we see two major warning signs: (1) they complain to other people about their partner instead of going to their partner with important issues; and (2) they minimize what they have and maximize what's missing. They're always looking around and thinking, "I could do better." Even with low-commitment couples, if we ask them, "Do you love your partner?" they'll say, "Yes." And they do! But there's no true commitment. They're not invested. They aren't thinking for two. There's no *us*. And that's the root of their struggle and the underlying reason they're in our office.

What we say to people in that circumstance: it *is* terrifying to commit to someone! We often enter relationships as a leap of faith. We sometimes commit to someone for all eternity before we really know them. And of course, over time, people change and grow. This person I married five, ten, twenty, forty years ago isn't the same person anymore. We discover surprising things about our partners over time and during conflicts. Life circumstances come up that put us under intense pressure. Nobody's perfect; we all have flaws. What commitment really means is that you are able to realize that while your partner isn't perfect (and okay, maybe they're a little bit crazy about this issue or that one), ultimately, nobody can replace them.

The good news here: you can work on rebuilding trust and commitment from any point. And everything we've been working on in this book builds trust: Turning toward. Softened start-ups. Listening closely and validating each other. Expressing empathy. Asking each other open-ended questions both in conflict and outside of it. Exploring your dreams together. *All* of this, over time, builds trust and commitment as well as that mindset of thinking for two, which is a mindset of cooperative gain. And it's a positive feedback loop: the more you practice these strategies, the more trust you build; the more you trust each other, the easier these conflict management strategies become.

Try It!

With your partner, decide on an area of conflict to tackle. You might choose a solvable problem that's been gridlocked; you might choose an issue you worked on in the last chapter, in the "dreams within conflict" activity.

Then go through the following steps:

- Get two pieces of paper and create a "bagel" for each of you, with an inner circle and a much larger outer circle. You can copy the image on page 247.
- In the inner circle, list the aspects of this issue that you can't give in on. These are the nonnegotiables: your minimal core needs, beliefs, values about this issue.
- In the outer circle, list your areas of flexibility. These are the aspects of this issue that—if you were able to have what's in the inner circle—you'd be able to compromise on.
- Now . . . talk about it!

- Share your diagram with your partner, and vice versa.
- Ask each other: *Why are the things in the inner circle so important to you?*
- Listen fully to the answers. If you need to, take notes to help you stay focused on the information your partner is offering.
- Ask each other: *Tell me more about these areas of flexibility. What does it look like to be flexible here?*
- Workshop some possible compromises! See what new ways forward you can find using these "maps" of core needs and areas of flexibility. Try answering the following:
  - What do we agree about?
  - What feelings do we have in common?
  - What common goals do we have?
  - How might we accomplish these goals?
- Finally, decide on a compromise—even if it's a partial or a temporary one that you'll reevaluate later to see if it's working—and articulate it here:
  - A compromise that honors both of our needs and dreams is:

    _____

    _____

FIGHT #5:
THE CHASM IN THE ROOM

Mistake: Stewing About the Fight

The past is never dead. It isn't even past.

~ WILLIAM FAULKNER

During the first year of the pandemic, Molly and Selena felt like they were doing all right. Months had elapsed since they'd gone into COVID lockdown with their two young kids—both moms worked from home and took turns doing the one grocery trip per week. They had no in-person contact with the families they used to mix with, trading kids for playdates and sleepovers, but they were getting by all right, just the four of them. It seemed like marriages were falling apart all around them under the stress of the pandemic and the sudden intensity of being thrown together twenty-four hours a day, seven days a week, with little reprieve or privacy—some of their friends, couples they'd known for years, were apparently realizing they didn't actually like each other all that much. Molly and Selena found themselves congratulating each other on how well it was all going, relatively speaking: *Hey, look at us, we still like each other—a lot! Wow, we're really crushing it!*

But then they had a fight. A big one.

It erupted over who was going to step away from work one morning to help their two daughters, ages five and seven, with remote learning. Remote learning had been tough. The kids were too young to be self-directed or even to stay at the computer screen for longer than ten minutes without one of their moms sitting next to them, keeping them engaged, explaining the things that just didn't translate through a Zoom screen. And Molly had been taking on the brunt of the work—as a freelance graphic artist, she had a more flexible job than Selena, who had to be at her desk and online at specific times with the activist groups she worked with (she was a program manager for an international nonprofit). But Molly had been pulling late nights to keep up with her workload—she was exhausted, and she wasn't getting enough time to keep on top of her projects. That morning, Molly told Selena she needed the morning for her own work: "Can you push off some meetings? I really need to get caught up. I've been doing this school stuff with the kids mostly on my own."

"Molly, I can't at this late notice," Selena said. "Anyway, you can do this stuff later, can't you? There's no such thing as a graphic art emergency, I don't think." She went into their bedroom, which doubled as her office, and shut the door.

Molly followed her in. The fight unfolded in there, in tense whispers so the kids wouldn't hear, with Selena's Zoom camera turned off and muted, people pinging into the Zoom waiting room. Molly said Selena was belittling her job—no, it wasn't an international rescue effort, but it was still important—to *her*. Selena said Molly was being a child, storming into her office in the middle of a meeting. Accusations flew: *You're being selfish. You're being unfair. You've never thought my work was as important as yours. Don't be ridiculous!*

Then Molly, frustrated and in tears, snapped, "Maybe you'd care about the girls' school more if you were the one who'd given birth to them."

There was a long silence. "I can't believe you would say that to me," Selena said finally. "I'm just as much their mother as you are."

"I know you are, I didn't mean—"

"I have to start this meeting," Selena said. "Please leave."

Later that night, Molly apologized for what she'd said. But she was still bothered by the way her wife had brushed off her work. Selena apologized too and suggested that in the future they make a clearer schedule for who would support remote school. But she was deeply wounded by what Molly had said about her role as nonbiological mother to their kids.

The conflict was, on its surface, resolved—they did make a schedule giving Molly more work time. But they fought again a few days later, and then again, and then again, about what they'd said to each other that morning. Neither could stop relitigating the details. They debated who had started it, who was more wronged, who had said what.

"You called me a terrible mother," Selena said during one late-night fight about the fight, in tears.

"I did not!" Molly yelled back. "I never said that!"

"You always make me feel like I'm not really a parent. You hold this birth thing over my head. You're the real mom and I'm just along for the ride. You made that very clear the other day."

"How did I do that? I was just asking for help. You can't have it both ways, Selena—you put more of the parenting on me and then complain that you're not doing more of the parenting. What do you want me to do here?"

"Well for one thing, you could stop throwing my infertility in my face every time you want to get your way."

"What are you talking about?"

"You know what you said! I didn't give birth to them, so I don't really care, right?"

"Oh, my God. You know what? I would be happy to be less of a mom so you can be more of one. How about I go back to work full-time and you stay home? You wouldn't last a day at home with the kids."

Molly and Selena are stuck—they just can't seem to stop fighting about the fight.

Where do these two go from here? They love each other and are committed to their family. But hurtful things were said (and then said again!), and if they can't address what happened without causing more damage, they're going to find themselves on an extremely rocky path. And they are not alone—this scenario is very common. Across all couples in our international study, 77 to 84 percent of couples reported failing to repair after a fight.[1] So many couples are like Molly and Selena, wondering, *Why can't we just move on?* when in fact, that's exactly the problem.

The Big Mistake: Trying to "Just Move On"

No matter how much we want to fight right, sometimes we hurt each other. Badly.

We've talked a lot in this book about the upsides of conflict—how our points of friction can become doorways into understanding each other better and becoming more connected, more intimate.

And that's true—they can, and we really want couples to understand that conflict is a normal, unavoidable, and often positive part of life and love. But the reality is that conflict can also be intense and even traumatic. Conflict is messy. *We* are messy. We're human, and we're each carrying our own heavy baggage—from life, from childhood, from previous relationships. We have triggers that get set off. Big emotions that grab us by the throat, or the heart, or the gut— wherever you feel it when you get flooded. We often don't know what we want or need; we don't express ourselves clearly; we misinterpret each other; we say things we don't mean, or we say them in the worst possible way. There's this ideal blueprint for conflict that we can try our best to follow, but sometimes we do get lost along the way. We fire off a volley of sharp verbal arrows at each other, and some of those land—right in the heart.

Every couple has regrettable incidents sometimes, where you both walk away after a conflict feeling angry, resentful, deeply hurt, even betrayed by things your partner has said. It happens to us all. It happens to the "masters" of love. But here's where we really go wrong: *not processing the fight.* We have not learned how to address regret-table incidents after they've happened, and so we just don't.

Instead, we apologize too fast, before we understand what we're really apologizing for.

We try to sweep it under the rug. That fight felt bad—let's not repeat it. We're still upset, but we keep it to ourselves.

Or we *do* talk about the fight, but we just get right back into it. We're back in full-blown, escalated conflict. A regrettable incident becomes yet another regrettable incident.

Over time, fights that go unprocessed force a wedge between the two of you either in the form of more conflict or in the form of less connection and avoidance. Intimacy breaks down. Everybody puts up walls—you were hurt, so now you're going to protect yourself. You can be sitting next to each other on the couch in our office, but emotionally, there's a gulf the size of the Grand Canyon between you.

The emotional wounds we end up with after a bad fight do not heal on their own. When we don't repair after a bad fight, those wounds endure. The negativity of the fight endures. And over time, like a caustic chemical, it begins to corrode the positive connection between us. It's hard to stay connected, stay close, when we have open wounds—when we're still walking around with those arrows sticking out of our hearts. When regrettable incidents occur, we have to process and heal from them. Otherwise, we'll be carrying the residue of that fight forward into our lives together.

Some Fights Are Forever...
If You Don't Process Them

When the influential psychologist Bluma Zeigarnik was a graduate student in the 1920s, working toward a doctorate in psychology at the University of Berlin and writing her thesis on memory, one of her professors mentioned something he'd noticed at a local restaurant. The restaurant was known for having a waitstaff that never wrote down the orders—the servers were able to remember the orders perfectly, even large tables with many guests. Talking with his waiter, the professor observed that the waiter had very sharp recall for the orders of tables that he hadn't passed on to the chef yet, but that once he delivered the order to the chef, he could no longer remember the details of the order. It seemed to imply that "unfinished business" of undelivered orders stuck in the waiter's mind more vividly than the orders he'd already completed.

Zeigarnik decided to test this idea in a lab setting. Over a series of experiments involving 164 participants, including students, teachers, and children, she brought people in one by one and gave them a simple instruction: *Complete this series of tasks as rapidly and correctly as possible.* Then each person had to start working their way through a list of about twenty small tasks—things like putting together a shipping box, solving a puzzle, making a small clay figure, working out a math equation. As each person worked, a research assistant would subtly interrupt them about half of the time—bustling into the room and insisting that something was wrong with the table setup or some other excuse—so that they were unable to complete that particular task in the allotted time and would be forced to move on to the next task without finishing.

Afterward, Zeigarnik asked each participant questions such as: What tasks did you just perform? Which ones did you enjoy? What do you remember about your work on each one? She found that participants could recall the details of the interrupted tasks *90 percent* more accurately than the ones they had been able to finish to their satisfaction.[2] It appeared that a desire to "finish" something, a sense that it was incomplete or unresolved, led to that event being retained much more vividly in memory. The act of *completing* something, then, was what allowed it to begin to fade, to be forgotten.

This finding was so significant and repeatable (it was backed up by subsequent studies) that it has come to be called "the Zeigarnik effect." And it has implications here, with our fights. When we have unfinished business with each other—when we haven't resolved a painful issue, when there are feelings we haven't been able to express, when hurtful things were said that haven't been addressed—we retain a blazingly clear memory of that fight. That fight is as vivid and sharp as if it happened yesterday. Plus, fights that get stored in long-term memory often contain traumatic incidents, and traumatic

memory is powerful. When that memory is accessed, all the different sensory aspects of that moment in time will come flooding
back—you're plunged back into that moment like a time traveler,
and your body responds accordingly: cortisol and adrenaline start
flowing; you experience flooding. As far as your body is concerned,
that original fight *is* happening again.

The Zeigarnik effect shows us that unless you fully process something, especially emotionally, it all stays in your memory. Then—and
here's a twist—that memory starts to get distorted. Modern neuroscience has found that memories, even those that remain vivid and
feel real and upsetting, aren't stable. Every time we access them, they
change. They get "edited." The way we remember things happening
becomes more and more biased toward *ourselves*,[3] meaning the
more we relive and ruminate, the more our memory of that event
may morph. We *felt* a certain way, and now our memory of events
and things said aligns more and more with that feeling. We end up
with one fight—an event we were both there for, a shared experience—
and yet we now have two very different memories of what happened.

In a fight, it's very likely that I'm going to have one perception of
events, and you're going to have a different one. I perceive your tone
of voice as dismissive and impatient; my version of events is that you
blew me off and that you have no interest in hearing about my life.
Meanwhile, your reality is that you're stressed, mentally consumed
with a problem at work, and all of a sudden, I'm pissed off and blowing up at you, acting totally irrational. Both of these realities are
valid. They both happened! That's what we each experienced.

There is no immaculate perception, no "God camera" looking
down and recording what "really" happened, that you can check
with to see who's right and who's wrong. There's just plain old
perception—there's the way you perceived things, and the way your

partner perceived things, and then there's our malleable, corruptible human memory. When it comes to "the facts" about what happened, there are no facts. There is only what we each experience.

And when it comes to our brain processing, it's as if there's no time in memory. These experiences can be as fresh as if they just happened and therefore just as upsetting—especially for things that feel unfinished or unresolved. And the longer we spend remembering and ruminating on those events, pulling them out of long-term memory and reexperiencing them, the more biased and distorted they may become.

So if you don't process this stuff with your partner—especially emotionally—it won't go away. It'll fester. You'll remember the words, the feelings, the adrenaline pumping through your body. You'll hyperfocus on all those nitty-gritty details, every critical or unfair thing your partner said, every contemptuous eye roll, just like that waiter remembering every item on the undelivered order. These sharp, potent memories are not something you want to hang on to. They're bad for your mind, your heart, your body, your relationship, your future. A bad fight you don't process will be like a pebble in your shoe—you can't just keep walking with it in there, limping along and in pain. You have to stop, sit down, and take it out.

Signs You Need to Address a Past Incident

When there's a regrettable incident in your past—recent or even distant—your relationship may exhibit certain symptoms. You might need to sit down and process something if . . .

- **Talking about it leads to more conflict.** Like Molly and Selena, you find yourself right back in heated, escalated conflict when you try to address it—a kind of Twilight Zone experience.

- **You're fighting about the fight.** You can't seem to stop relitigating the fight, battling over who said what and how they said it, who was to blame the last time around, whose "version" of events is correct. It becomes a pattern. Fighting about the fight leads to more fights about the fight, a sort of daisy chain of conflict.

- **You're avoiding the topic entirely and talking and connecting less in general.** Talking about this issue went so poorly last time, you don't want to attempt it again; you keep your feelings to yourself and likely start feeling distant or disconnected from your partner. Often, sex life wanes.

- **You're fighting more about (seemingly) unrelated stuff.** Disagreements about other issues may escalate faster; you're harsher with each other as pent-up resentment over the past incident leaks out. This can look like . . .

- **Big reactions that appear to come out of nowhere.** You say, "Can you run to the grocery store and get some milk?" Your partner replies, "I'm not doing anything for you! You've been horrible to me!" *Whoa.* These kinds of off-the-wall or overblown responses to things that seem totally innocuous in the moment are often signs of some subterranean burning lava flow under the surface from a past incident that has not been addressed.

All of these responses to a bad fight that still hurts are perfectly normal and perfectly human. But they don't help anything. What to do instead? The answer is *processing,* which essentially means being able to talk about what happened *without* getting back into the conflict. And this is a specific skill with specific steps.

How to Process a Fight

Like the waiters in Bluma Zeigarnik's restaurant, you need to put down the plate of food so you can move on. Until you do, you're going to be walking around carrying this hurt, this resentment, these feelings of anger, betrayal, confusion, and more.

The blueprint for successfully processing a fight emerged from one of our own fights. (Whatever mistakes we make in love and conflict, we tend to funnel into lab research in the hopes of developing interventions for others—and this one paid off!) Here's how it went down: One morning as we were both getting ready for work, Julie told John about a bad dream she'd had the night before. In the dream, John had betrayed her—he'd been unfaithful. She was really rattled and upset by the dream, and she talked about the terrible things "Dream John" had done to her as she turned on the water in the shower and stepped in.

Listening to this, John got angry. "I'm not that person," he snapped. "What have I ever done to suggest any of this? That's not who I am!" He said some critical things about how she was always accusing him of stuff, that he could never do anything right. "Why did you even tell me this?" He stormed out of the bathroom.

Julie was, by now, crying in the shower. He'd implied she was a bad person for bringing this up, which was exactly what her dream had been about: him turning against her. She turned the water off, threw on a towel, and ran out after him.

"You're proving my dream to be true!" she cried.

A little while later, when we were both calmer (and drier, in Julie's case), we sat down and talked about it.

"Don't you understand?" Julie said. "I was trying to tell you. In the dream, you're just a stand-in for my mom, who always treated me terribly, with contempt. It's just symbolic. It's not about you. I thought you would understand that."

We talked it through, and we did all this processing of the moment in the bathroom—why Julie had brought up the issue the way she did, why John had responded the way he did. Julie had these feelings left over from childhood, vestiges of a childhood relationship that got superimposed onto this one. We can have these feelings in the here and now, in the present moment, that don't quite make sense. So subconsciously, we scan our environment for something or somebody that will loosely fit with the theme of your feeling. And then you point the gun and *fire*. It's not about that person, but you imagine it is.

This is a *trigger*.

And it's a huge part of why conflicts start and why they escalate.

We all come into adulthood with baggage. And we carry that baggage into our relationships. We have these soft, tender spots, these old wounds that have left behind scars. Scar tissue is more brittle than healthy tissue; it tears easily. Sometimes, we press on each other's scar tissue and it tears open again. And it hurts. We lash out. We have a big reaction that our partner doesn't understand. And it fans the flames of a conflict, like pure oxygen. *Whoosh.*

After we talked through our own conflict, we thought: *This is so common. How do we help other couples process moments like this?* So we started putting together an intervention for processing, modeled after what had worked for us, along with the data-based strategies from the lab that we knew worked.

The Key to Successful Processing:
Both Realities Are Valid

We especially wanted to address the way people remember fights so differently—how in conflict, they each have their own "reality" of how the fight unfolded.

We filter everything through our own perceptions, emotions, assumptions, interpretations, and extrapolations. Your partner enters the room with an upset expression on her face and you think, *She's mad at me.* That may not be her experience at all—she's upset about something wholly unrelated to you. She's mad because the mail is late. Because the cat peed on the floor. Because she lost her wallet. Who knows! But when we try to talk to each other about this stuff, our assumptions get baked right into our language. *(Partner 1: You were angry with me the minute you walked in the door! Partner 2: What? No I wasn't! You always accuse me of stuff like this!)* To understand what happened and to repair the hurt that was done, we really have to understand what our partner saw, heard, and felt even if—and *especially if*—it's different from what we experienced during the incident.

We knew this part had to be carefully structured so that people didn't get back into the fight. What we don't want is for the repair conversation to devolve into arguing over whose reality is more correct, who remembers the fight better. When we come together to process, we have to work from the common assumption that *both realities are valid* and that each subjective reality holds some truth. The goal is not to agree on a set of facts about "what happened." It's to understand your partner's experience so you can empathize with them and understand where they were coming from.

So when we talk about what happened, it is critically important to talk about our *own* perceptions and experiences using "I" descriptions. We don't assign blame, assume intent, or tell our partners what they did or said. Instead, we describe what we perceive happened. This takes some work and practice! Check your language as you speak, and any time you can flip your rhetoric so that you state what *you* saw, heard, or felt instead of what your partner did or said, flip it. Instead of "You were angry with me the minute you walked in the door!" you say, "You came into the room, and I saw an angry expression on your face. I thought you might be upset with me." Try phrases like:

> I imagined . . .
>
> I assumed . . .
>
> It seemed to me that . . .
>
> I saw . . .
>
> I remember . . .
>
> I heard you say . . .

We can use this kind of first-person, self-descriptive language to truthfully describe our own experience without accusing or criticizing or forcing our version of events onto our partners. This leaves them, in turn, much more open, receptive, and able to empathize with our experience.

Once we've shared our experiences with each other—inviting

each other into *our* subjective reality to see how events unfolded through our eyes—we need to validate each other. We need to say to each other: *That makes sense. If that's what you were hearing, I get why you responded that way.* You don't have to agree with it! Validation simply means that you understand a small part of your partner's experience.

Now, *triggers*. Triggers were the hot spark of our fight that inspired this process, and we knew they had to be addressed. Triggers are so powerful. People needed to go back into the past and figure out what this fight in the present moment was dredging up for them. Partners needed to reflect and then talk to each other about what parts of *this* fight triggered a big emotional reaction in them. When else had they felt that way? Did they have those feelings (of being abandoned, misunderstood, criticized, etc.) before this relationship? In a prior romance, in childhood, in school?

And then—How do we apologize for real? We always want to apologize right away. To immediately make it better. But when you apologize right away, you don't even know yet what you're apologizing for—you haven't heard, from your partner, what it was that affected them, and you haven't had the chance yet to express your own experience of the fight. For people to be able to take responsibility for their own part in the fight and to *really* apologize to each other and repair the hurt they've caused, it needs to come after everything else. We really need to understand each other's experience and the impact we've had on each other before we can say "I'm sorry" and have it mean anything.

Finally, we talked about how couples can move forward after conflict. How do we deliver that food order to the chef and then leave it behind?

In the end, we developed a five-step process. We're going to give you the basic instructions here and then take you through it in more detail afterward.

THE FIVE STEPS

1. **Feelings:** Share how you felt. Don't say why you felt that way, and don't comment on your partner's feelings. Simply describe your own.

2. **Realities:** Describe your "reality." Take turns. Summarize and validate at least a part of your partner's reality.

3. **Triggers:** Share what memories or experiences you've had that might have escalated the interaction and the stories of why these are triggers for each of you.

4. **Responsibility:** Acknowledge your own role in contributing to the fight.

5. **Constructive planning:** Together, plan one way that each of you can make it better next time.

We wrote up the five steps into a little guidebook and began refining the steps. But before we even had a final draft, our little "Aftermath of a Fight" booklet experienced its own trial by fire when we had one of the worst fights of our entire married lives.

Beta-Testing the Five Steps...on Ourselves

It began with the ring of the telephone—our daughter, Moriah, calling from college. She was a sophomore, just a few weeks into her fall semester. Her freshman year had been tough. She'd gone through a breakup, had lost the friend group associated with that boyfriend, had felt isolated and depressed, and then had gotten extremely sick with strep throat—to the point where when she came home for the summer, she was still ill. She recovered and went back in September, but we both worried about her.

Lately, though, it seemed things had been looking up! She'd joined a cooking club, where she made a new group of friends who seemed sweet and supportive. She loved her classes. Whenever she called, she sounded happy. It was such a relief. We still worried (we *are* parents, after all), but we were hopeful for a good year. And then that afternoon, she called. Julie picked up.

From here, we'll give you the two different narratives of events: first Julie's, then John's.

Julie's Reality

As soon as she picked up the phone, Julie could tell that her daughter was sick. Moriah's voice had that soft, weak sound. A little red flag went up in her mom-brain—her daughter had always been the kind of kid who struggled with her health.

But at the same time, she sounded so happy! Julie had been very worried about how depressed Moriah had been and then sick too. She was really glad she was happier now. Still, had her strep throat returned? As her daughter gushed about learning a new Thai dish in her cooking club and talking until late at night with her new friends, Julie held herself back from saying anything that might sound controlling and domineering. *Don't be a helicopter parent,* she told herself. *She's nineteen years old, she can take care of herself.* Julie wanted to say, "Sounds like you're getting sick; you should take it easy," but instead she said, "Wow, sounds like you're having an amazing time—I'm so happy for you!" Moriah went on, talking about staying up until three and four in the morning with her study group, and Julie bit her tongue even harder. It was truly a feat of Olympic strength not to scream, *You need your sleep!*—but she did it. Instead, she listened and said, "I'm so glad you're loving these classes; it all sounds so interesting."

When she hung up, she was proud of herself for keeping her worry inside and just being supportive. *She'll be okay,* she told herself. *Staying up late and talking is what college kids do.*

As she and John were getting ready for bed, she started recapping the phone call to him. She mentioned that though their daughter sounded happy, she was worried about her health, with all the late nights. At that point, John had interrupted her.

"Stop trying to control her," he said. "Back off, just let her be! This is what college is all about. I wish you would just leave her alone and stop telling her what to do."

Julie felt like she'd been slapped. She was deeply insulted—she imagined that John had automatically assumed she'd been controlling and domineering, when that was exactly what she had tried so hard not to be. She thought that John clearly didn't trust her as a parent to have the wisdom to edit her words, when in fact that was exactly what she had done. She felt anger rise up in her hot as lava, and words leapt into her head that she knew she shouldn't say, but they flew out anyway.

She remembered saying, "Well, *I* wish I had a mature partner for a co-parent."

Wham. John's face had turned bright red. He shouted something back—she couldn't remember what—then he grabbed his pillow and left the room, slamming the door.

She didn't feel sorry for what she'd said—not yet. She was still furious. *Fine,* she thought. *I get the bed all to myself tonight!* She went to bed, turned off the light, and fell asleep.

John's Reality

To this day, he could remember Moriah in her freshman year, sobbing on the phone that nobody liked her, that she felt unlovable, that her friends had shunned her. It was awful. She was so far away, and there was so little he could do. When she came home for the summer, sick and depressed, he had tried to reassure her over and over that she was the most lovable creature on the planet as far as he was concerned. When she went back to school, joined a cooking club, and made new friends, he was delighted—this is what college is all about! Staying up late, talking into the night, forming irreplaceable bonds. He didn't want her to lose that.

He knew that Julie had a lot of influence on Moriah—they were very close—and when Julie started talking about how worried she was about these late nights, he felt alarmed, worried that she'd try to steer her away from those experiences.

"Give her a little space," he remembered saying, "and stop trying to control her. College is a time for having deep conversations all night—talking about God and the meaning of life. Let her find her own balance."

Then, out of nowhere, he heard Julie accuse him of being immature. A bad parent.

He started to fight back—he yelled something harsh, he couldn't remember what—then decided to get out of there before he said something he really regretted. He stomped out of their room and threw his pillow down on the couch, but he couldn't sleep. He tossed and turned all night, too agitated to sleep.

What Now? Processing Our Own Fight

We're love researchers, well schooled in the science of relationships. Anything that can be charted and graphed about how to be successful in love and long partnerships—we've analyzed it. But at the end of the day, we're still just two humans in a relationship, each with our own past lives that have shaped us—and wounded us.

The more we get to know each other in a relationship, the more we learn about each other and map each other's inner worlds, the more aware we become of each other's triggers or "enduring vulnerabilities." But knowing your partner is a lifelong process—not an "early relationship only" type of thing. Look at us: at the point when we had this fight, we managed to stomp on each other's triggers without really realizing we were doing so. And we'd been married twenty years!

Now, we might have four decades of research on love and conflict, but we're still as vulnerable to a bad fight as any couple out there. But after this incident, we did have a leg up. We had our newly mapped out blueprint for how to process a fight. So once we both cooled off, we decided to sit down and use it.

Cooling off first is critical here. You'll notice that we did not try to process our fight that night, right after we had it. We were both still too furious to do that! If you're angry and flooded, the five steps are not going to work. You need to be able to zoom out and observe your fight as if you're in the audience at a play, sitting up in the balcony, looking down at the action on the stage. You have to be calm and capable of witnessing and describing what happened in that play, act by act, as you remember it. So it needs to be a time when you've been able to reflect a little bit. We still often hear people trading the advice *Don't go to bed angry.* Not true! Sometimes going to bed angry is exactly what you need to do to calm down and get that necessary distance from the fight so you can be sitting up there on that balcony, looking down.

The next day, we were both calm and we had that perspective. So we took some time to talk. We got out our little prototype booklet, and we followed the five steps. We've listed them below for you.

Step 1: Feelings

Share what you felt but not why. Take turns describing what you felt during the fight. You can choose from the list below or come up with your own description. Read *aloud* the descriptions that were true for you. Keep your comments simple, and stick to the format "I felt . . ." Avoid statements like "I felt like *you* . . . " Don't comment on your partner's feelings. (Below is an abbreviated list of feeling descriptors; the full list appears in the Quick Guide at the back of this book.)

I felt . . .

defensive / not listened to / like my feelings got hurt / totally flooded / angry / sad / unloved / misunderstood / criticized / like you didn't even like me / not cared about / worried / afraid / unsafe / tense / I was right and you were wrong / both of us were partly right / out of control / frustrated / righteously indignant / morally justified / unfairly picked on / unappreciated / unattractive / stupid / morally outraged / taken for granted / like leaving / like staying and talking this through / powerless / like I had no influence / lonely / alienated / ashamed / abandoned / exhausted / remorseful

We both used the list of feelings, scanning down it until we hit on the words or phrases that best described our experiences. (You can name as many feelings as you want—as many as you felt.)

"I felt defensive," Julie shared. "Not listened to. Angry. Sad, a little. Misunderstood and criticized. Unsafe, tense, frustrated. Unfairly picked on. Unattractive . . . I always feel unattractive. Powerless. Like I had no influence. Lonely. Abandoned. And remorseful."

"I felt defensive too," John said. "My feelings were hurt. I was flooded and angry. I felt I was right and you were wrong. I felt righteously indignant. Morally justified. Unappreciated. Lonely. And tired."

Step 2: Realities

A. Take turns describing your perceptions, your own reality of what happened. Don't describe your partner. Avoid attack and blame. Describe your perceptions like a reporter, giving an objective description. Say, "I heard you saying . . ." rather than "You said . . ."

B. Summarize and validate your partner's reality. Use empathy by saying something along the lines of "I can see why this upset you." Validation does not mean you agree, it means you can understand even a part of your partner's experience.

C. Do both partners feel understood? If yes, move on. If no, ask, "What do I need to know to understand your perspective better?" After validating, ask your partner, "Did I get it? Is there anything else?"

Julie began.

She described her reality—talking to Moriah, biting her tongue so hard to keep from interfering with her daughter's new independence, then hanging up feeling proud that she'd given her daughter space to do her own thing. Then sharing with John her worry about Moriah's health . . . "and the first thing I remember you saying was *Stop trying to control her, back off!* Or something very similar. And I thought—*he thinks he has to tell me what to do, that he has to instruct me.* I felt like I was being criticized and put down . . . like you didn't trust me as a parent. And my anger just came from the ground up. And I said the words . . . *I wish I had a mature partner as a co-parent.*"

"Oh yeah," said John wryly. "I remember those words."

(We did both laugh.)

John summarized Julie's experience back to her: "So here's what I heard. You were really worried about her health, but you didn't try to control her. You weren't being a helicopter mom. And when you talked to me that night, you wanted me to join you in being worried . . . and when I didn't and instead suggested you back off, that was insulting. Because you weren't being a helicopter mom. So you were really offended. Did I get that right?"

"Yes," Julie said. "You got it."

"Well, it makes sense to me that you'd be upset," John said, shifting into validating. "You wanted support in being worried about her health, which is a concern for both of us, and you didn't get that from me. And I get that you'd be offended that I suggested you were being a helicopter parent when you actually weren't."

Next, it was John's turn. John described *his* reality—especially how excited he'd been about Moriah finding a new group of friends and joining this cooking club.

"My mom was a hotel chef," John explained. "She was really talented with food, and I love cooking, too, so Mom and I used to talk about it and trade recipes all the time. It was a bond I had with my mom. And I've been so happy to have it with my daughter. I knew you were worried about her health and that she listens to you—I was afraid you'd influence her to quit the club, and I'd lose that connection. And when you said that thing about me not being a mature father, I really lost it. Because there's nothing I've done in my life that's as important to me as being her dad. Everything else pales by comparison. So when you said that . . . well, if I'd stayed in the room, I would have regretted what I said. I was really angry."

"I can understand why you felt that way," Julie said, after she summarized John's experience and he confirmed she got it right. "I can really see how that would have been a big fear for you. Especially because when she was in high school, you two weren't as close. So you wanted to keep this bridge to her. You didn't want to lose any bricks in that bridge."

"Yes," John said. "That's exactly right."

Step 3: Triggers

A. Share what escalated the interaction for you. What events in the fight triggered a big reaction in you?

B. Scroll back through the video feed of your memory and stop at a point where you had a similar set of feelings in the past. Now tell the story of that past moment to your partner so they can understand why it's a trigger for you.

C. Share your stories—it will help your partner understand you. As you think about your early history or childhood, is there a story you remember that relates to what got triggered in you, your "enduring vulnerabilities"? Your partner needs to know you so that they can be more sensitive to you.

For us, in this particular processing session, this was the most revelatory step: identifying our own triggers.

For Julie, her trigger was this pervasive feeling that health is so fragile, and the consequences for inaction are so high. When she was a little girl, her dad was a cardiologist who took good care of his patients—but not his family.

"We were basically not allowed to be sick," Julie told John. "It was somehow offensive to him, like we'd done it on purpose."

When she was about ten years old, she and the rest of the family were set to get their polio vaccine, which had been newly rolled out. It was a live vaccine, given in a little bit of sugary syrup. The night before the appointment, Julie's cheek had swelled up—odd. She went to her dad, but he said it was no big deal, probably just an insect bite.

Two weeks later, Julie suddenly experienced incredible pain in one leg at school.

"It was the worst pain I've ever felt," Julie said, "including child-birth!"

She had a high fever for weeks. She finally recovered. But her leg didn't. She got out of bed one morning, and it just wouldn't work. She had to drag it. She didn't tell her parents—"Remember, we weren't supposed to be sick!" Developing a lot of balance, she hid it for three months before someone noticed. Then there followed many doctor appointments, neurologist appointments, daily shock ther-apy on her leg, and wearing a big heavy metal brace—still, nobody could figure out what was wrong. Finally, the CDC did. Julie's swol-len cheek that day wasn't an insect bite; it was the mumps, and it had interacted with the vaccine, activating it into a full-on disease. Julie was one of four people in the entire country who had actually con-tracted polio from the vaccine.

"Before that, I'd been really athletic," she said, "but all of that stopped, of course. I wore a brace for a year and a half. And even when it came off, I was never 100 percent again."

It was a nightmare. And Julie carries, to this day, the feeling that, had her father been paying closer attention as a medical doctor and hadn't let her get the vaccine that day, when she was sick, none of it would have happened. The moral of the story: Julie was now wired very strongly that if she had a sick kid or anyone was sick around her, for that matter, she was going to address it. And there she was being told to *ignore* it by John—or so it had seemed. This was her trigger: her own parents had missed something that was going on with her health, and the ramifications had been huge—lifelong.

John's trigger was from childhood too. He talked about growing up in Brooklyn—he was a smart, bookish kid and skipped grades twice in elementary school. The year he started high school, his family moved to a new town in New Jersey. He started the ninth grade at age twelve, surrounded by fourteen-year-olds who immediately singled him out—the bookish, small, Jewish, new kid—for bullying and abuse. The bullying and the name-calling, and the constant daily stress and feelings of low self-worth that went along with it, persisted for the entire four years of high school.

"I went through a lot of what Moriah went through her first year at college," John told Julie. "Depression, loneliness, doubting myself. Then, at sixteen, off I went to Fairleigh Dickinson University for college . . . and it was a whole different universe."

John lived with his parents and worked a part-time job to cover his tuition, but he still had an incredible college experience. At university, it was okay to be smart. It was okay to be passionate about intellectual pursuits. People wanted to talk about things! They wanted to stay up all night discussing philosophy and the meaning of life. John loved it. For the first time in his school life, he thrived.

"For me, it was a kind of renaissance—a rebirth," he said. "Everything changed. I could believe in myself. I had confidence. I had a community. It was a huge turning point for me, for my life, and I wanted so badly for Moriah to have the same experience—I just couldn't stand the thought of anything derailing that."

It was this stage of processing, Step 3, where we both realized—with a bit of surprise, honestly—how intensely this old childhood stuff had triggered us emotionally. Yes—on the surface, the whole fight was about our daughter staying up a bit too late. But the situation had brought up some really deep stuff that we'd both been carrying around our entire lives and had breathed life into these old hurts. In Julie, this had activated a drive to be vigilant and not let a potentially damaging illness slip by the attention of a parent. For John, it was this urgent need to protect a fragile, burgeoning experience that could be life changing and positive. This wasn't a fight about a phone call or whether Julie was a helicopter mom and John an immature dad (neither true!)—it was about this old stuff from childhood that had marked both of us. The fascinating thing was, we'd spoken to each other of these histories before. Remember, we'd been married for two decades! Of course, John had mentioned being bullied; Julie had described her experience with polio. But we hadn't ever connected the dots in this way before, where we realized the impact these histories had had on us and the influence they continued to exert in our lives . . . and our fights.

Ultimately, it was because of these intense triggers that our fight had gotten so nasty—and it was understanding each other's triggers that was so healing. We were both able to validate each other, genuinely. And it was amazing how much easier the next step was—taking responsibility for our part in the incident—once we understood each other and felt understood.

Step 4: Take Responsibility

A. Under ideal conditions, you might have done better at talking about this issue. What set you up for this miscommunication? Share how you set yourself up to get into this conflict. Read aloud the items that were true for you on this list (short sample below; a full list to choose from appears in the Quick Guide at the back of this book):

- I've been very stressed and irritable lately.
- I've been overly sensitive.
- I've not shared much of my inner world.
- I haven't been emotionally available.
- I've been depressed.
- I've had a chip on my shoulder lately.
- I've not made time for good things between us.
- I've not asked for what I've needed.
- I've been feeling like a martyr.
- I've needed to be alone.
- I have been very preoccupied.
- I haven't felt much confidence in myself.
- I've been running on empty.

B. Specifically, what do you regret about this fight or regrettable incident?

C. What do you wish to apologize for?

- I'm sorry that . . . (you don't have to pick something off the list—these are just examples. Make your apology specific like your regrets above.)
  i. I overreacted

   ii. I was so negative

  iii. I attacked you

  iv. I didn't listen to you

   v. I wasn't respectful

  vi. I was unreasonable

 vii. (your own, or more options in the back of the book)

"You know I've been stressed and irritable lately," John said, choosing the first option off the list above. "And I've had a big chip on my shoulder—I've had a number of grants that have been turned down recently, and I just heard the National Institute of Mental Health decided not to fund research on relationships anymore. And so . . . I've been feeling like a martyr. I was definitely spoiling for a fight. I've been in such a crappy mood—angry in traffic, stuff like that. But what I regret is insulting you as a mom. Because you're a fabulous mom. I love you as a mom. And I apologize for assuming you wanted to control her. And I want to apologize also for not knowing that you must have been triggered—that there was something behind your strong reaction. So—I'm sorry. I'm sorry I overreacted and that I didn't ask you any questions."

Now, after Julie accepted John's apology, it was her turn.

"Well," she said, also using the list above (that first list is so helpful!), "I've probably not expressed much appreciation toward you. I've been overly sensitive . . . which I always am. I think I haven't made much time for good things between us. I've been working really hard and long hours—so have you. And I've been very, very preoccupied. I probably needed to be alone, as an introvert, to process my worry. So what I really regret is saying those terrible words to you about being an immature partner or co-parent. God, I feel so bad about that. You didn't deserve one syllable of that. You are an amazing father and an amazing partner. And besides that, you're pretty cute."

John, as you can imagine, accepted this apology.

Step 5: Constructive Plans

Share one thing your partner can do to make a discussion of this issue better next time. (It's especially important to remain calm as you do this.) Then, while it's still your turn, share one thing *you* can do to make it better next time. What do you need to do to be able to put this behind you and move on? Be as agreeable as possible to the plans your partner suggests.

John: "One thing I can do is when you get really emotional, that's the time for me to ask questions rather than react. And one thing you could do differently is you could tell me: 'This is a stress-reducing conversation.' That would help me be a better listener."

Julie: "I think one thing I could do differently is bite my tongue for the seventy-*sixth* time and not say something awful in the heat of the moment. Really, I need to work on exercising that muscle, because I do say things I don't mean. And John, one thing you could do differently is realize . . . *every* conversation we have is a stress-reducing conversation!"

At the end of the processing, we were both laughing. We both felt better. Closer. And the things we'd said to each other would not go on to haunt us. We'd taken the stones out of our shoes.

Closing the Chasm

We were so grateful, after that bad fight, to have the five steps we'd worked on to fall back on. Those steps are in the Fight Right Quick

Guide at the back of this book so that you can quickly flip to it when you need it. Honestly, we *still* use it. Even if you've been researching love and conflict for your entire career, there's really something helpful about having the steps clearly laid out for you—a blueprint to follow. When the words for your feelings don't come effortlessly, you have somewhere to turn to for help.

When we first introduced the five-step process in an intensive workshop, the therapists who were helping support the group were terrified. They took one look at it and started shaking their heads. They had concerns: People wouldn't be able to handle their torrent of emotions! This process would bring out even more issues! It would make things worse!

It was the exact opposite.

We've been teaching this booklet for ten years now. When we do any kind of intervention in our workshops, we closely observe the effects and how people are doing. We walk around from couple to couple, listen, check in. And what we see constantly with this process is that people are not getting back into the fight. They're not getting flooded. They are listening. They are empathetic. They can sometimes get emotional, but they are calm. And a lot of the time, they're making major breakthroughs in this conversation.

And here's an amazing thing: there is no time limit on repair.

It's never too late to process a regrettable incident. It could have happened yesterday or twenty years ago. You can still process it. In one workshop, we had a couple who'd been married forty years who processed something that happened on their honeymoon.

In fact, this was the case with Molly and Selena. Almost a year went by before they processed their fight—a year that went by in a blur. A pandemic year. A year of handing the kids off to each other like batons while one went to work and the other cooked macaroni and cheese, put babies to bed, folded laundry. A year when they started talking to each other a little bit less. Keeping their worries and emotions a bit closer to the vest. When they stopped turning to each other first for closeness and support and started turning to others. They'd said, "Sorry," but they were losing track of each other.

They came to a workshop because they felt the chasm growing between them. They were aware of the distance, but they didn't know how to fix it. However, when we introduced the "repair a regrettable incident" intervention and asked everyone to choose a recent or past fight that had caused wounds that hadn't yet healed, they looked up at each other and locked eyes—they both knew exactly which fight they needed to process.

So much time had passed, they wondered if they would be able to remember how they'd felt, specifically. But they did. It was fresh and vivid, as if it had happened yesterday. They were still able to viscerally recall exactly how they felt (Molly: *flooded, worried, taken for granted*; Selena: *defensive, unappreciated, shocked*). They were able to walk each other through their subjective realities. Molly described how she perceived what had unfolded: she'd gone to her wife for support, making what seemed to Molly to be a very reasonable request, that her wife shift her schedule to make room for Molly to meet her deadline, the same way Molly had been flexing her work to accommodate Selena's for the past year. She shared how worried she'd been that she was getting squeezed out of her career by parenthood—because her job was more flexible, she was always the one to push off work. And now this deadline felt like an emergency, even though the project itself wasn't a big deal—she'd dropped so many balls lately, it seemed that if she didn't hit it, she'd lose her credibility completely. "I saw you walk away from me into the bedroom and close the door, ending the conversation, and I imagined that was you telling me, 'Your work doesn't matter. You don't matter.' "

Selena described her own reality: her whole team waiting for her on Zoom, a meeting she'd been meticulously preparing for for months, about to launch a major new initiative at her organization to support activists in the field who were counting on them . . . then Molly out of the blue—and seemingly casually—was asking her to cancel. And then, when she couldn't, was throwing the thing she was most insecure about in the whole world—that she hadn't given birth to her own babies—in her face. She expressed that she had a lot of grief about not being able to carry a baby herself, to have that full experience.

They explored their triggers—for Molly, growing up with a mother who had given up her own career to stay home with her kids and then had always resented it, letting the kids see and feel that resentment. "When we decided to have kids, I vowed I would never do that." For Selena, a prior relationship—a long one that almost became a marriage—where she often felt manipulated into "proving" her love. "I had to give stuff up that I really cared about in order to show her she was more important," Selena said, "and it just kept escalating. Nothing was ever enough. Sometimes even now I feel I have to hold a line, because if I don't, I'll give up too much."

When they got to the apology stage, everything was different. This time, *I'm sorry* really meant something.

Selena: "I regret not seeing how much you were struggling. I should have offered you more support before we even got to this moment. I'm so sorry I left you hanging."

Molly: "I deeply regret what I said. I have regretted it every day for the past year. I didn't mean it, and it isn't true—I just said it out of desperation, I think, trying to get something to change. You are a wonderful mother to our children, and you've given them so much. They didn't need to grow inside you to be just like you. I mean, they both have your sense of humor. Just yesterday they were farting and laughing about it."

"Excuse me," said Selena, "that's *your* sense of humor!"

They could finally move on from their terrible fight.

Doing Repair Right: The Ten Most Common Pitfalls to Watch Out For

When you're ready, process a fight of your own. Remember—it can be a recent one or something from long ago. There is no time limit! You can use the instructions in this chapter or flip to the Quick Guide at the back of the book for the full five steps, all in the same place.

Now, a few reminders and troubleshooting tips.

Don't try to have this conversation too soon! This is a very common mistake. Don't leap right into processing immediately after the fight. You cannot do these steps immediately on the heels of a regrettable incident. You need to be able to zoom out, be calm, and review the fight from a distance. Imagine you're in a balcony in a theater, looking down at the stage, where the fight is unfolding. You're going to describe the play act by act, as you remember it. You can observe it and describe it (or at least your reality of it), but you don't get back into it. You're not walking down there and hopping on the stage. If you feel that happening, it's a sign you should stop and process later.

You have to go step by step. No skipping! No switching the order around! No sliding or halfway completing the steps! If you're skipping things like validating each other, fully exploring your triggers, et cetera, you're going to have the same problem when you try to apologize, where it doesn't really heal the hurt.

Remember that there are two realities. We've said this a number of times, but we say it again here . . . because it can be *hard.* You're listening to your partner describe something that you do not remember that way or that you didn't experience. But your work in this processing exercise is not to relitigate events. The "truth" is irrelevant here—it's simply not accessible. Perception is everything, and there are always two points of view.

Imagine you're sitting across the room from your partner and you're both looking at the same potted plant. If you both draw the plant, those two pictures are going to look very different from your two vantage points. And that's really the point here—when your partner describes what they perceived, and you don't remember it that way, *that doesn't matter.* You accept that's what they perceived. That is useful information for you! Your goal is to understand your partner's point of view at a deeper level, including the old triggers that informed their behavior.

Don't misunderstand what a trigger is. Remember: a trigger is an event from the past, from your life *before* this relationship, that generated a similar set of emotions. It was *not* from this relationship. If there was an event in the relationship that was similar to this one, it should be processed separately, using these same steps.

Remember that you must do these steps without criticism or blame. Be attentive to your language as you're describing your fight act by act. Describe yourself. Use "I" language wherever possible. If you need to describe your partner's words or actions, use "I saw you," "I heard you say . . ." You're not assigning intent or meaning to their words or actions here. Instead of "And then you said that incredibly mean thing to me," you say, "What I remember is you saying *x*, which felt horrible, and I imagined in that moment that you hated me." You are using your words to paint a picture of your own *inner world,* not describing the badness of your partner.

If the apology still does not land . . . During the apology phase, you can accept your partner's apology or not, and vice versa. Usually, if you go through the steps thoroughly, you probably won't feel like rejecting your partner's apology. But if one person cannot accept the other's apology, ask that other person, "What else do you need to hear in order to accept my apology?" Hopefully, the first person will describe what they need so that the apology feels more complete (e.g., "I need to talk more about *x*" or "I feel like I haven't expressed the impact of *y* so that you really understand").

No piling on of other things! That means no "kitchen sinking" (dumping other issues or other fights into this one) and no *patterns.* You are not going to sit down to process a fight and point out, "And you did the same thing to me last week, and last year, and in 1985!" Look, it's natural—people will want to point out a pattern of behavior that's been bothering them. But it won't work. Patterns are formed over a number of incidents, and you can't process them all at once. If you try to, your partner will feel like they're getting buried under an avalanche. Bring up only *one* incident at a time. And sometimes, if you address a single incident in a pattern of behavior, that will end up being enough.

If it's not enough, there may be other work to be done. If you're trying to process a particular regrettable incident, and you or your partner are having issues trusting each other through the process, then you may have what psychologist Susan Johnson calls an *attachment injury.* Attachment injuries happen when one-half of a couple violates their partner's expectation that they will be there for them and be supportive through times of difficulty or distress. If an attachment injury has occurred, it can throw a wrench into the repair process. This could sound like one partner not being able to accept an apology no matter what or not accepting that their partner will be able to change something moving forward. "Yeah, but there was this other time . . . when you really weren't there for me." You may not be able to repair until you've addressed the attachment injury and rebuilt trust. For this, we recommend professional support—the Gottman referral network (www.gottmanreferralnetwork.com) is a good place to start.

When it's something really big, ask for help. This process can handle really terrible fights, where nasty things were said, where there was turning away or turning against, lashing out, unfairness, blame, yelling and screaming. This framework can heal quite a lot in that department. But it can't handle major, long-term patterns of secrecy or betrayal. If there's been an affair, or financial betrayal, or a pattern of dishonesty, you're going to need professional support from a therapist to work through it. This repair process is limited to one event. So if you and your partner are facing something more extensive, you're going to need more help. One place to start is the Gottman Referral Network (www.gottmanreferralnetwork.com), a database of Gottman-trained therapists that is free to access and can point you to clinicians who practice the Gottman Method for Couples Therapy in your area.

Finally, stay focused on the goal: You are not trying to resolve the issue; you are processing *how your communication about the issue went wrong.* Remember, as always, that many of your conflicts will be unsolvable. So while you both will, in Step 5, articulate something you can do differently in the future to hopefully avoid another incident like this one from happening again, your processing of the fight is not about finding a fix or a solution for the issue itself that you were discussing when the regrettable incident took place. It's about fixing the way you communicate about the issue in order to avoid future regrettable incidents like this one, through understanding each other better, repairing hurts, and restoring your trust in each other.

We're all human. And we make mistakes. But we can get better. We can turn a regrettable incident into an incredible learning opportunity and a way to love each other better. Our conflicts are endless mirrors of our deeper humanity. They compel us to see and accept the full and complex humanity of our partner—both the wonderful parts and the deeply human flaws. That means accepting their vulnerabilities, their baggage, their trauma, and their weaknesses—all the nuances that create the whole individual, the heart and soul, of this person you fell in love with.

CONCLUSION:
THE GOOD FIGHT

Megan and Abdul met on a bus. It was headed inland from Mombasa, into the heartland of Kenya. Megan, a Peace Corps volunteer on her weekend off, boarded the bus carrying a cup of chai and an orange. It was sweltering hot, the first day of Ramadan.

Abdul boarded with his father and his younger brother, who had just failed his exams and did not want to sit next to their dad for the long bus ride home. Abdul had agreed he'd sit next to their father and spare his brother the torture of being lectured to for six hours. But as they walked up the aisle, he saw Megan sitting there with an open seat beside her. As soon as he saw her, he says, he felt warm inside. He grabbed his brother's arm.

"If we're in that row," he said, "I'm sitting next to that girl."

They were indeed in that row. His brother sighed and joined their father in the other pair of seats, resigned to his fate.

For six hours, they talked. She started by pointing toward the roof of the bus and saying the Kiswahili word for "sun." It was so hot! He noticed right away that her accent was good. But he spoke perfect English. He worked as a law clerk for the Kenyan Supreme Court. They switched to English; she offered him part of her orange.

"It's Ramadan," he said. "I'm fasting."

She was embarrassed. She knew it was Ramadan. And now, she looked like this oblivious American. But when they got off the bus all those hours later, he gave her his phone number. He put a wish out into the universe: *Let me see her again.* For the next two days, his phone did not leave his hand. He carried it everywhere. He checked it a thousand times. He slept with it under his pillow. Finally, she texted.

On their second date, they walked the beach and talked about everything: religion, children, family, geography, all the things you talk about when you're planning a life together.

"We didn't get officially engaged until the next year," says Megan, telling the story of how they met, "but that was the night we both knew we'd get married."

They've been married for seventeen years. And they've always been sure: this is the person for me. Yet they had a bad patch—one that made them really consider if they might not make it.

They had just moved from Kenya to Washington, D.C., where Megan had landed a job and Abdul had been admitted to a graduate program. He'd given up his position with the Kenyan Supreme Court to move with her; he hoped the degree he was pursuing would help him find his place in the United States. But he didn't like D.C. When they were in Kenya, he'd had a clear path: he'd been a lawyer, on track to advance, and he understood what was expected of him as a Kenyan man. Here, he felt scared and overwhelmed just by going out into the world. The racism and judgment were intense, and he felt he was constantly missing the mark in social interactions because of different cultural norms.

"Every interaction would terrify me," he says. "The only place I felt safe was in a classroom."

"Wow," she says, ten years later. "I'm not sure I even fully knew that until you said it just now."

"The only place of power I really had was fighting with Megan," he says. "But it was over nothing. Little things, and my anger was coming out sideways."

"We were really, really off track," she agrees.

They were fighting constantly. Every day felt like a struggle. The effortless, instant, and deep connection that they'd always had since the beginning seemed now to be hard to find. To him, she was becoming an enemy—someone who'd pulled him into a life he didn't want. To her, he was becoming a stranger—Who was this combative person? This was not the open, optimistic man she'd met on that bus. It was wearing them both down in every way.

"When we were fighting, I would be physically exhausted from it," Abdul says. "I could tell that she was too. We'd be fighting as we lay in bed, and all of a sudden, she'd be asleep—right in the middle of a fight. Snoring!"

Their fights had all the warning signs of a relationship headed in the wrong direction: harsh start-ups. Escalations. The Four Horsemen. They'd both get flooded; Abdul would yell, Meghan would flee and slam the bathroom door.

One day, they say, they woke up and looked at each other and realized, "We're not enjoying this relationship anymore. We can't keep having these terrible fights about nothing, about everything, about who knows what, and just keep on going. We have to stop and figure this out."

In that moment, they made a conscious decision: *We want our relationship back.*

They sat down and talked it through. For hours. It was like that first six-hour bus ride, except this time, they weren't beginning their relationship—they were saving it. They made a mutual agreement: they were going to shift the way they engaged with each other. They were going to approach conflict differently.

"It was the first time in our relationship that we realized that we didn't have to be controlled by these patterns that come up," Abdul says. "We could create a new pattern."

When they started to feel a fight over "nothing" escalate—they'd stop and ask: Why is this escalating? What are we really fighting about? What's underneath this? What can we shift about the way we're speaking to each other?

They started to use each squabble that started to spiral out of control as a kind of window, or microscope: like archaeologists, they looked under the layers to ask, What's really going on? A fight about who was supposed to have sent in the paperwork to renew their lease was underpinned by Abdul's unhappiness in this city and regret at leaving his previous career. A fight about the messiness of the living room was sparked by cultural gender expectations regarding who did domestic labor. A fight about using a turn signal really was about nothing—it came from the two of them not spending enough time together lately, away from the kids and the logistics of life, just connecting. It was nice to realize, in that instance, that there wasn't some huge issue lurking under the surface—to be able to turn to each other in the car and say, *We need a date.*

It wasn't always linear. Fights don't always proceed in a straight line, from soft start-up, to dreams, to compromise, to repair. They can cycle through those phases multiple times. They backtrack, go sideways; they get put on pause when the kids come barreling in the door from school, when life intrudes in all kinds of ways. They had to keep coming back to the dreams conversation when they realized they'd skimmed over it; had to keep reminding themselves to start softly—even midfight, when they introduced a new issue or thought.

It didn't change the fact that there were still problems coming at them, like balls in a batting cage—that's life! But now it started to feel again like they were fielding those balls together instead of slinging them at each other.

We know now from our research that we're going to have the same fights perpetually, over and over, and somehow we just have to wrap our minds around the fact that they're not going to get resolved. One of you will always be messy; the other a neat freak. One of you will always be loose and free, driven to enjoy this precious fleeting time on Planet Earth; the other will always be driven to find safety, craving the calm and steadiness of future security. One of you will always want to go to the party, the other will always want to stay home. There will be issues with kids. With jobs. With in-laws. There will be tough financial times. There will be dishes in the sink. Bills forgotten. Big emotions and careless things said. There will be doubts. There will be times when you want too much sex or times when you don't want enough. And there will be *change*. None of us are static creatures; we grow and evolve and regress and grow again. Sometimes you give your partner exactly what they said they wanted . . . and that's not what they want anymore.

So . . . you're gonna fight.

But now, you're going to have good fights.

This book has taken you through five major shifts you can do to break out of old patterns and have good fights. Let's recap what we've learned across the last five chapters.

Recap: The Good Fight

What a healthy fight looks like, in a nutshell:

- **When you're upset about something, you describe yourself.** Describing our partner rather than ourselves is one of the first mistakes couples make, and it's what lands us squarely in a harsh start—we begin by describing the personality flaws or the terrible qualities of our partner. Instead, describe your own feelings and describe the *situation* you're upset about.

- **You explain your *positive need*.** Your positive need implies what your partner can do to shine for you rather than what you resent. Launching an attack will only ever yield one possible response: *defensiveness.* Instead, offer a doorway into collaboration.

- **You talk about your dreams and theirs.** You slow things down. You ask each other open-ended questions that have to do with your histories on this issue. You find out what your partner's core needs, core beliefs, core dreams are—the aspects of their position on an issue that are so important to them, they can't give them up; and you figure out what's most important to you.

- **You compromise without giving up too much.** In a good fight, we separate out what is core and essential to our identities, what we could never sacrifice, and what exists outside that, what we can be flexible on. There are always details we can flex on that don't prevent you from fulfilling your core need or dream.

- **Finally, you process past regrettable incidents** and put them in the rearview mirror. Once you've delivered that food order, you can release it from the steel trap of your memory so that it won't leak into future fights. The next fight you have can be a good fight—without the built-up resentment and emotion of an unprocessed incident from the past.

We all arrive in relationships with beliefs and feelings about conflict that we carry with us—from childhood, past relationships, and other formative experiences. We each have our own conflict style; each relationship has its own conflict culture. When we set out to help couples who are stuck in conflict, who are gridlocked and unhappy, we don't set out to change who they are. The point is not for you to become a completely different person or even to change your "conflict style." Avoiders, to a certain extent, may always tend to avoid; the more volatile among us will tend to seek passion and high emotion. But what we *can* change is the patterns of our fights. We don't have to keep making the same mistakes.

No matter who we are, no matter what our past, no matter what our conflict style, or what gridlock we are stuck in with our partner, we can instead learn to make these shifts. And the more we do it, the more it will become our habit and our "default setting" to bring up our agenda in a gentler way, to respond nondefensively, to explore what's going on underneath it all and really get down into those depths that are so, so important, and to get to what's *flexible* while honoring each other's areas of inflexibility. An enormous amount of being a master of conflict is having compassion for each other's enduring vulnerabilities—to see and accept our partner's weak and tender spots and take care of them, even through disagreement, and allow them to take care of us too.

Do Megan and Abdul still fight? Sure. But it feels completely different.

"When we start to feel it going wrong, we stop and talk about it," Megan says. "That's the foundation. We've hit the wall many, many times, but now we make a different choice when we get to that point of being angry or frustrated. We don't just let it escalate into what it's becoming."

"We don't always hit the mark," he says. "But once we overcome resentment and reconnect, everything else kind of falls into place."

Megan and Abdul say they feel closer than ever instead of estranged and at odds—even when they're fighting.

"Talking to him is exhilarating," says Megan. "It was on the first day and it is now."

"She's incredibly smart," he says. "We spark ideas for each other."

"Also, I like his butt."

"We laugh a lot," he says, laughing. "We laugh all the time."

Having good fights, as Megan and Abdul discovered over years of trial and error, is a process. It's not a one-time conversation. It's an ongoing one.

So, to help with your good fights, we've compiled our most successful conflict interventions into a short section here, at the back of the book. This guide collects all of the strategies from each of the five fights in one place. Essentially, it's a map you can follow to walk your way through a fight from start to finish. There is nothing wrong with pulling this book out and flipping to the "Quick Guide" section in the heat of the moment! Don't be afraid to stop the action and open to the "Stating Needs" list of phrases, or to the "Repair Checklist," so you can remember all the ways there are to say *I'm sorry* and get back on track. Never hesitate to own up to a misstep in conflict and reach for this guide. There's no shame in asking for a do-over. *That came out wrong—can I try again?* Then flip to the "Softened Start-Up" script.

Even certain individuals who've been studying love and conflict for forty years still frequently flip to these resources and follow the step-by-step guidance. But we won't name names.

FIGHT RIGHT QUICK GUIDE

Going into a conflict conversation, remember:

Conflict Can Be Upsetting and Uncomfortable

We have to wrestle with the negative emotions we generally try to avoid, like anger, sadness, and fear.

But conflict is an opportunity to learn how to love our partner better.

In fact, we need conflict in order to grow and continue to know each other intimately.

The goal of any fight is not to win.

It's to understand your partner more deeply.

1
Start Right

If You Need to Raise an Issue...

Mistake to avoid: Starting harshly with criticism.

How to fight right: Start softly even if you're upset.

Why It Matters

- 97% of the time, how a conflict begins is also how it ends. The first *three minutes* of a fight set the tone for the rest of the conversation.

- A harsh start feels like an attack and only gives our partners one option in terms of how to reply: *defend*.
- Open up a conflict conversation to all the possibilities for how it might go—learning, creative solutions, collaborative problem-solving, connection—by starting more gently.

What to Do: The Softened Start-Up

"I feel (emotion) about (situation / problem) and I need (your positive need)"

- <u>(emotion)</u>: Describe *yourself* and *your* feelings.
- <u>(situation / problem)</u>: Describe the problem without criticizing or blaming your partner for it. You're talking about the *situation* not about your partner.
- <u>(your positive need)</u>: State your *positive* need—identify what your partner can do to help this situation get better. You're not fixating on the negative or listing the ways they've failed. You're telling them specifically how they can shine for you.

FIGHT RIGHT REMINDERS

No "kitchen sinking"! Don't pile in other issues or instances. Focus on *this situation* only, even if the issue is a pattern that repeats itself.

If Your Partner Raises an Issue...

Mistake to avoid: Defending, explaining, rebutting
   How to fight right: Postpone bringing up your perspective on this, and just listen.

Why It Matters

- In studies, the "masters of love" were those who could truly *listen* while their partner described a concern without bringing up their own perspective right away.
- Most people rush too quickly into the "persuasion" phase of a conflict, skipping over a critical phase of information-gathering about the issue.
- Successful couples make sure they have fully understood an issue from their partner's point of view before moving on.

What to Do: Be a Great Listener

- Listen closely, without bringing in your own perspective. When your partner brings an issue to you, your first job is to fully understand what their complaint or need is. Tune in to their world. Hear your partner's pain, even if you don't agree with the details.
- Ask clarifying or open-ended questions to understand the issue better. *"Sounds like it wasn't the fact that I wasn't home, but that I didn't call until the last minute?" "Is there anything else going on with this issue for you?"*
- Summarize what you heard. Make sure you understood and that your partner *feels* understood. *"So, you're feeling like all of the kids' logistics have been on you—is that right?"*
- Offer validation. Step into your partner's shoes and show them that you understand, empathize, and can see things from their point of view. *"That makes sense." "I understand why you'd feel that way." "I get that."*

FIGHT RIGHT REMINDER

Validation does not mean you agree. It just means you can empathize with any part of your partner's experience.

> If needed, refer back to the Feelings and Needs list on page 149.

2
Stay Collaborative

If You're Getting Flooded...

Mistake to avoid: Staying in the fight
   How to fight right: Don't fight when flooded! Take a break.

Why It Matters
- We can't fight right while flooded—in fight or flight, we don't have access to the healthy processes of conflict resolution, emotional regulation, and information processing—and are likely to escalate to a regrettable incident that causes damage and needs to be processed.
- Flooding might *feel* like: racing heart, shortness of breath, tightness in the body, spinning thoughts, heat anywhere in the body.
- Flooding might *look* like: lashing out, attacking, criticizing (outward); shutting down, stonewalling (inward).

What to Do: Take a Break!

- <u>Tell your partner.</u> Don't just walk away—communicate that you're feeling overwhelmed and upset and that you need to take a break. If your partner seems to be getting flooded, don't ever say, "I think *you're* getting flooded." Say, "Let's take a break and come back to this conversation in (agree on a time)."

- <u>Take at least twenty minutes . . .</u> This is the minimum amount of time that your body needs in order to process norepinephrine, the stress hormone, out of the bloodstream.

- <u>. . . but no longer than twenty-four hours.</u> It's fine to take a longer break if needed. Don't come back to the conflict if you're still flooded. But once you've calmed down, reconvene to resume the conversation—don't just sweep it under the rug and move on (see also: *Processing a fight*).

- <u>Get out of visual range.</u> When we're flooded, we need to remove ourselves from our partner's circle of energy. On a break, be with yourself and nobody else.

- <u>Do something soothing that takes your mind off the fight.</u> A break is not a break if you engage in distress-promoting thought loops like *I can't believe she said that!* Or *I'm going to get even.* Take your mind off the fight! Do something that brings down your physiological arousal. Try:

  - A long walk while listening to music, a podcast, or paying attention to your sensory experience (birdsong, trees in the wind, other sounds of the natural world)

- Lie down and practice deep breathing (activates the vagus nerve, will bring your nervous system down out of its state of arousal)
- Meditation practice (move thoughts *away* from distress-promoting thoughts about the fight)
- Read a book or magazine
- Housework, gardening, organization, answering emails, any other chore or task on your to-do list
- What else do you find calming, engaging, relaxing? Write your ideas here in case you need the reminder in the future:

  _____

  _____

- <u>Come back when you've agreed to.</u> If you're still feeling flooded, come back and let your partner know you need more time.

FIGHT RIGHT REMINDER

There is no shame in asking for a break. There is nothing wrong with stopping a fight and returning to it later when you are both calmer. It's okay to go to bed, even if the issue is not resolved. Communicate your needs clearly, tell your partner if you need to leave and take a walk or attend to other matters, and say when you'll be back. Breaks are a good thing!

If You're Getting Polarized...

Mistake to avoid: Trying to solve the problem
How to fight right: Solve the moment.

Why It Matters

- Most of our conflicts are perpetual not solvable—these issues will be with us for the entirety of our relationships.
- In conflict, we often need to reframe the goal: the goal is not to win. The goal is not to persuade our partner of anything. The goal is not even to arrive at a solution.
- The goal is only to make *this* conversation about the issue a positive one.

What to Do: Solve the Moment

- Talk about *yourself* and *your* needs. Just as with the softened start-up, continue to describe yourself and the situation rather than describing your partner's behavior or faults.
- Don't fight flooded. Self-soothe and take breaks. Help each other stay calm.
- Make repairs. The masters of love are the couples who make repairs throughout conflict. Shoot for the Magic Ratio! In conflict, we need *five* positive interactions for every *one* negative interaction to keep the conversation on the right track. Don't try to count, but remember that negativity packs a big punch—fill your conflict conversation with lots of small repairs and other positives.
  - Affection
  - Appreciation
  - Validation
  - Loving touch
  - An apology
  - A smile
  - A nod of understanding

- Humor
- Empathy
- Open-ended questions to find out more about what your partner thinks and feels about this issue

FIGHT RIGHT REMINDER

If you feel yourself getting polarized from your partner during a fight, practice *the assumption of similarity*. This simply means that if you identify a positive quality in yourself (*"I am rational"*), then try to see some of that quality in your partner. If you identify a negative quality in your partner (*"He is so rigid"*), try to see the ways that you can be that way too.

If needed, refer back to the Repair Checklist on page 187.

3
Get Down to the Dreams

When You're Getting Stuck...

Mistake to avoid: Staying on the surface
    How to fight right: Figure out what you're really fighting about.

Why It Matters
- Sometimes a problem we thought was solvable turns out to be perpetual, and even though we start softly, talk about our own feelings and needs, make repairs, we can't

arrive at a way forward, and it feels like we're banging our heads against a wall.

- Perpetual fights like these can get *gridlocked,* which is when they start to feel big, heavy, cause a lot of flooding, and leave us feeling rejected, betrayed, and hurt.
- If you have a gridlocked problem—or even before you do—interrupt the cycle by getting down to the roots of this conflict.

What to Do: Dreams Within Conflict

- <u>Discuss a perpetual or gridlocked problem.</u> Ask each other the questions below. Help each other understand the dreams, values, beliefs, or history behind your position on this issue. One person should be the speaker first, the other the listener; then switch.
- <u>The speaker's job:</u> Talk honestly about your feelings and beliefs about this issue. Explore what this position means to you, what the dream might be behind your position; tell the story of the source of this dream or belief—where it comes from, what it symbolizes. You must be clear and honest. What do you *really* want? <u>*Don't try to persuade your partner of anything right now.*</u> Just explain how you see things clearly so they can understand.
- <u>The listener's job:</u> Your job is to make your partner feel safe enough to tell you this dream or story. Toward this end, you will listen the way a good friend would listen. Suspend judgment; focus on learning more about your partner's story. Don't try to solve anything—it's much too soon for that. Your only job now is to understand your partner's dream.

The Dream Catcher's Magic Questions

1. What do you believe about this issue? Do you have some values, ethics, or beliefs that relate to your position on this issue?

2. Does your position relate to your history or childhood in some way?

3. Why is your position on this issue important to you?

4. What are your feelings about this issue?

5. What is your ideal dream here? If you could wave a magic wand and have exactly what you want, what would that look like?

6. Is there some underlying purpose or goal in this for you? What is it?

FIGHT RIGHT REMINDER

If you find you can't answer some of these, say, "I wish I could answer that, but I need more time." And then reflect: When else have you felt this way? Have you been in this situation before? Why is this so important to you? Sometimes dreams take a while to surface. Give them space to do so.

Remember that the goal in talking about dreams is not to solve the problem. The goal is to move from gridlock to dialogue. The goal is to know each other more deeply and understand each other's position more deeply. The goal is to learn something.

If needed, refer back to the list of questions and sample dreams on page 219.

4
Find Your Areas of Flexibility

When You Need to Work on Compromise...

Mistake to avoid: Competing to win
    How to fight right: Get on each other's side.

Why It Matters

- To truly compromise, we need to feel safe, which means we first need to figure out what we *cannot* compromise on—the core needs within this issue that are so important to us we can't give up on them without giving up too much.
- For this to work, we must practice the principle of Japanese aikido: *Yield to win.* We try accepting the parts of our partner's request that seem reasonable or possible surrounding our core needs. The more we can say yes, the more they can, and the problem becomes something you are working on together instead of against each other.
- For compromise to be successful, we have to find a way forward that honors both partners' deepest dreams and core needs.

What to Do: "The Bagel Method"

- Use the bagel image to map out your core needs and your areas of flexibility.
- In the inner circle, list the aspects of this issue you can't give in on. These are the nonnegotiables: your minimal core needs, beliefs, values about this issue.

- In the outer circle, list your areas of flexibility. These are the aspects of this issue that—*if* you were able to have what's in the inner circle—you'd be able to compromise on.
- Now . . . talk about it! Ask each other:
  - Why are the things in the inner circle so important to you?
  - How can I support your core needs here?
  - Tell me more about these areas of flexibility. What does it look like to be flexible here?
- Compare your "maps" to find a way forward:
  - What do we agree about?
  - What feelings do we have in common?
  - What shared goals do we have?
  - How might we accomplish these goals?
- A compromise (even if temporary, that we'll reevaluate later) that honors both our needs and dreams is . . . .

FIGHT RIGHT REMINDERS

Don't be the rock! If all we do is say "no," then we become an obstacle our partners start to go around instead of collaborating with. We lose all power in the relationship. Partners who have the most influence are the ones who can *be* influenced.

Compromise never feels perfect. Everyone gains something and everyone loses something in compromise. The important thing is feeling understood, respected, and honored in your dreams.

COMPROMISE OVALS

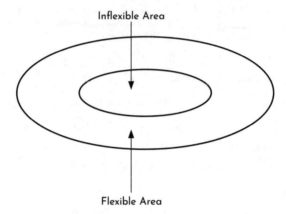

My inflexible area or core need on this issue is:

My more flexible areas on this issue are:

5
Process Past Fights

When a Fight Hasn't Been Addressed...

Mistake to avoid: Sweeping it under the rug
  How to fight right: Know how to process regrettable incidents.

Why It Matters

- We all have fights where we say the wrong thing, do the wrong thing, end up hurting each other. This is inevitable!
- The big mistake we make is when we try to move on from the incident without addressing it—unprocessed fights can become like a pebble in our shoe, rubbing us raw as we try to walk on without stopping to take it out.
- We have to address past incidents *without getting back into the fight.* We don't want to fight about the fight. We want to process what happened so we can make a discussion about the same issue better the next time.

What to Do: Process the Fight

Prep: Before You Begin

Take your seat in the balcony.
Make sure you're calm and have some distance from the events. You should be able to look back on the fight as if looking down at a play unfolding on the stage from

balcony seating. You need to be able to observe what happened without getting back into it.

Let go of "the facts."
Remember that there is no God camera. There is no factual transcript of what occurred. Each of your realities has validity—perception is everything.

As always, talk about yourself.
Remember to talk about yourself and your feelings. Don't say: "You were angry at me." Say: "You looked upset and I felt you were mad at me." It's a small but critical pivot.

Step 1: Feelings

Share how you felt but not why. Choose as many as apply.

- [ ] Defensive
- [ ] Out of control
- [ ] I wanted to win
- [ ] Not listened to
- [ ] Frustrated
- [ ] My opinions didn't even matter
- [ ] Feelings got hurt
- [ ] Righteously indignant
- [ ] There was a lot of give & take
- [ ] Totally flooded
- [ ] Morally justified

- [ ] I had no feelings at all
- [ ] Angry
- [ ] Unfairly picked on
- [ ] I had no idea what I was feeling
- [ ] Sad
- [ ] Unappreciated
- [ ] Lonely
- [ ] Unloved
- [ ] Disliked
- [ ] Alienated
- [ ] Misunderstood
- [ ] Unattractive

- ☐ Ashamed
- ☐ Criticized
- ☐ Stupid
- ☐ Like you didn't even like me
- ☐ Guilty
- ☐ Morally outraged
- ☐ Took a complaint personally
- ☐ Not cared about
- ☐ Like leaving
- ☐ Like staying and talking it through
- ☐ Worried
- ☐ Culpable
- ☐ Overwhelmed with emotion
- ☐ Afraid

- ☐ Abandoned
- ☐ Disloyal
- ☐ Unsafe
- ☐ Not calm
- ☐ Exhausted
- ☐ Tense
- ☐ Stubborn
- ☐ Foolish
- ☐ Remorseful
- ☐ Powerless
- ☐ I was right and you were wrong
- ☐ Shocked
- ☐ I had no influence
- ☐ Both of us were partly right

Step 2: Realities

We assume all realities are valid.

- <u>First</u>: Take turns describing your perceptions—your own reality of what happened during the fight. Describe only what YOU saw, heard, and felt, not what you think your partner meant or felt. Avoid attacking or accusing. Talk about what you might have needed from your partner. Describe your perceptions like a reporter, giving an objective moment-by-moment description.
- <u>Next</u>: Summarize and then validate your partner's reality. Say something like, "It makes sense to me why you saw it that way," or "I can see why this upset you." Validation doesn't mean you agree but that you can understand even a part of your partner's experience.

- <u>Finally</u>: Check in. Do both partners feel understood? If yes, move on. If no, circle back. Ask: "What do I need to know to understand your perspective better?" After summarizing and validating, ask you partner: "Did I get it?" and "Is there anything else?"

Don't...

assign blame, assume ill intent, or tell your partner what they were thinking or feeling.

DO...

say, "I imagined..." "It seemed to me..." "I saw..." "I thought..."

Step 3: Triggers

"Trigger," definition: *An old bruise that gets pressed on. Something from before the relationship, an event from your past, that generated a similar set of emotions.*

- <u>First</u>: Share what escalated the interaction for you. What events in the interaction triggered a big reaction in you?
- <u>Next</u>: As you rewind the video of your memory, stop at a point where you had a similar set of feelings triggered in the past. Now, tell the story of that past moment to your partner so your partner can understand why that is a trigger for you.
- <u>Keep going</u>: Continue to share your stories—it will help your partner understand you. As you think about your past relationships, early history, or childhood, is there

another story you remember that relates to what got triggered in you, your enduring vulnerabilities? Your partner needs to know this in order to know you and to be more sensitive to you.

Some triggers might be:

I felt judged. I'm very sensitive to that.

I felt excluded. I'm very sensitive to that.

I felt criticized. I'm very sensitive to that.

I felt flooded . . .

I felt ashamed . . .

I felt lonely . . .

I felt belittled . . .

I felt disrespected . . .

I felt powerless . . .

I felt out of control . . .

Your own: _____

Validation:

- Does any part of your partner's triggers and story make sense to you? Say so.
- Example: "It makes sense that you felt attacked in that moment, given what you went through in your previous relationship."

Step 4: Take Responsibility

Under ideal conditions, you might have done better at talking about this issue. What set you up for the miscommunication? What was your state of mind? Share how you set yourself up to get into this conflict:

I'd been very stressed and irritable.

I'd not expressed much appreciation toward you.

I'd taken you for granted.

I'd been overly sensitive.

I'd been overly critical.

I'd not shared very much of my inner world.

I'd not been emotionally available.

I'd been turning away more.

I'd been getting easily upset.

I'd been depressed.

I'd had a chip on my shoulder.

I'd not been very affectionate.

I'd not made time for good things between us.

I'd not been a very good listener.

I'd not asked for what I needed.

I'd been feeling like a martyr.

I'd needed to be alone.

I'd not wanted to take care of anybody.

I'd been very preoccupied.

I hadn't felt very much confidence in myself.

I'd been running on empty.

Read aloud the items that were true for you on this list.

Then: *Specifically, what do you regret, and specifically, what was your contribution to this fight or regrettable incident? What do you wish to apologize for? Make your apology specific to what you regret saying or doing. "I'm sorry that . . ."*

> I overreacted when (I said or did) . . .
>
> I was really grumpy when I . . .
>
> I was defensive when I . . .
>
> I was so negative when I . . .
>
> I attacked you when I . . .
>
> I didn't listen to you when I . . .
>
> I wasn't respectful when I . . .
>
> I was unreasonable when I . . .
>
> Your own: _____

If you accept your partner's apology—say so! If not, say what you still need.

Step 5: Constructive Plans

What is one thing your partner can do differently to avoid an incident like this from happening again? Share one thing your partner can do to make a discussion on this issue better next time. Then, while it's still your turn, share one thing YOU can do to make it better next time. Be as agreeable as possible to the plans suggested by your partner.

FIGHT RIGHT REMINDER

It is never too late to process a fight or regrettable incident. You can process a fight after a day or after decades.

The moments of conflict and being out of sync are ultimately opportunities in every relationship:

To know our partner better over time.

Explore more resources for
turning conflict into connection here.

ACKNOWLEDGMENTS

This book would not have been possible without the incredibly important help we've received from so many of our friends and colleagues. First, we begin by recognizing the nearly 100,000 couples to date who have voluntarily contributed to everything we know about love relationships. You courageously volunteered to reveal the most intimate part of your lives for our scientific review. Without you, we would have nothing to offer the world.

We begin by acknowledging the essential, vital contributions of our lifelong great friend, Dr. Robert Levenson, of the University of California, Berkeley. Without Bob, none of this research and thinking would have ever seen the light of day. Despite the best advice from John and Bob's older colleagues, who firmly advised them to stop doing research together and to stop the foolhardy practice of investigating two interacting people at once, Bob agreed to follow his and John's unstoppable curiosity about what makes love relationships succeed or fail. Bob and John began doing research together with absolutely no hypotheses, which is a definite violation of good research practice. Almost fifty years later, they can proudly claim that they began together happily in complete ignorance. Fortunately, still in complete ignorance, John and Bob both got lucky and met the loves of their lives in Dr. Julie Schwartz and Dr. Michelle (Lani) Shiota.

Using all the vast time-series data that Bob and John generated, we want to acknowledge the enormous contributions of Dr. James Murray and his students for helping us create nonlinear dynamic mathematical models of couples' interaction, which resulted in many papers and the MIT Press book *The Mathematics of Marriage* in the year 2002.

For the last thirty years, we have benefitted from the contributions of many of our colleagues working at the Gottman Institute (TGI), the Relationships Research Institute (RRI), and Affective Software, Inc. (ASI), which has now been joined in one company, called Gottman, Inc. (GI). We wish to recognize our valiant co-founder of TGI and our dear friend, Etana Kunovsky; our highly esteemed prior CEO and dear friend, Alan Kunovsky; and our current amazing CEO of TGI and also our dear friend, Ed Sargent—who is now also head of all learning. We wish to acknowledge the huge contributions of Dr. Renay Bradley, who brilliantly led our nonprofit Relationships Research Institute for many years, conducting several critical clinical trials. We also want to acknowledge the invaluable contributions of Dr. Sybil Carrere, John's former lab director at the University of Washington; and the vast contributions of John's former students, Dr. Lynn Katz, Dr. Jim Coan, Dr. Janice Driver, Dr. Howard Markman, Dr. Cliff Notarius, Dr. Regina Rushe, Dr. Amber Tabares, and Dr. Dan Yoshimoto. We also want to recognize our late colleague, Dr. Neil Jacobson, and his widow, Dr. Virginia Rutter, for their invaluable support, especially regarding the study of domestically violent couples.

Our TGI staff, both past and present, have supported our mission to bring relationship help to over a million individuals. They include: Erin Cox, professional development and tech support for TGI; Dr. Carrie Cole, our current Love Lab research director; Dr. Don Cole, clinical director; Crystal Cressey, early couples department support for TGI; Emily Cripe, social media for TGI; Jen Dalby, early online learning; Caitlyn Donahue, marketing for TGI; Katelyn Ewen, beautiful graphics for TGI; Michael Fulwiler, director of marketing for TGI; Beth Goss, master trainer of our worldwide Bringing Baby Home program; Belinda Gray, early director of products department for TGI; Walter Guity, past head of customer service for TGI; Kendra Han, director of couples department for TGI; Laura Heck, early director of professional clinical development and Certified Gottman Trainer (CGT) and 7 Principles for Making Marriage Work Program; Stacy Hubbard, CGT, development of 7 Principles for Singles (with Dave Penner); Kennedy James, head of operations for TGI; Sean Jeffries, inventory management for TGI; Amy Loftis, director of professional development for TGI; Jennifer Luu, graphic design for TGI; Vivian Lu, marketing assistant for TGI; Torsten Oberst, marketing director; Sadie Peterson, professional development, operations for TGI; Joni Parthemer, development and teaching of BBH; Dr. Dave Penner, the amazing clinical director and master trainer for twelve years (he developed the 7 Principles Program and 7 Principles for Singles with Stacy); Carolyn Pirak, development and teaching of Bringing Baby Home (BBH) and emotion coaching programs for TGI; Katie Reynolds, public and media relations for TGI and Gottman, Inc.; Becca Sangwin, marketing for TGI; Aziza Seykota, director of product development; Therese Soudant, couples department support for TGI; Janani Subramanian, head of finance and accounting; Weston Triemstra, website development and tech support; Keeley Trygstad, tech and operations support for TGI; and Linda Wright, early director of couples department for TGI.

For the last six years, our close friend Rafael Lisitsa has been the valiant and endlessly persevering CEO of first, Affective Software, Inc. (ASI), and now that ASI and TGI have merged into Gottman,

Inc. (GI), GI's brilliant leader and CEO. He is a man of multidimensional vision and talented leadership in many areas of life and is far ahead of the curve in the new revolutionary world of artificial intelligence. We also want to thank Ed Sargent, past CEO of TGI and now current chief of learning for Gottman, Inc. Ed brings amazing skill, team building, and a profound understanding of our mission that has helped spread our work across the globe. Ed is also a dear beloved friend and endless supporter of our work. We also bow to the genius and hard work of Dr. Vladimir Brayman, who first served as our chief technology officer at Affective Software, Inc., and now at GI. He has been the architect of all our algorithmic creations and programming, including our validated Trust Metric, and he has become a treasured friend besides. Dr. Brayman has pioneered all our ML and AI technological development as it carves out a never-before-achieved AI pathway into emotionally intelligent AI assistance. Together, Rafael and Vladimir have created revolutionary new patent-winning innovations and remarkable technological inventions. These include creating the online validated questionnaires of the Gottman Relationship Checkup, and using AI machine learning to create our online Love Lab, with its amazingly automated Specific Emotion Coding (SPAFF), automated heart rate detection for any skin tone using only videography, and the enormously powerful mathematics and software of GottmanConnect for assessing relationships. Brayman and his team have also integrated thirty-seven modules and assessment recommendations to fine-tune assessment and interventions.

Our goal in creating a web-based platform has been to democratize help for couples so that anyone, regardless of geography, sexual orientation, gender, or socioeconomics, can access the best scientifically based help for their relationships. We are proud to announce that it is now possible for any couple in the world to fully assess *and* *treat* their relationship issues on their phones, pads, or computers in the comfort and privacy of their own home. Rafael and Vladimir have had a great staff to assist them. Therefore, we also wish to acknowledge the contributions of Connor Eaton to our AI development, Steven Fan for the Gottman coach videos, as well as current ongoing videography projects: Dr. Dmitriy Drusvyatskit of the University of Washington for his mathematics; Alexander Elguren for his brilliant leadership in content development; Inna Brayman, our calm and patient head of customer service; plus numerous others, including John Fantell, Dr. Yuriy Gulak of Rutgers University for his mathematics, Sam Hage, Kendra Han, Sean Jeffries, Raleigh Keagan, Frans Keylard, Brianne Korthase, Alexander Miropolsky, Torsten Oberst, Letha Penhale, Vadim Popov, Philippe Post, Alexandra Spangler, Braeden Stamas, Janani Subramanian, and Lisa Tashjian. If we have neglected to mention any of our current dedicated staff, please forgive our error, which is solely our own.

We want to also express endless gratitude for the unique contributions of our housemates and wonderful friends, master trainers, and clinicians: Dr. Don Cole, our esteemed clinical director, and Dr. Carrie Cole, our research director and the head of our new Seattle social psychophysiology Love Lab. Don and Carrie Cole courageously moved from Houston to Seattle to become the new clinical and research faces of the Gottman Institute, as John and Julie someday (but not in the near future) plan to recede into the sunset in their Seaward double kayak. Carrie had to master so many things at once, including learning psychophysiology and how to run a very complex laboratory, while simultaneously getting her PhD. There is nothing that woman cannot do. We are forever grateful to Don and Carrie.

From our partners in doing-good-in-the-world (Tikkun Olam),

and from the company Idea Architects, first we acknowledge our brilliant and visionary dear friend and literary agent, Doug Abrams; our agent and fearless leader, Rachel Neumann, who gave all of her deep experience and razor-sharp vision to this project; and our incredibly gifted writing assistant, Alyssa Knickerbocker. With all her magic, Alyssa waved her wand to help create and perfect the book you now hold in your hands. Without brilliant Alyssa, this book would not exist. We also want to acknowledge Bella Roberts, our assistant literary editor, who helped with the proposal and scheduling, and executive assistant Mellisa Kim, who helped with the notes. We also wish to acknowledge Brockman Inc., particularly our agent, Katinka Matson, who first shepherded our *New York Times* bestseller, *The Seven Principles for Making Marriage Work,* written with Nan Silver, as well as other subsequent books.

And to our editor, Shannon Welch—we are so grateful to you for seeing the potential in this project and sharing our vision for helping couples connect through conflict. The entire team at Harmony has been indispensable: Theresa Zoro, president; Diana Baroni, publisher; and Gail Gonzales, deputy publisher, for their leadership; Mia Pulido, editorial assistant, for steadfast problem-solving and support; Christina Foxley, Odette Fleming, and Tammy Blake, for their tireless and creative marketing and publicity; Anna Bauer, Irene Ng, and Andrea Lau for the incredible design work that made this book a beautiful object; and Joyce Wong, production editor, and Dustin Amick, production manager, for shepherding this book across the finish line.

We could never have created this book without our stalwart friends, life stewards, and fellow journey men and women: Cara and Phillip Cohn, for their spiritual guidance and wisdom; Alison Shaw and Derk Jager, for their undying decades of love, support, and Alison's incredible cooking; and Mavis Tsai, for her enduring friendship both as a fellow researcher and creator, lifelong wise companion, and Julie's favorite partner in all things adventurous.

Last, but not least, we thank our beloved and endlessly working almost-a-doctor daughter, her precious husband who is a long-sought son, and our most amazing grandchild ever, whom they've thankfully brought into our lives. How can we thank you enough for wanting to raise your child in a multigenerational family? We are so profoundly honored. We love you so much.

Without all of you, we would have failed utterly. Therefore, to all these partners in our lifelong venture, we bow our heads in deeply heartfelt gratitude.

NOTES

INTRODUCTION

1. Roi Estlein, Ateret Gewirtz-Meydan, and Eugenia Opuda, "Love in the Time of COVID-19: A Systematic Mapping Review of Empirical Research on Romantic Relationships One Year into the COVID-19 Pandemic," *Family Process* 61, no. 3 (September 2022): 1208–28. https://doi.org/10.1111/famp.12775.
2. Lynn Gigy and Joan B. Kelly, "Reasons for Divorce: Perspectives of Divorcing Men and Women," *Journal of Divorce & Remarriage* 18, no. 1–2 (October 18, 2008): 169–88. https://doi.org/10.1300/J087v18n01_08.
3. J. M. Gottman, "The Roles of Conflict Engagement, Escalation, and Avoidance in Marital Interaction: A Longitudinal View of Five Types of Couples," *Journal of Consulting and Clinical Psychology* 61, no. 1 (February 1993): 6–15.
4. John Mordechai Gottman and Robert Wayne Levenson, "The Timing of Divorce: Predicting When a Couple Will Divorce over a 14-Year Period," *Journal of Marriage and Family* 62, no. 3 (August 2000): 737–45. https://doi.org/10.1111/j.1741-3737.2000.00737.x.
5. John M. Gottman, Janice Driver, and Amber Tabares, "Repair During Marital Conflict in Newlyweds: How Couples Move from Attack–Defend to Collaboration," *Journal of Family Psychotherapy*, 26, no. 2 (June 2015): 85–108. https://doi.org/10.1080/08975353.2015.1038962.
6. John Gottman and Julie Gottman, "The Natural Principles of Love," *Journal of Family Theory & Review* 9, no. 1 (March 2, 2017): 7–26. https://doi.org/10.1111/jftr.12182.
7. Gottman and Levenson, "The Timing of Divorce," 737–45. https://doi.org/10.1111/j.1741-3737.2000.00737.x.
8. Gottman, Driver, and Tabares, "Repair During Marital Conflict in Newlyweds," 85–108. https://doi.org/10.1080/08975353.2015.1038962.
9. John M. Gottman et al., "Gay, Lesbian, and Heterosexual Couples About to Begin Couples Therapy: An Online Relationship Assessment of 40,681 Couples," *Journal of Marital and Family Therapy* 46, no. 2 (April 2020): 218–39. https://doi.org/10.1111/jmft.12395.

WHY WE FIGHT

1. James Coan and John M. Gottman, "The Specific Affect Coding System (SPAFF)," in *Handbook of Emotion Elicitation and Assessment,* ed. James A. Coan and John J. B. Allen (New York: Oxford University Press, 2007), 267–85.

2. John Mordechai Gottman, *Marital Interactions: Experimental Investigations* (New York: Academic Press, 1979).
3. John Mordechai Gottman and Robert Wayne Levenson, "A Two-Factor Model for Predicting When a Couple Will Divorce: Exploratory Analyses Using 14-Year Longitudinal Data," *Family Process* 41, no. 1 (Spring 2002): 83–96. https://doi.org /10.1111/j.1545-5300.2002.40102000083.x.
4. Claus Wedekind, Thomas Seebeck, Florence Bettens, and Alexander J. Paepke, "MHC-Dependent Mate Preferences in Humans," *Proceedings: Biological Sciences* 260, no. 1359 (June 22, 1995): 245–49.
5. John Mordechai Gottman, *What Predicts Divorce? The Relationship Between Marital Processes and Marital Outcomes* (Mahwah, NJ: Lawrence Erlbaum Associates, 1994).
6. A. F. Shapiro, J. M. Gottman, and S. Carrére, "The Baby and the Marriage: Identifying Factors That Buffer Against Decline in Marital Satisfaction After the First Baby Arrives," *Journal of Family Psychology* 14, no. 1 (March 2000): 59–70. https://doi.org/10.1037//0893-3200.14.1.59.PMID:10740682.
7. Nicole A. Roberts and Robert W. Levenson, "The Remains of the Workday: Impact of Job Stress and Exhaustion on Marital Interaction in Police Couples," *Journal of Marriage and Family* 63, no. 4 (November 2001): 1052–67, https://doi .org/10.1111/j.1741-3737.2001.01052.x.
8. Lowell J. Krokoff, "The Correlates of Negative Affect in Marriage: An Exploratory Study of Gender Differences," *Journal of Family Issues* 8, no. 1 (March 1987): 111–35. https://doi.org/10.1177/019251387008001006.
9. J. M. Gottman and L. J. Krokoff, "The Relationship Between Marital Interaction and Marital Satisfaction: A Longitudinal View," *Journal of Consulting and Clinical Psychology* 57, no. 1 (February 1989): 47–52.
10. Richard J. Davidson et al., "Approach-Withdrawal and Cerebral Asymmetry: Emotional Expression and Brain Physiology," *Journal of Personality and Social Psychology* 58, no. 2 (March 1990): 330–41. https://doi.org/10.1037/0022-3514.58 .2.330.

WHY WE FIGHT THE WAY WE FIGHT

1. J. M. Gottman, "The Roles of Conflict Engagement, Escalation, and Avoidance in Marital Interaction: A Longitudinal View of Five Types of Couples," *Journal of Consulting and Clinical Psychology,* 61, no. 1 (February 1993): 6–15.
2. P. G. Ashford et al.,eds., *The Collected Papers of Lewis Fry Richardson,* vol. 1. (Cambridge, UK: Cambridge University Press, 2009).
3. Graham B. Spanier, review of *Communication, Conflict, and Marriage,* by Harold L. Rausch, William A. Barry, Richard K. Hertel, and Mary Ann Swain, *Journal of Marriage and Family* 37, no. 1 (February 1975): 236–38, https://doi.org/10.2307 /351050.
4. Gottman, *Marital Interactions.*
5. John M. Gottman and Robert W. Levenson, "Marital Processes Predictive of Later Dissolution: Behavior, Physiology, and Health," *Journal of Personality and Social Psychology* 63, no. 2 (1992): 221–33. https://doi.org/10.1037/0022-3514.63 .2.221.
6. Rachel Ebling and Robert W. Levenson, "Who Are the Marital Experts?," *Journal*

of Marriage and Family 65, no. 1 (February 2003): 130–42. https://doi.org/10 .1111/j.1741-3737.2003.00130.x.

7. John Mordechai Gottman and Robert Wayne Levenson, "What Predicts Change in Marital Interactions over Time? A Study of Alternative Models," *Family Process* 38, no. 2 (June 1999): 143–58. https://doi.org/10.1111/j.1545-5300.1999.00143.x.

8. Rand Conger et al., eds., *Families in Troubled Times: Adapting to Change in Rural America* (New York: Aldine de Gruyter, 1994).

9. Gottman et al., "Gay, Lesbian, and Heterosexual Couples About to Begin Couples Therapy: An Online Relationship Assessment of 40,681 Couples," 218–39.

10. John Mordechai Gottman, *Principia Amoris: The New Science of Love* (New York: Routledge, 2014).

11. Gottman, *What Predicts Divorce.*

WHAT WE FIGHT ABOUT

1. Gottman, *What Predicts Divorce.*

2. John M. Gottman, *The Science of Trust* (New York: Norton, 2011).

3. Belinda Campos et al., "Opportunity for Interaction? A Naturalistic Observation Study of Dual-Earner Families After Work and School," *Journal of Family Psychology* 23, no. 6 (December 2009): 798–807. https://doi.org/10.1037 /a0015824.

4. Gottman, *What Predicts Divorce.*

5. Gottman and Gottman, "The Natural Principles of Love," 7–26. https://doi.org /10.1111/jftr.12182.

6. N. S. Jacobson et al., "Psychological Factors in the Longitudinal Course of Battering: When Do Couples Split Up? When Does the Abuse Decrease?," *Violence and Victims* 11, no. 4 (Winter 1996): 371–92.

7. Renay P. Cleary Bradley and John M. Gottman, "Reducing Situational Violence in Low-Income Couples by Fostering Healthy Relationships," *Journal of Marital Family Therapy* 38, no. 1 (June 2012): 187–98. https://doi.org/10.1111/j.1752 -0606.2012.00288.x.

8. Neil Jacobson and John Gottman, *When Men Batter Women: New Insights into Ending Abusive Relationships* (New York: Simon & Schuster, 1998).

9. U.S. Department of Health & Human Services, Center for Behavioral Health Statistics and Quality, *2020 National Survey on Drug Use and Health (NSDUH): Methodological Summary and Definitions.* Rockville, MD: Substance Abuse and Mental Health Services Administration. Retrieved from https://www.samhsa.gov /data/.

10. U.S. Department of Health & Human Services, *2020 National Survey on Drug Use and Health (NSDUH).*

11. Julia C. Babcock et al., "A Component Analysis of a Brief Psycho-Educational Couples' Workshop: One-Year Follow-Up Results," *Journal of Family Therapy*, 35, no. 3 (August 2013): 252–280. https://doi.org/10.1111/1467-6427.12017.

12. Debra Trampe, Jordi Quoidbach, and Maxime Taquet, "Emotions in Everyday Life," *Plos One* 10, no. 12 (December 23, 2015): e0145450. https://doi.org/10 .1371/journal.pone.0145450.

13. Jennifer S. Lerner et al., "Emotion and Decision Making," *Annual Review of Psychology* 66 (2015): 799–823. https://doi.org/10.1146/annurev-psych-010213 -115043.

FIGHT #1: THE BOMB DROP

1. John M. Gottman, "The Mathematics of Marital Conflict: Qualitative Dynamic Mathematical Modeling of Marital Interaction," *Journal of Family Psychology* 9, no. 2 (1995): 110–30.
2. S. Carrère and J. M. Gottman, "Predicting Divorce Among Newlyweds from the First Three Minutes of a Marital Conflict Discussion," *Family Process* 38, no. 3 (Fall 1999): 293–301.
3. Gottman et al., "Gay, Lesbian, and Heterosexual Couples About to Begin Couples Therapy: An Online Relationship Assessment of 40,681 Couples," 218–39. https://doi.org/10.1111/jmft.12395.
4. Anatol Rapoport, *Fights, Games, and Debates* (Ann Arbor: University of Michigan Press, 1970).
5. Gottman, *What Predicts Divorce.*

FIGHT #2: THE FLOOD

1. Gottman, *What Predicts Divorce.*
2. Gottman, *What Predicts Divorce.*
3. Gottman et al., "Gay, Lesbian, and Heterosexual Couples About to Begin Couples Therapy," 218–239. https://doi.org/10.1111/jmft.12395.
4. Eugene T. Gendlin, *Focusing: A Step-by-Step Technique That Takes You Past Getting in Touch with Your Feelings—To Change Them and Solve Your Personal Problems,* 2nd rev. ed. (New York: Bantam, 1982).
5. Gottman, Driver, and Tabares, "Repair During Marital Conflict in Newlyweds," 85–108. https://doi.org/10.1080/08975353.2015.1038962.
6. Gottman, Driver, and Tabares, "Repair During Marital Conflict in Newlyweds," 85–108. https://doi.org/10.1080/08975353.2015.1038962.

FIGHT #3: THE SHALLOWS

1. Statistic is from couples surveyed after our workshops.
2. Kim T. Buehlman, John M. Gottman, and Lynn F. Katz, "How a Couple Views Their Past Predicts Their Future: Predicting Divorce from an Oral History Interview," *Journal of Family Psychology* 5, nos. 3–4 (March 1992): 295–318.

FIGHT #4: THE STANDOFF

1. Daniel V. Meegan, "Zero-Sum Bias: Perceived Competition Despite Unlimited Resources," *Frontiers in Psychology* 1, no. 191 (November 2010): 191.

2. Claudia M. Haase et al., "Interpersonal Emotional Behaviors and Physical Health: A 20-Year Longitudinal Study of Long-Term Married Couples," *Emotion* 16, no. 7 (October 2016): 965–977. https://doi.org/10.1037/a0040239.
3. Gottman, *The Science of Trust*.
4. Gottman et al., "Gay, Lesbian, and Heterosexual Couples About to Begin Couples Therapy: An Online Relationship Assessment of 40,681 Couples," 218–239. https://doi.org/10.1111/jmft.12395.
5. J. M. Gottman et al., "Predicting Marital Happiness and Stability from Newlywed Interactions," *Journal of Marriage and Family*, 60, no. 1 (1998): 5–22.
6. J. M. Gottman et al., "Predicting Marital Happiness and Stability from Newlywed Interactions," 222.
7. John Mordechai Gottman et al., "Correlates of Gay and Lesbian Couples' Relationship Satisfaction and Relationship Dissolution," *Journal of Homosexuality*, 45, no. 1(2003): 23–43.
8. Gallup, "Americans' Self-Identication as Lesbian, Gay, Bisexual, Transgender or Something Other Than Heterosexual, 2012-2022." Gallup 2022 telephone poll.
9. David Graeber and David Wengrow, *The Dawn of Everything: A New History of Humanity* (New York: Farrar, Straus, and Giroux, 2021).
10. John Nash, "Two-Person Cooperative Games," *Econometrica* 21, no. 1 (January 1953): 128–40. https://doi.org/10.2307/1906951.

FIGHT #5: THE CHASM IN THE ROOM

1. J. M. Gottman et al., "Gay, Lesbian, and Heterosexual Couples About to Begin Couples Therapy: An Online Relationship Assessment of 40,681 Couples," 218–39. https://doi.org/10.1111/jmft.12395.
2. B. Zeigarnik, "On Finished and Unfinished Tasks," in *A Source Book of Gestalt Psychology*, ed. W. E. Ellis (London: Kegan Paul, Trench, Trubner, 1938), 300–314.
3. G. H. Bower, "A Brief History of Memory Research," in *The Oxford Handbook of Memory*, E. Tulving and F. I. M. Craik, eds. (New York: Oxford University Press, 2000), 3–32.

INDEX

ABOUT THE AUTHORS

World-renowned researchers and clinical psychologists Drs. John and Julie Gottman have dedicated their careers to the research and fostering of healthy, long-lasting relationships. Dr. John Gottman is professor emeritus in psychology at the University of Washington, where he founded the Love Lab and was named one of the top ten most influential therapists of the past quarter century. Dr. Julie Schwartz Gottman, cocreator of the immensely popular *The Art and Science of Love* workshop, was named Washington State Psychologist of the Year and received the 2021 Lifetime Achievement Award from *Psychotherapy Networker*.

Available from
New York Times bestselling authors
JULIE SCHWARTZ GOTTMAN, PhD, and JOHN GOTTMAN, PhD

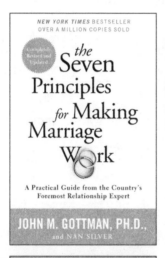

Learn more here:

Available wherever
books are sold